On Gladsmuir Shall The Battle Be!
The Battle of Prestonpans 20-21 September 1745

Arran Paul Johnston

Helion & Company Limited

Helion & Company Limited
Unit 8 Amherst Business Centre
Budbrooke Road
Warwick
CV34 5WE
England
Tel. 01926 499619
Email: info@helion.co.uk
Website: www.helion.co.uk
X (formerly Twitter): @Helionbooks
Facebook: @HelionBooks
https://helionbooks.wordpress.com/

Published by Helion & Company 2017. Reprinted in paperback 2024
Designed and typeset by Mach 3 Solutions (www.mach3solutions.co.uk)
Cover designed by Paul Hewitt, Battlefield Design (www.battlefield-design.co.uk)

Text © Arran Johnston 2017
Illustrations © as individually credited
Maps © Arran Johnston 2017

Cover: 'The wounding of Lt. Col. Whitney at the Battle of Prestonpans (Painting by Peter Dennis © Helion & Company 2017)

Every reasonable effort has been made to trace copyright holders and to obtain their permission for the use of copyright material. The author and publisher apologise for any errors or omissions in this work, and would be grateful if notified of any corrections that should be incorporated in future reprints or editions of this book.

ISBN 978-1-804515-67-9

British Library Cataloguing-in-Publication Data.
A catalogue record for this book is available from the British Library.

All rights reserved. No part of this publication may be reproduced, stored in a retrieval system, or transmitted, in any form, or by any means, electronic, mechanical, photocopying, recording or otherwise, without the express written consent of Helion & Company Limited.

For details of other military history titles published by Helion & Company Limited, contact the above address, or visit our website: http://www.helion.co.uk

We always welcome receiving book proposals from prospective authors.

In memory of
Derrick Charles Flintstone
1931-2017

Contents

List of Illustrations	vi
List of Maps and Plans	viii
Preface	ix
Acknowledgements	xi
Introduction	xii
1 Prestonpans	19
2 'The King's Friends in the North'	39
3 'Very Troublesome Neighbours'	57
4 The Race to the Capital	73
5 The Road to Prestonpans	96
6 The Battle: Day One	124
7 The Battle: Day Two	153
8 Beyond the Battle	184
Epilogue	205
Appendices	
I Orders of Battle for the Opposing Armies at the Battle of Prestonpans	213
II Letter from Lieutenant Colonel Shugborough Whitney to Lieutenant Archibald Campbell, aide-de-camp to Major General Humphrey Bland	215
Bibliography	217
Index	221

List of Illustrations

Detail from John Slezer's 1693 'Coast of Lothian from Stony Hill', which looks eastwards over Musselburgh towards Prestonpans. (Reproduced with permission of the National Library of Scotland, Edinburgh)	19
A view of Prestonpans from Dolphinston. (Author's collection)	23
The original haven at Cockenzie, to the east of the later harbour. (Author's collection)	27
Preston Cross and Tower, the heart of the old medieval village. (Author's collection)	30
Rev William Carlyle's church at Prestonpans. (Author's collection)	34
Sir John Cope, by Kate Hunter. (Reproduced with permission of the Battle of Prestonpans 1745 Heritage Trust)	42
Edinburgh Castle from the south, showing the half-moon battery. (Author's collection)	53
Charles Edward Stuart, by Kate Hunter. (Reproduced with permission of the Battle of Prestonpans 1745 Heritage Trust)	63
Glenfinnan, where the Jacobites raised their Standard on 19 August. (Author's collection)	74
General Wade's road, at the western end of the Corrieyairack Pass near Fort Augustus. (Author's collection)	80
Ruthven Barracks, Badenoch, which successfully defended against the first Jacobite attempt. (With thanks to David Beards)	87
The Royal Palace of Holyroodhouse, where Charles Edward held court and council from 17 September until 1 November. (Author's collection)	97
The Cromwell Harbour at Dunbar, where Cope landed the British army. (Author's collection)	103
Hunter's Bog, 'the hollow between the hills', where the Jacobite army camped on 17 September. (Author's collection)	107
View over Linton Bridge towards the village, where Carlyle re-joined the redcoats. (Author's collection)	114
View of Traprain Law from the Dunbar-Haddington road as it crosses Pencraig Brae. (Author's collection)	117

LIST OF ILLUSTRATIONS vii

Haddington Cross. The blue and white castellated building is the George Inn, where Carlyle dined with the dragoon officers before the false alarm on 19 September. (Author's collection)	119
The Causeway, Duddingston, where Charles Edward Stuart held his Council of War on 19 September. (Author's collection)	122
'A Plan of the Battle of Tranent', a contemporary illustration showing the various redeployments of the British line. (Reproduced with permission of the National Library of Scotland, Edinburgh)	125
View from the Gladsmuir, looking north-west towards the actual site of the battle.	133
The Roman Bridge, Musselburgh. The Jacobites crossed from right to left on the way to Prestonpans. (Author's collection)	135
View from the Jacobite's first position, on Birslie Brae, across to Cope's position in the north-east. (Author's collection)	139
The ridge west of Tranent, Birslie Brae being to the right, as viewed from the Tranent Meadows. Walter Grosset observed the Jacobites' initial position from near here. (Author's collection)	142
The Heugh, from which Walter Grosset was attacked on his scouting mission. Tranent church is on the left, with its defensible walled churchyard. (Author's collection)	145
Looking north-east across Cope's position at the end of day one. The Jacobites would appear off to the right the following morning. (Author's collection)	147
Colonel Gardiner's home, Bankton House, viewed from north through the avenue of trees along which it was once approached. (Author's collection)	149
The Waggonway heading north across the plain. The British army slept in the field to the left, marching over the tracks the following morning to deploy. (Author's collection)	154
The Riggonhead March, by Andrew Hillhouse. (Reproduced with permission of the Battle of Prestonpans 1745 Heritage Trust)	158
View from just forward of the British left towards the Jacobite right. The MacDonald regiments would have charged over this stubble field straight towards the camera. (Author's collection)	162
The view of the charging Camerons and Stewarts as they headed towards the artillery and Gardiner's Dragoons. (Author's collection)	163
The Surrender of Cockenzie House, by Andrew Hillhouse. (Reproduced with permission of the Battle of Prestonpans 1745 Heritage Trust)	172
Thorntree Fields, later the site of Thorntree Mains farm. The fallen are believed to be buried in this area. (Author's collection)	181
Memorial to Captain John Coltrane Stewart of Lascelles' Regiment, Prestonpans churchyard. (Author's collection)	192
The Colonel Gardiner Monument at Bankton, viewed from the south. (Author's collection)	198
The *Battle Bing* viewpoint pyramid at Meadowmill. (Author's collection)	202

List of Maps and Plans

1	Prestonpans and vicinity in 1745.	21
2	The distribution of the British army in Scotland immediately before the Rising.	47
3	Phase One of the northern campaign: the race to the Corrieyairack Pass.	76
4	Phase Two of the northern campaign: the race to Edinburgh.	91
5	Edinburgh in September 1745.	101
6	The British army's march from Dunbar to Haddington.	110
7	The Jacobite army's march from Edinburgh to Tranent.	129
8	The British army's march from Haddington to Preston.	131
9	Positions on the afternoon of 20th September.	138
10	Positions on the night of 20 September.	151
11	Positions at dawn on 21 September.	160
12	The collapse of the British right wing.	165
13	Events following the main engagement.	175

Preface

> I cannot let slip this occasion of giving a short account of the Battle of Gladsmuir, fought on the 21st of September, which was one of the most surprising actions that ever was. We gained a complete victory over General Cope, who commanded 3,000 foot and two regiments of the best dragoons in the island, he being advantageously posted with also batteries of cannon and mortars, we having neither horse nor artillery with us, and being to attack them in their position and obliged to pass before their noses in a defile and bog. Only our first line had occasion to engage, for actually in five minutes the field was cleared of the enemy, all the foot killed, wounded or taken prisoner, and of the horse only two hundred escaped, like rabbits, one by one. On our side we only lost a hundred men between killed and wounded, and the army afterwards had a fine plunder.
>
> Charles Edward Stuart, Jacobite Prince of Wales

The victor of Prestonpans was almost as surprised at the scale of his success as everybody else was. Even ten days after the battle, in this letter to his father from their ancestral palace at Holyroodhouse, Charles Edward Stuart could not hide his amazement. His account does not boast of the courage of his men, the brilliance of his officers, or of his own inspired leadership; instead it lists the reasons why the Jacobite army should have failed. He writes of the number of his enemies, their advantages in cavalry and firepower. He recalls the strength of their position and the obstacles which had to be overcome in order to get to grips with them. And yet, despite the odds being so clearly stacked up against them, the victory of the Highlanders was total. If Charles Edward Stuart was surprised, how much more so were his opponents!

The young Prince was right to be impressed by his army's achievement. His army had been pulled together in just a few short weeks and then forced to cut its teeth against trained soldiers after marching to the other side of the country. So on paper the outcome of this engagement ought never to have been in doubt; only the most reckless gambler would have predicted the outcome to be as it was. But the Jacobites were nothing if not gamblers, and Charles Edward had won. In so doing he had turned a local insurrection into a serious challenge to the government of King George II.

But had the Jacobite army really won the Battle of Prestonpans, or had the British army lost it? Was the outcome, which put so much heart into the Jacobite cause, down to the strengths of the victors or the errors of the vanquished? To answer, we must immerse ourselves in those dramatic, bloody, and confusing events of 21 September 1745.

Acknowledgements

I wish to thank all those in the communities surrounding the battlefield who cherish this heritage and who have been so supportive of efforts by myself and others to understand, promote and protect this important historical site.

I am especially indebted to the Battle of Prestonpans (1745) Heritage Trust and its founder Gordon Prestoungrange. In the ten years that I have so far been involved with the trust I have met many fascinating people, discovered many new skills, and shared the story of this remarkable battle with a wider audience than I could ever have found alone. I am grateful to all those who have helped along the way, and look forward to many more such years.

This seems an appropriate place to thank Martin Margulies for his transatlantic friendship, and for his annual visits to the regimental dinner of the Alan Breck's Prestonpans Volunteer Regiment. The Brecks themselves deserve special mention for their passion and commitment to keeping the history of this battle alive. In that vein, I must also acknowledge Ed Bethune and his colleagues at the 1722 Waggonway Project.

For their permissions to reproduce images I am grateful to the Battle of Prestonpans (1745) Heritage Trust, Andrew Hillhouse, and the National Library of Scotland. I would also like to thank Peter Dennis for his powerful cover illustration showing the wounding of Lieutennat Colonel Whitney, and Roddy Tulloch for permission to publish a letter written by Whitney from his private collection.

I am grateful to Helion for providing me with this opportunity to lay out the results of my work at Prestonpans, and I hope the resulting volume proves valuable to others who might one day wish to build upon it.

Most importantly of all, I would like to thank my wife Fiona for her patience and support, and our daughter Charlotte for keeping me smiling.

Arran Paul Johnston
Dunbar, July 2017

Introduction

'On Gladsmuir shall the battle be!' prophesied Thomas the Rhymer of Erceldoune in the thirteenth century. Like all good prophecies, the verses are sufficiently obscure to invite plenty of interpretation, denial, and belief. Thomas' were popular and well-known in Scotland, so when a Highland army swept away its red-coated opponents within a few miles of Gladsmuir village in East Lothian, it appeared to some as if the ancient promise was being fulfilled. Thus the Jacobites of 1745 began to speak not of the Battle of Prestonpans, but of the Battle of Gladsmuir. The name had other advantages too: it avoided association with Preston in Lancashire, scene of Scottish defeats in 1648 and 1715. But to most non-Jacobites the link between the battlefield and Gladsmuir was weak: they named the engagement after the nearby settlements of Preston or Prestonpans. The latter soon became the norm.

There is no battlefield quite like Prestonpans. Although relatively small numbers of men were involved, they fought within a fascinatingly rich landscape of settlement, agriculture, and early industry; a landscape representative of Lowland Scotland on the cusp of the Industrial Revolution. On this little battlefield was also an engaging concentration of influential people and evocative names, from the Bonnie Prince of legend to the earls, lords and chieftains who stood on that day for all of Scotland's many faces: Highland, Lowland, and Borders; urban and rural; law lord and feudal chieftain; Jacobite and Hanoverian. There were men who were already famous and men who would become famous in the near future, from politicians and military commanders to some of the leading doctors, clerics, and historians of the Scottish Enlightenment. Here was a battle which would inspire poetry and song in Scots, English, and Gaelic – songs as diverse as *Hey Johnnie Cope* and *God Save the King* – and would form the centre-piece of the first great historical novel, Walter Scott's *Waverley*. This cultural legacy of the Battle of Prestonpans continues to this day, with artists, playwrights and hundreds of volunteer embroiderers all creating new works in recent years. Monuments on the battlefield have been raised in stone in three different centuries. This battlefield means something.

In the short term the battle mattered because, as with most great battles, its immediate ramifications were significant. It saw, for a time at least, the government of Scotland change hands. It ruined some reputations and made others, destabilised a government and threatened to overthrow a king. Without the political and military credibility that Prestonpans gave to the Jacobites, without the materiel of war which it placed in their hands, and without the room it gave them to freely recruit across much of Scotland, there would have been no march on London and no decision to be made at Derby. The name of Culloden would not chime so many melancholy chords, as no battle need ever have taken place there. But this does not mean, as is so often assumed, that the clan system of the Highlands would have survived and flourished if the last Jacobite Rising had never happened or else had been defeated in its infancy: the road may well have been longer and perhaps less painful, but the direction of travel had already been determined. It is however possible that if the Jacobites had been defeated at Prestonpans, then the aftermath of the Rising would have been more moderate as the threat that they posed would never have become so acute.

Without the victory at Prestonpans then, it is doubtful whether the '45 would be any more famous today than its inglorious predecessor in 1719. The name and face of Charles Edward Stuart would not be recognised the world over, would not appear on so many classroom walls, and would not form a central pillar supporting Scotland's tourism industry. If the outcome at Prestonpans had been different, perhaps some of the sad laments spawned in the wake of Culloden might instead recall the blood stained field of Prestonpans, but it is doubtful that they would be so many or so famed. Perhaps there might still be a folk song or two about Lieutenant General Cope, but they would be of a rather different tone to *Hey Johnnie Cope*. Certainly the Prince's cause could not have survived an early battlefield defeat, and the Rising would have been dead in the water.

It is also worth wondering whether a Jacobite defeat at Prestonpans would have held any great interest to the military historian. The defeat of a hastily raised, untrained, and indifferently equipped force of Highlanders by a professional army with an advantage in firepower and horse; the vain endeavours of an inexperienced exile starting out with a few friends and several crates of supplies, overwhelmed by the resources of an advanced state already mobilised for large-scale warfare. These are not even the ingredients of a good story, far less the cause for ongoing interest and in-depth investigation. But that is not what happened.

In fact, nothing that happened in this month-long campaign seems to have happened the way it should have done. A recently-built network of modern roads and fortifications failed utterly in their purpose to contain local disturbances; a supposedly disarmed population produced an army the same size as the government's within a few weeks; an experienced general found himself wrong-footed and outmanoeuvred by a plucky amateur; a capital city fell without a shot being fired; and a regular army was scattered in minutes by an enemy it thought contemptable. For the Jacobites this was a victory against the odds, and that makes for inspiring reading whatever the final outcome of the war seven months later.

To explain these events, the British army in Scotland has been presented as raw and under-prepared, badly led by an incompetent and timid general, and abandoned in the moment of crisis by its senior officers. The soldiers fled in abject terror from a fierce warrior-race with rippling muscles and savage weapons, led by chieftains who represented an older, purer Scotland that was soon to be extinguished forever. Of course the Prince himself has both fans and critics, so much so that it seems that one must hold to one extreme view or the other, but he is still commonly perceived as staying in the background whilst wiser heads – Lord George Murray's in particular – engineered him a stunning victory. Prestonpans, it seems, was a heroic fluke, doomed never to be repeated.

But is there actually any truth in all this? The Battle of Falkirk suggests that Prestonpans was no pure fluke, yet the outcome at Culloden is usually considered inevitable. What we find at Prestonpans are two armies which, whilst very different in many ways, were surprisingly well matched in both numbers and capacity. Together we are about to explore how that situation came about, and how the battle came to be fought in Prestonpans and not in some other noble spot further north (the Battle of Snugborough?). Then by following closely in the footsteps of the armies as they cross East Lothian we will look for the subtle hints in those final days which shed light on why events played out the way that they did. For that last week of the campaign we must therefore look in detail at the movements and moods of the armies, and the fascinating little episodes which for all their apparent absurdity might have affected the outcome of the coming battle.

In doing all this we will seek out some of the real people involved in these momentous events, soldiers and civilians alike, so as to gain a sense of what *they* thought happened. Thus we not only find the best evidence for what actually occurred, but we also remind ourselves not to see battles merely as shaded blocks drawn across two-dimensional contour-lines; instead we see them as live and unpredictable events, experienced by real people in real time. Perhaps that way we can get a truer sense of what the Battle of Prestonpans really was like.

We are immensely fortunate that so many voices from Prestonpans can still be heard. This book draws its material almost entirely from the letters, narratives, and memoirs of people who were close to the story. From amongst the Jacobites we are blessed with narratives by senior figures such as John William O'Sullivan, Lord George Murray, Lord Elcho, and John Murray of Broughton, as well as from lower ranking officers like John Maclean and James Johnstone. On the other side, the official inquiry into the defeat provides us with an unprecedented richness of material from all ranks of the British officer corps: Sir John Cope himself, Thomas Fowke, Peregrine Lascelles, the Earl of Loudoun, the Earl of Home, and countless aides and other officers give testimony covering the details of the campaign. Others wrote about their experience in private correspondence.

There are also numerous civilian accounts, including those of Patrick Cricthon, John Home, Andrew Henderson, Alexander Carlyle, and Hew Dalrymple, Lord Drummore. All of these listed were hostile to the Jacobites, but as civilians had little reason to cover the failings of the military. Carlyle is particularly important to this study, despite the fact that his memoir was written many years after the battle, because he lived on the battlefield as well as participating in it; he therefore knew the landscape and the community intimately. We also have maps and plans drawn at the time from personal or eye-witness experiences, as well as contemporary newspaper accounts and official documents. Few primary sources are without fault or bias of course; most are openly partisan and some are aggressively so. On both sides, writers were influenced by the need to claim credit or deny responsibility, to protect friends or to finger enemies. But it is better by far to have a wealth of such sources, with all their annoying inconsistencies, faulty memories, and confused chronologies, than to suffer like so many battles do from a paucity of detailed first-hand evidence.

This is not of course the first book to cover the Battle of Prestonpans, nor do I expect it will be the last. Most books on the '45 will give you the bones of the story, and the better ones will devote a chapter to the battle rather than a just section or a few paragraphs. But this book is for those who believe the Battle of Prestonpans deserves more than that. Those who think so are already blessed with Martin Margulies' excellent study and his balanced conclusions, which is one of the reasons why I have not written this book sooner. I am fortunate in counting Martin a friend and so I hope he will pardon my trespassing on his ground. I hope also that he can see the value in my own contributions, written ten years on from his own and incorporating some fresh insights based on my intimacy with the battlefield itself. Like Margulies I have concluded that Sir John Cope has been badly maligned for two and half centuries, and it is hard not to feel a pang of sympathy for him. But unlike others I do believe that Cope's career was derailed by the disaster, and that, regardless of any face-saving tactics that may have occurred, he lost the support of the King as a result of his defeat.

Margulies has taken the lead amongst contemporary historians in rehabilitating Cope – who is usually treated with more clemency now than at any time since the battle, at least by historians. This is a process which really began with the Victorian general Sir Robert Cadell, who lived in Cockenzie House a century after Cope's baggage was captured there. I do not have Cadell's experience in battlefield command but I do share his ability to draw on a personal familiarity with the landscape in which the engagement was fought. I have the very good fortunate to live in East Lothian and to travel the routes of these two armies on a daily basis. I see their shadows everywhere I go, and I hope this comes through in my writing. For those less familiar with the area, I have prepared several new maps and plans which I hope will prove useful.

Maps have been very important to the creation of this book, as they have greatly aided my attempts to reconstruct the landscape of East Lothian (or Haddingtonshire) in 1745. Unsurprisingly to any researcher of the period, the most valuable has been General Roy's Military Survey of Scotland which provides an unprecedented snapshot of the country in the decade immediately after the battle. Thanks to the National Library of Scotland, who have now made it freely available online as a digital overlay on satellite images of the modern landscape, it is possible for any inquisitive researcher to peel back the layers of time and rediscover some lost worlds. Although not entirely faultless, Roy's map is an immense achievement and is vital to studies such as this. An interesting aside is that Roy's brother lies buried in the churchyard at Prestonpans. Other helpful maps have included: Taylor and Skinner's 1776 road survey; several late eighteenth and early nineteenth century maps and town plans which have aided my attempts to understand the settlements and communities through which the armies passed; and the first edition Ordnance Survey map from a century after the battle, which nevertheless holds open a window onto the landscape prior to any major twentieth century infrastructure interferences. I have also scoured the Name Books, the catalogues of place-names and their possible origins collated by early Ordnance Survey researchers, in pursuit of hidden clues and lost local traditions. This was a task which provided plenty of enjoyable diversions as well as useful information.

The archaeology of Prestonpans battlefield has also been important in informing this book. The archaeological study of the site is by no means comprehensive or complete, but a key survey by Glasgow University in 2008-9 offered significant insights which have been incorporated into my narrative, whilst locally reported finds have also offered further clues to where the critical areas of action might have been. A 2016 survey of a part of Thorntree Fields has revealed the surprising limits of the ground disturbance there, hinting that there might yet be more to be found in some of the areas which are yet to be systematically surveyed, and the community continues to offer up anecdotal evidence and remembered knowledge which cannot be ignored. As a result of all this I have moved, shuffled, and tweaked the deployments at Prestonpans more times even than Johnnie Cope, but based on all the evidence I am confident that my conclusions are at least sound even if not perfect. There are some degrees of accuracy which cannot be achieved, and it would be foolish to claim otherwise.

The same applies to the fraught issue of numbers at Prestonpans. Estimates of the numbers engaged, captured, killed and escaped are rarely consistent except within loose margins, even from those that one might expect to be best placed to know. Whilst some writers, both at the time and subsequently, have taxed themselves over the single digits, I find that since none of the variables can be stated with certainty, the best conclusions we can expect are carefully considered estimates. This is what I have tried to present, and I hope those who enjoy the micro-detailing will forgive my occasional tendency to round up when the evidence is simply too thin for confidence. In fact it is not just numbers which remain uncertain, as, despite the wealth of eye-witness evidence, some of these events happened so fast and were so traumatic to experience that even the best memories were clearly rendered fallible. This makes it occasionally difficult to piece together the true sequence of events, but I have nevertheless tried to present a narrative which is fluent and clear as well as true to the sources. Where there is room for doubt I have said so.

But it is not only the past which can be uncertain. It is important to acknowledge that Prestonpans is a battlefield under threat. Over time, of course, the battlefield has changed, but it has not changed beyond recognition. Far from it, as will be explained in the final chapter of the book. Recent years have, however, brought in a succession of proposals which would go well beyond nibbling at the site's edge. Many in the community, supported by thousands more beyond, have been active in trying to hold back this tide. I therefore hope that what I have set out on these pages not only explains what happened at Prestonpans and why, but also where. Is it really important, I have been asked several times, to micro-study battlefield landscapes? Well, yes it is. It is not always possible, and even a well-documented battle requires margins of error, but where the archaeological record cannot help us the historical often can and *vice versa*. It is the marriage of the two that provides the fullest picture, and that is what is attempted here. So I truly hope, firstly, that this book can serve as a guide for those who wish to understand and explore the battlefield in detail; and secondly, that by expressing clearly what happened and where, there might be less confusion (or wilful ignorance) as to what areas of the site are historically sensitive.

It is time now to offer a light-hearted apology to those local residents who petitioned the *Scots Magazine* in 1745 demanding that the battle be named only after one of the nearby settlements. In defence of my title therefore I offer only this: Gladsmuir is the name by which Charles Edward Stuart referred to the battle, and he did so deliberately and knowingly. The Jacobite army earned its victory, and so the name they chose to give it is important for us to remember too. In reality, of course Gladsmuir is by far the least geographically reasonable of a host of possible names, and I therefore comply with the normal practice and refer to the engagement as the Battle of Prestonpans throughout the book as I have throughout this introduction. Any descendants of those first petitioners who pick this up should therefore forgive its title! I should also add that I occasionally use the word Prestonpans to mean the whole battlefield area, including Cockenzie and Tranent for example.

My use of Gladsmuir on the cover of this book should not of course be assumed to reveal any personal prejudice of my own any more than the fact that I often grant Charles Edward his royal title, or that when I am writing from the perspective of Cope I occasionally refer to the Jacobites as rebels and insurgents. However many parallels it is tempting to draw, the politics of today are not those of 1745 so please do not look for them in these pages.

On the subject of names and titles, there are number of points I ought to clarify in advance. It should be obvious in the text whether the king I am referring to is a George or a James. I have opted to refer to Cope's army as 'the British army' rather than the rather stodgy 'Government forces' or the technically erroneous 'Hanoverian army'. I occasionally refer to them as redcoats too, but mainly for variety and reader familiarity. I use the term Jacobites and Highlanders more or less interchangeably when discussing the Prince's army, which is neither to deny the presence of Lowlanders in the ranks (although still very much a minority in this campaign), nor to assume universal Highland support for the cause. Those from the north who fought for George II are usually identified as 'Highland Companies' or 'Government Highlanders'. When it comes to William Murray, I have titled him 'Tullibardine' until he recovered his estates at Blair and thereafter have tended to use 'Jacobite

Duke of Atholl'. Since his brother (the recognised Duke) is only a minor player in our narrative, that should not become too confusing. The only other names likely to confuse are George Murray and John Murray, one a lieutenant general and the other Charles' secretary of state. These I usually distinguish as 'Lord George' and either 'Secretary Murray' or 'Murray of Broughton'. If I ever refer simply to Murray then it is to be taken as Lord George. To add to the Murray confusion, there were technically two Murray's Regiments in Cope's army since their colonels shared a surname. They are easily distinguished however as one of them was the Highland regiment also known as the Black Watch, and so that is the name I use. As was the custom at the time, and to avoid the confusions created by repeated military reforms, I refer to all other infantry regiments by their colonels' name rather than by their number.

There is one final point I would like to address in this introduction. I was once asked after a presentation whether the fact that the Jacobite cause ultimately failed means that Prestonpans in fact had no lasting effect on history and therefore no great importance. This approach is erroneous for several reasons, most of which I hope are self-evident. For one, it assumes that ultimately a Jacobite defeat was inevitable, and that assumption prevents us from understanding those who took part. For the men who stood on that battlefield the stakes could not have been higher, and the outcome of the battle created a real opportunity for the course of history to be changed. That the potential was never fully realised, for better or worse, must not detract from the importance of the battle in setting in motion the train of events which led to Derby and eventually Culloden. I also believe that even if a battle can indeed be proven to have been utterly pointless and without any serious effects, we still owe it to those who died to care about it. We should be kinder to the memories of those who have fought and died in the long succession of conflicts that have forged our nations. And as Lord George Murray would write after it was all over: 'I believe it will be thought more surprising that we did so much than that we did not do more.'[1]

It is time then that we commence our journey onto the battlefield at Prestonpans. We will view it first in peacetime, in the summer of 1745, when few of its residents could have imagined what was heading their way. By exploring it at the outset, we should later be able to follow the flow of events without the need to break into the narrative for detailed descriptions of the buildings and landscape features which make up the battlefield: we will all by then be equally familiar with them. I hope this is a journey which you can enjoy, as I have tried to make my account as accessible to those with no prior knowledge as to those with an existing interest in the Jacobite wars. And when the smoke of battle has cleared once more and the final pages have been read, I would encourage all of you to put this book in your bag, put your boots on your feet, and make your way to Prestonpans Battlefield to see for yourself.

---

1 Murray, G., 'Marches of the Highland Army', in Chambers R. & Forbes. R (eds), *Jacobite Memoirs of the Rebellion of 1745* (Edinburgh: W & R Chambers,1834), p.30.

1

Prestonpans

In the summer of 1745 the villagers of Prestonpans and its surrounding settlements go about their busy lives without any inkling that events are being set in motion which will bring civil war to their doorsteps and lasting fame to their community. Less than ten miles from the capital of Scotland, the Prestonpans area is full of life and industry, already developing a distinct character from much of the rest of the county. The old medieval market village of Preston is yielding primacy to the burgeoning coastal settlement of Prestonpans immediately to the north, and, although separate still, their communities are closely interconnected. To the south is the mining village of Tranent; to the east the salt making

Detail from John Slezer's 1693 'Coast of Lothian from Stony Hill', which looks eastwards over Musselburgh towards Prestonpans. (Reproduced with permission of the National Library of Scotland, Edinburgh)

community of Cockenzie; and to the west, the larger village of Musselburgh and the road to Edinburgh.

Our journey through the area begins on that road, five miles to the east of the capital's Netherbow Port. Here the road crosses the River Esk by means of a high three-arched bridge, bringing the traveller properly into the county of Haddingtonshire or East Lothian. It is a particularly fine county. It sends two representatives to the Westminster parliament in London, one for the rural county and one for the main burghs of Haddington, North Berwick, and Dunbar. The current burgh Member is Sir Hew Dalrymple, of an illustrious and productive family, whose uncle and namesake will play a supporting role in the coming battle. The county Member is the no-less-distinguished Lord Charles Hay, who fought with King George II at Dettingen in 1743 and then with the king's son Cumberland at Fontenoy in May 1745. There it was Hay who famously invited the French Guards to give the first fire if they so wished. His brother, whose fine tower house at Pinkie stands on the eastern end of Musselburgh, is none other than John Hay, Marquess of Tweeddale and Secretary of State for Scotland. Charles Hay's own property at Linplum House, just to the south of Haddington, is just one of many worthy estates and fine houses which stud the East Lothian landscape.

East Lothian's terrain is varied. It softens from the high moorland tops of the Lammermuirs in the south, through rolling folds of rich and fertile farmland in the centre, to the long arced coastline blending cliffs and crags with open bays and sandy beaches, and a number of good harbours which are fair for fisherman and trader alike. Across the width of the shire runs a line of natural beacons, great rocky remnants of former geological ages: North Berwick Law, gazing out to its off-shore neighbour, the Bass; Traprain Law, ancient capital of the Votadini, with its ringed ramparts as yet unsliced by quarrying; the hump-backed Garletons keeping watch over Haddington; and Falside's long ridge, capped at its western end by the castle keep from which it takes its name. In the extreme east, thirty miles as the crow flies from the old bridge at Musselburgh, the county is bounded by a deep ravine traversed only at the zig-zagging Pass of Pease. It will be another forty-one years before the Pease is bridged, with what will then the world's highest bridge, so for the time being the road still climbs up the steep far slope before it heads along the coast towards the Border, Berwick and England.

To Drummore and Dolphinston

Descending the eastern ramp of the Roman Bridge, we follow the main branch of the road into Musselburgh.[1] This is the main post road to England, an important and busy route which leads past Secretary Tweeddale's tower-house at Pinkie

---

1 Alternatively known as the Old Bridge. There is nothing Roman remaining, although the medieval bridge probably stands on the site of an ancient predecessor which led to the important fort at Inveresk.

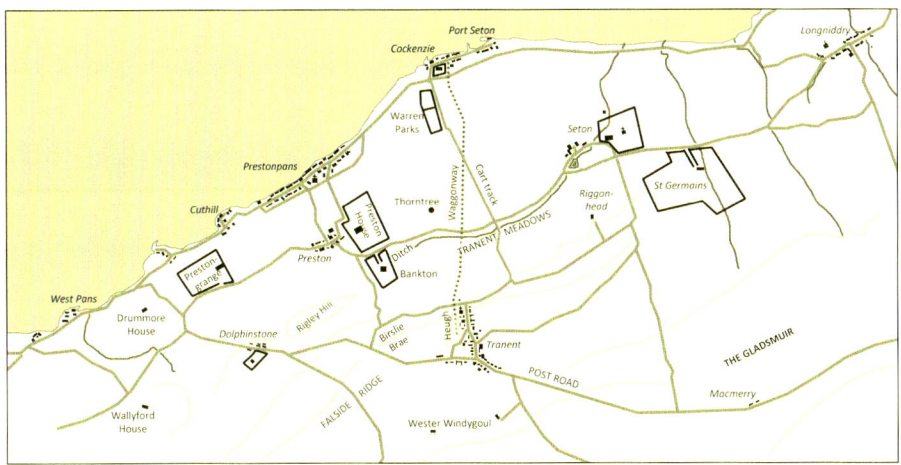

Map 1 Prestonpans and vicinity in 1745.

and continues parallel with the coast until it crosses the little Ravensheugh Burn to reach the agricultural estate called Drummore. At the centre of the estate is a pleasant if not grand house which was known until recently as West Pans, after the little cluster of houses on the coast to the north of it. There you can find men like John Finlayson and Robert Angus working in the salt pans, their wages dependent on the quantities of precious salt which are produced by their labours.

The estate house, just inland of the village, has just been renamed by its new owner Sir Hew Dalrymple, uncle of the Member of Parliament. Just this very year Dalrymple has become a Lord of the Justiciary: Lord Drummore. He is the second son of the late Lord North Berwick, whose brother was the late Master of Stair who was notorious for his hand in the Glencoe Massacre of 1692. His successor, the current Earl of Stair, is therefore Drummore's cousin. This is the famous commander who had led the Pragmatic Army, including Lord Hay of Linplum of course, to victory over the French at Dettingen in 1743 in the presence of King George himself.[2] Another cousin of Drummore – the Dalrymples were certainly prolific – is the master of Newhailes House, a fine place on a plateau overlooking Musselburgh from the west, and which he was busy improving considerably. Drummore does not lack for influential relations.

But at fifty-five, Lord Drummore is not only politically and socially well-connected but also shrewd and intelligent in his own right. He is stout in body

---

2   The Pragmatic Army was so-called because it was assembled from the forces of the allied states which stood by the Pragmatic Sanction of 1713, the edict which allowed for the accession of Maria Theresa to the Austrian throne in 1740.

and possessed of a penetrating gaze, features which the great portraitist Allan Ramsay will soon capture. He is also generous and good spirited, popular in the community for his informal arbitration of local disputes and his charitable giving. Drummore also keeps on his payroll one Geordy Sym, said to be the best bagpiper in East Lothian, although the infamous Simon Fraser, Lord Lovat, criticised Sym's performance when he made a visit to Prestonpans in 1741.[3] Agricultural improvements were underway at Drummore's estate in 1745, and in just a few years the house itself would be replaced with a larger dwelling which better suited his status and would stand the test of time. In short, Lord Drummore comes across as a something of an ideal representation of his type of Enlightenment gentry; for all his local geniality it would not do to forget that he and his extended family are major power-players on the national stage.

Beyond the Drummore estate the road offers two main choices: one branch leads on to the coastal village at Prestonpans, but the main road forks right in search of higher ground, turning sharply south before dog-legging south-east and crossing open farmland towards Dolphinston, a small agricultural village on the western edge of Wygtrig Hill. The ancient name of this low eminence, barely distinguishable from the general slope upwards towards Falside Ridge, has since been corrupted: sometimes it is called Whiggery Hill, of which some residents might approve more than others, but more commonly it is known as Rigley Hill, which is less charming but easier on the tongue. The origins of the settlement name, Dolphinston,[4] are also curious as the little village here seems to have been known as Cowthrople (or Cowthropple) until the seventeenth century. It may be that the name was changed when a new lordly manor house was built here over the top of its more ancient predecessor, to give it a rather grander feel than Cowthrople. The rebuilt castle is, perhaps dubiously, reputed to have housed Oliver Cromwell as he passed through after victory at Dunbar in 1650. If that is so then Cromwell chose it over a number of other appealing options nearby, although Dolphinston did at least boast a prime location on the main London road.

This house or castle was certainly large and stood in a walled enclosure which still survives on the south side of the road, along with the lonely seventeenth century doocot (the Scots word for a dovecote) which is the sole surviving piece of the property. By 1745 Cowthrople/Dolphinston Castle is in poor shape, and it is not singled out on contemporary maps and plans, although that is true of some other nearby properties too. The sixty-four acre estate had been added to the lands of Prestongrange, and so the house had become surplus to requirements. By 1802 it will be a total ruin; only fragments will be visible when the Ordnance Survey came by fifty years later; and just a part of a wall and vault remained visible in 1914. Half

---

3   Carlyle, A. *Autobiography of the Rev. Dr Alexander Carlyle* (Edinburgh: Blackwood & Sons, 1860), p.59.
4   Alternatively Dolphingston or Dolphinstoun.

A view of Prestonpans from Dolphinston. (Author's collection)

a century on and these too had disappeared.[5] But sorry as it might appear in 1745, Dolphinston's decaying castle is still visible as the road passes through the little farming village and continues uphill.

Tranent to St Germains

The road climbs up the rising ground, heading eastwards onto crest of Falside Ridge and running on to Birslie Brae, site of some early medieval coal pits. This shoulder of hill looks down across partially enclosed farmland towards Preston village in the north, but the road itself continues along the crest into Tranent. This is a coal mining community, as digging here on the hilltop brings none of the flooding challenges which are still delaying efforts to mine the coastal seams safely or profitably. Tranent therefore enjoys a beneficial position up on the ridge, straddling the main road between Edinburgh and London. Although part of the village runs either side of the road, however, most of it twists off northwards at a right angle to it. This orientation was probably determined in no small part by the presence of a deep ravine on the western side of the town, known as the heugh. Its steep sides were no doubt a useful defence in former, more dangerous times,

---

5 To view the fragmentary evidence, begin with the reports at https://canmore.org.uk/site/53715/ cowthrople.

and in 1745 we find the heugh to be wooded on each side. Along the bottom runs a waggon road, wooden rails with earth lain between to give the ponies a good footing. This is the Tranent-Cockenzie Waggonway, which was installed in 1722 and is effectively Scotland's first railway line. Its carts carry large quantities of coal down to the salt pans and harbours on the coast below.

On the eastern side of the heugh stands Tranent parish church, the tower peering over the treetops. It marks the northern tip of Tranent and on its northern face the churchyard is supported by a strongly-buttressed retaining wall beneath which runs a hollow way. Across the track, and therefore outside of the walls, stands a tall lectern doocot dating to 1587 which offers a fine view across towards the Firth of Forth. Beneath the north-west corner of the churchyard wall there is something of a crossroads, where the waggonway path is crossed by a west-east track which allows pedestrians approaching from Birslie Brae to bypass the high road to approach the church or to descend along the waggonway route to Prestonpans. There is a gate in the wall to give access from the crossroads into the churchyard, with steps or a ramp to reach the higher ground of the church itself. Most of the congregation, however, come from Tranent and so approach from down the main street, past the old and obsolete Tranent Tower, accessing the churchyard from its south-east corner.[6]

In 1745 this church is far from looking its best. It is an old medieval structure but its architectural integrity has been much hindered by centuries of patchwork alterations. Along with most buildings of any interest or worth in the area, Tranent church had been burned in 1544 by English soldiers on a mission for King Henry VIII to punish the Scots for refusing to marry their infant queen to Henry's young son. The church had then been put back together and re-roofed, unlike its neighbour in Preston which had to be abandoned altogether. For over half a century the villagers of Preston and Prestonpans were obliged to walk to Tranent for divine service, hence the need for that northern gateway, although so few were making the effort that they were eventually given a minister of their own again. But although Tranent church had survived the Rough Wooings, the repairs were probably none too sympathetic to the original structure as the political situation remained very volatile and the Reformation was gaining ground. The building itself comprises of a central nave flanked asymmetrically on either side by shorter aisles. Two pairs of side-by-side buttresses support the north and south walls of the main nave. The long aisles have only narrow windows which admit little light into the centre of the church, above which there rises a squat tower. The interior is dark and gloomy therefore, which only adds to the general sense of neglect. It will be half a century before the whole structure is razed and redesigned. In the meantime, amongst those who warm the pews of this uninspiring setting are

---

6   The north-west entrance port has since been closed up and the churchyard extended partially into the heugh. The only access to the churchyard is via the south-east corner now.

the stonemason Henry Davidson, Robert Penston the gardener, a farmer called Alexander Henderson, and the Gardiners of Bankton House.

Reverend Charles Cunningham's manse stands on the south side of the churchyard, with its windows looking over the graves and the church itself. Houses and cottages line Tranent's main street which runs past the old tower and over the brow of the hill where it joins the high road as described. Much of the land around the village is enclosed with dykes and hedges, or else is pitted with surface coal workings. To the south-west is Wester Windygoul, the home of one John Anderson who had been out in 1715 for the Jacobites. His son Robert runs the family estate at Whitburgh a few miles further out, whilst relations of theirs farm other land in the area. Until recently a branch of the Andersons had also leased the farm at Riggonhead to the north-east of Tranent, where there sloping ground peters out towards the plain. Beside the farmhouse here is a curving defile, like a gash in the otherwise open ground. The farmland is good, but the ground along the base of the ridge is marshy along the whole distance from beyond Riggonhead all the way back to the shadow of Birslie Brae. The water running off the ridge gathers at its base, unable to drain away naturally, creating a morass. In an effort to drain some of this ground, known benignly as the Tranent Meadows, a deep ditch has been cut running parallel with the ridge, nearly one and a half miles in length. This helps make at least parts of the meadows usable, and so some areas are enclosed. Young Robert Anderson finds it good ground for shooting snipe. An old cart track leads from eastern Tranent down across the meadows and over the plain, crossing the waggonway line close to Cockenzie.

Back in Tranent, the main road continues eastwards along the ridge through the village of Make-Merry (Macmerry) and then over the Gladsmuir. Here it traverses a broad stretch of moorland on which there sits a hamlet of the same name and a modest seventeenth century church which is being ably ministered by Reverend William Robertson, a young man with a bright future ahead of him.[7] Apart from an old prophecy by Thomas the Rhymer that a great battle would one day be fought at a place called Gladsmuir, there is nothing remarkable about the moor at all. It is high and open enough to offers views across the river estuary to Fife in the north, or back westwards to Arthur's Seat, the volcanic crag which rises up beside the old royal palace in Edinburgh some twelve miles away. Barely three miles in the opposite direction is Haddington, the county town, towards which the main road now continues. Just beyond Gladsmuir village there is a turning onto a more minor route heading north, and it is this which we now follow as it strikes out directly past Elvingston. In former times it was this road, which soon turns to the left towards St Germains, which formed the main route from Haddington

---

7   Robertson would become Principal of the University of Edinburgh, chaplain to King George III, and a renowned historian. He took over at Gladsmuir parish in 1741, aged twenty. He was a friend of Alexander Carlyle.

to Edinburgh, before the road on the ridge assumed pre-eminence. This original route of the great post road is shown on the Pont and Hondius map of 1573 running through the plain rather than along the ridge. It is still a useful road in 1745 however, bringing the traveller back onto the coastal plain. The medieval hospital of St Germain, established in the twelfth century, had become ruinous even before the 1573 map had been drawn, although the chapel remained in service until the Reformation finally finished it. Now the site has been transformed into a pleasant country estate, and St Germains House will be again be remodelled several times in the coming generations.

Seton and Cockenzie

A short distance along the road westwards from St Germains stands the vast turreted magnificence of Seton Palace.[8] This was once a building which spoke of power and confidence; its high walls, towers, and chimney stacks dominated the skyline of the plain. In its grounds is a fine collegiate chapel whilst to the west of the palace is the humble hamlet which shares its name. But the Palace's days of power are over. This extraordinary house is already in a serious state of disrepair, missing roofs telling clearly of the neglect the building is enduring. This was the seat of the Seton earls of Winton, once powerful magnates and the dominant landowners in this part of Scotland. The Setons had been staunch supporters of the ill-fated Queen Mary throughout the crises of her reign, and their successors were no less loyal to her grandson Charles I during his. True supporters to the last, George Seton had then followed the family tradition in 1715 by supporting Charles I's grandson in his turn. He would be the last of the Seton earls.

Loyalty to both the Royal Stuarts and to the Old Faith was so deeply rooted in the Setons that when the Earl of Mar raised the standard of King James VIII in 1715 it seemed a given that the Earl of Winton would support him. The partisans of George I were so sure of it that Government troopers ransacked Seton Palace even before the earl had declared one way or another, desecrating the family chapel. With provocation added to conviction, Winton duly came out for the Jacobites. He raised a local troop of horse and headed into the borders to link up with supporters both there and in England. He was not at home, therefore, when a large force of Highlanders arrived at Seton that autumn. With the main armies in deadlock at Stirling and Perth, the Jacobites had detached a party under Mackintosh of Borlum and undertaken a daring night-time crossing of the Forth. Their aim was to seize Edinburgh whilst the Government forces were still in Stirling, but the city authorities were unimpressed by Borlum's mere 2,000 men and so closed the gates. The Jacobites had briefly occupied Leith before withdrawing to Seton Palace

---

8 Also known as Seton Castle. Its successor, on the same site but dating to the late 18th century, is known today as Seton House.

The original haven at Cockenzie, to the east of the later harbour. (Author's collection)

and digging in behind its walled enclosures. The enemy then marched out to meet them and the two small armies formed their battle-lines in the open cornfields west of the Seton estate. It must have been a tense encounter, but after only a few desultory shots the Government forces withdrew.

The Jacobites did not stay around much longer either, and they marched south to link up with Winton for an ill-conceived marched into England. In November 1715, on the same day as the Earl of Mar's advance on Stirling was halted at Sheriffmuir, this second army laid down its arms after a day of dramatic street fighting at Preston in Lancashire. Winton was taken prisoner and in due course was sentenced to death. But his time was not yet through: he escaped from the Tower by cutting through his bars, fleeing into exile in France and then Rome. Although the Earl of Winton had survived, his estates and titles were forfeited and his hopes of returning to Scotland were negligible. By 1745 he is sixty-eight years old and living in obscure exile. His mighty palace at Seton stands bare and empty, a tragic memorial to the sacrifice of a remarkable family, and a warning to all of the risks of rebellion.

The Setons had not just been powerful magnates; they had also been important and innovative local landlords and employers. Many local families and businesses were dependent on their successes, and so the effects of the '15 must have been felt keenly by those who lived in the shadow of the great palace. The Winton lands and interests were taken over by the York Buildings Company, a

London-based business specialising in buying up forfeited Jacobite estates and exploiting their assets. Thus there might still be work for men like Christian Ramsay, a labourer living in the village, or his neighbour John Anderson the carpenter, but this sudden replacement of an ancient noble family by a London-based commercial enterprise severed a psychological link in the community. Perhaps some of the Winton's old loyalties still linger amongst their former tenants. After all, the old earl is still alive. He might one day return to reclaim his rights. In the meantime, however, the York Buildings Company has been busy stepping up the commercialisation of the earl's coal and salt assets in an attempt to make the estate profitable.

The 1722 waggonway is the most obvious symbol of this process, the cartloads of coal rumbling along the wooden rails down from the heugh at Tranent, over the marsh on a raised dry bed, and across the farmland until they reach Cockenzie. Here the coal can be used for the salt works or else taken into the harbour for export. Once unloaded, a horse or pony draws the flat-nosed cart back up the waggonway to begin the process again. Cockenzie sits on the coast a little to the north-west of Seton and its Palace, and whilst there is a newer harbour at Port Seton, that of Cockenzie (Cockenny) is of deeper antiquity. The name means the Cove of Kenneth, and his original natural haven survives just a short walk from the harbour. A man-made harbour was created to the west, and in due course this will become the main hub for the exports. Vast quantities of coal are required for the salt pans in Cockenzie itself, however, as these are the drivers of the Cockenzie economy. Buckets on swinging arms draw water up from collection ponds to feed the great iron pans, some perhaps the length of three tall men, beneath which the coal fires burn. Men and boys operate the pans, their women gathering in the salt once the water has boiled off. Working the pans is a family affair, as the Mitchells, Reids, Chrightons and Mackenzies could no doubt tell us.

The manufacture of salt at Cockenzie was such a success by the late seventeenth century that the Setons had a fine house built behind the pans for their manager. A large warehouse was adjoined to the house shortly afterwards, a clear indication of the quantities being produced. The house itself also speaks of prosperity. It faces southwards, many windows looking out over a pleasant garden complete with decorative turrets. The waggonway passes down the eastern side of the property before reaching the coast to feed both the salt pans and the harbour. Later in the eighteenth century its route will change slightly to instead pass down the western side of Cockenzie House, around which a new perimeter wall would be built, stubbing up against the waggonway where it cannot quite complete its right angle. In 1732 a shrewd businessman had moved into the village and leased Cockenzie House from the York Buildings Company after sensing the potential of this busy and productive community. This was William Cadell, whose family would have a long and distinguished association with the property. In the future, with the Company struggling to make sufficient profits from Cockenzie, the Cadells would take over their coal and salt interests and take the industrialisation to a whole new level. But fine though the house and grounds at Cockenzie are, a stroll in William Cadell's garden is not altogether peaceful, with the rumble of coal carts and the whinnying of horses to the fore and the bustle of the harbours and hiss of the pan fires behind. Small though it is, Cockenzie is a village at the forefront of the industrial revolution.

In front of Cockenzie House runs the coast road from Prestonpans, which continues eastwards past Port Seton around the hump of the coastline to Aberlady, North Berwick, and eventually Dunbar. Immediately across this road from Cadell's house is a large area, on the western side of the waggonway, which is set aside for the controlled breeding of rabbits and hares. This warren park is enclosed by hedges and it produces both meat and fur; another addition to the diverse local economy. Within the enclosures is a network of low humps and mounds, and the warren-keepers work hard to encourage their residents to live in ordered communities: it makes them easier to catch. The warren park intrudes into an otherwise open area of good farmland, gently sloping down as it leans towards the sea. These fields fill the space between the coast and the Tranent Meadows drainage ditch to the south, and separate Cockenzie from Prestonpans and Preston in the east. There is a slight depression through part of this field, which tends to become a little boggy, but otherwise the ground is unobstructed. This is fertile and productive land, unenclosed and unwooded except for a single hawthorn tree which stands in the south-western quadrant of the field, visible from the roadside as the traveller makes their way from Seton into Preston.

It is to this road that our attention now returns, the old post road which reaches Seton village after passing St Germains. Beside this village is an unremarkable pool which marks the eastern end of the drainage channel from the Tranent Meadows. The road runs past this little loch, although on its western side it is also possible to cross the ditch by use of a small wooden footbridge. A little further on there is a narrow track which somehow finds a dry route across the marshland to Riggonhead Farm, passing through the defile around the side of the farm before making its way up the slope to Tranent. This is not a route which sees much activity, but it is useful for those who live locally. It is this path which Robert Anderson of Whitburgh uses when visiting relatives or when going for a shoot in the wetlands. The old road prefers to follow the drainage ditch, running along its north side and separating the marshlands from the good farmland beyond. About half way between Seton and Preston the road is crossed by the waggonway as it heads northwards towards Cockenzie. The road falls into line parallel with the Falside Ridge to the south, the tower and doocot of Tranent church clearly visible, and just a short distance further that solitary thorn-tree can be seen off to the right. Beyond this run the long stone walls of another grand estate: Preston House.

Preston and Bankton

Those long stone walls enclose the magnificent formal gardens of Preston House. The grounds and their labyrinthine walkways are a pet project of their owner and are much visited by the gentlefolk of his society. Nor is the house itself unworthy of its charming setting, boasting a subtle grandeur to its main body and to the elegant projecting pavilions to both east and west. One of these houses a fine library, although it was also useful in providing convenient egress for Lord Grange's visiting mistresses. James Erskine, owner of this fine plot and receiver of these nocturnal visitors, is a considerable figure on both a national and local level. He is the brother of the now-exiled Earl of Mar, 'Bobbing John', who had led the Jacobite Rising in 1715. The year before the '15 had seen the death of Queen Anne and the accession of George I, and the latter had snubbed Mar's initial overtures

Preston Cross and Tower, the heart of the old medieval village. (Author's collection)

and dismissed him as Secretary of State for Scotland. Lord Grange had initially shared his brother's misfortunes and was sacked from his legal office. But it was when Mar raised the Standard of the Stuarts in 1715 that Grange discovered his interest in landscaping, keeping his head out of trouble. As the '15 staggered into stalemate and then failure, the brother of its leader worked diligently on improving his gardens at Preston.

In early 1716 the unfortunate Mar headed into exile with his king, who had arrived in Scotland too late to affect the outcome. But Grange had survived and was left with the task of rescuing the family name and fortune: he petitioned hard but vainly for his brother's pardon, and did all he could to keep Mar's Alloa estates in the family. In that he was more successful. His own career recovered for a while, and in 1736 Grange had made his maiden speech at the Westminster Parliament on a subject close to his heart: witchcraft. He opposed the repeal of witchcraft legislation, drawing for his evidence on the large collection of works he had gathered in his pavilion library at Preston. But Grange's interest in the subject was not shared by his fellow members, and the speech inspired more mirth than awe. He was not, it seems, destined to make a name for himself in parliament, and perhaps in part he was limited by the possible taint of Jacobitism lurking at his shoulder. Grange was not entirely free from suspicion in London and this proved to be a political Achilles heel. It is even possible that these career frustrations did indeed lead him into some degree of Jacobite intriguing, although he of all people must have appreciated the appreciate the risks. All told, the last thing a man in Lord Grange's position needed was a major scandal.

Until 1745, his main problem had been his own wife, Rachel Chiesley. Her parents had been unhappy in marriage too, and when the Lord President of the Court found in favour of her mother during their separation, John Chiesley had murdered him. Rachel was just ten years old at the time, but the hanging of her father would not be the last scandal of her life. In time her charms drew Lord Grange's attention and they probably married quickly after an indiscretion, possibly in 1707. Their marriage produced nine children but little lasting happiness. Instead it became an open sore: he had affairs; she drank heavily and publicly embarrassed him. Alexander Carlyle, son of the minister in Prestonpans, remembered how as children they took turns to act as sentry whilst playing at Preston House, lest the lady of the house approach. Carlyle thought the vigil unnecessary, since she always made such a racket that she could be heard coming.[9] The lord and lady separated, but Rachel continued to harass and harangue her husband until even their sons had lost patience with her. Grange despaired of a solution, perhaps afraid that his wife might make the sort of accusations which could ruin him politically. He had to lock up his papers at Preston for fear of what his wife might steal or reveal.

9   Carlyle, *Autobiography*, p.13.

In 1732 Grange and his friends came up with an extraordinary remedy. Rachel was forcibly kidnapped from her townhouse in Edinburgh and rushed first into the Highlands then on to the lonely island of St Kilda. Simon Fraser, Lord Lovat, was deeply involved in the abduction. Lady Grange's volatility had been well known in Edinburgh society, most of which now acquiesced in the assumption that she was being confined in some comfortable castle in the north. Her increasingly scandalous behaviour had ensured that no great efforts were made to rescue her. But Rachel managed to slip letters out of St Kilda and by early 1745 harder questions were being asked. But then she died in May of this momentous year, before her fate could become commonly known.

Lord Grange will be remembered most for the outrageous fate which befell his wife, and however much he might have been provoked the solution applied to his problems was surely extreme. But the fact that he was able both to execute such a scheme and to survive any ramifications shows just how much influence he is able to draw upon in Scotland. In London, on the other hand, greatness still seems to evade him. He finds solace in the company of a Scottish coffee-house owner in Haymarket, and shortly after hearing the news of Lady Grange's death they marry. Now he spends less and less time in Preston. Despite the treatment of his wife, it is hard to take a dislike to James Erskine. He certainly comes across as a big personality, perhaps pompous and certainly a little eccentric, combining a heartfelt faith with a love of good company and even better claret. It is not just female company that slips through those pavilion doors: at the manse in Prestonpans, Mrs Carlyle can often be heard to mutter that her husband enjoys the drinking at Preston House at least as much as the theological discourse!

In laying out those fine gardens of his, Lord Grange had moved the old post road slightly to the south off its original course. The new enclosures might even have brought the former market place of Preston into his grounds, inadvertently preserving the fine mercat cross from later interference. Another result is that the road now has to squeeze into a narrow strip of land between Preston House grounds on the one side and Bankton estate on the other. Since the high road over Birslie Brae is now the main road to England, this was shift was presumably seen as unimportant even though it creates a bit of a bottleneck and obliges the road to dogleg back into Preston village. Since Bankton House stands on the south side of the road, amidst grounds which extend into the Tranent Meadows, that property falls into the parish of Tranent. Its owners do not therefore attend Preston church along with the Granges, their nearest neighbours. This is perhaps as well: the straight-laced Colonel James Gardiner probably approves little of the minister's claret-fuelled doctrinal debates.

Gardiner is a hero of Marlborough's wars, his martial reputation somewhat now at odds with his rather severe and godly demeanour in his later life. He purchased Bankton House in 1733 and set up home there with his wife Frances, daughter of the Earl of Buchan. As an Erskine, Frances Gardiner is also related to the exiled Earl of Mar and his brother across the road at Preston House. It is unclear when the name Bankton was adopted for their home, and in 1745 it is still have been common to hear the estate referred to as Olivestob or Olliestob. This is probably a corruption of Holy Stop, the name given to a medieval property which may once have stood on the site of the present house. This had been a stopping point on the Salters' Road for monks making their way from Newbattle Abbey to Preston Grange, who perhaps slaked their thirst at a well here. Their lands had later passed to the Setons and then to the Hamiltons. At the end of the seventeenth century, around the same time as the erection of the salt manager's house at Cockenzie, the Hamiltons built a fine new mansion at Olivestob with distinctive Dutch gables and orange harling. They were themselves related by marriage to the Lord Grange of Preston, but they were later obliged to sell their estate. Hew Dalrymple briefly took up residence before purchasing West Pans (Drummore). Then the Gardiners had moved in. Their estate is bounded by hedged enclosures, and off to its eastern side begins the drainage ditch which runs from here all the way back to its terminus in the pond at Seton, a mile and a half to the east.

The venerable old village of Preston is still in 1745 a distinct settlement from Prestonpans, although their communities are of course inter-connected. Preston had once been the more senior of the villages, benefitting from the advantage of the main London-Edinburgh road. The traffic along this route allowed medieval Preston to develop into a prosperous little market community, and even in 1745 its architecture speaks of that heritage. There is a very fine mercat cross, topped with a splendid royal unicorn, from which important proclamations had once been read and around which the commerce of the village was once focussed. The uninhabited remains of Preston Tower rise above the other residences, once the seat of the local Hamiltons before they built Lord Grange's current abode. Beside the tower also stands the family's pleasant early seventeenth century dower house, whilst on the western edge of the village rises the turreted white mass of Northfield House.

But the glory days of Preston have already passed, and the old market centre has been subsumed into Lord Grange's enclosures. The main road between the capitals had shifted onto the ridge, taking away the trading traffic. The important Chapman's Fair had then moved out of Preston in 1732, following the shift in economic focus to Prestonpans to the north. The 'Priests' Town' did not even have a church of its own any more: the original building had been utterly destroyed in the Rough Wooings and had never been rebuilt, the parishioners being obliged to walk to Tranent for services. It had probably once stood in the vicinity of Northfield House, the latter structure removing any trace of its ruins. When a new church was finally erected after more than half a century, it was built in Prestonpans rather than Preston. So its large houses and walled gardens made the old village of Preston somewhat quieter and more genteel than its northern, economically more diverse, neighbour.

Prestonpans and Prestongrange

Prestonpans, or Salt Preston, is a coastal village formed of a long high street running east to west parallel with the rocky shoreline. The street is not truly straight but kinks in the middle, and at its heart is the spot still known as Aldhammer after the shipwrecked Viking who is said to have set up home here after the loss of his ship. At the start of the eighteenth century a large new dwelling had been erected

Rev William Carlyle's church at Prestonpans. (Author's collection)

in the centre of the street, Aldhammer House, ensuring that the name and the legend would live on. Behind Aldhammer are the salt pans after which the town became known. It is here that the Berries, Rannies, Sinclairs and others perform the labour-intensive process of drawing buckets of sea water up to the shore and into the pans for boiling over coal fires. They work under the watchful eyes of salt officers like William Brown and Thomas Redpath. It takes great quantities of water to make a decent return in salt, and great quantities of coal too, but the effort pays off and the industry has long been integral to the local economy. It even helped the oyster trade, as the best crops are the renowned Pandores oysters, supposedly collected from near the salt pan doors! On the eastern end of Prestonpans stands a windmill, presumably to help draw water up to the pans as a similar structure would later do across the Forth at St Monans.

It is not just the panners and their families who populate Prestonpans of course: there are wrights, gardeners, cobblers, weavers and sundry other trades. There are also brewers, like Andrew Sherriff, who have already established one of the other industries for which Prestonpans would soon become famous, and a growing middle class. The latter includes the Hogg, Mathie, and Young families; Robert Keith of Craig, who would serve on embassies to Vienna and St Petersburg; Colin Campbell, a Commissioner of the Board of Customs; and the customs collector George Cheap. In later life Alexander Carlyle would recall these respectable families and the abundance of playmates they provided for a child growing up in the midst of a modest, safe and pleasant society.

These are the people, rich and poor alike, who make up the flock of Alexander's father, Reverend William Carlyle. His church stands on a rise on the south side of Prestonpans, overlooking the main street. It has a stubby steepled tower on its west end and a fine graveyard about it, while the Carlyles themselves live in a large manse immediately to the east. This is the church which had been built at the very start of the seventeenth century to replace the long-lost church of Preston. Reverend Carlyle is a lively and popular minister, who once bought everyone in The Whale tavern a drink in return for a promise that they would attend church on Sunday. He had preached to a packed house that week. He had been invited to the parish by Lord Grange and had moved up from the south-west with his young family. The existing stipend was found to be grossly inadequate until Grange and Drummore interceded on Carlyle's behalf; in 1732 it had been doubled to £140 a year.[10] This is the minister who enjoyed those long evenings of theological debate with Lord Grange over a tipple or two, to the chagrin of his wife. Their son Alexander, whose later memoir offers such valuable gossipy insights into this community in the 1730s-40s, has not yet begun his own illustrious career in the church, being just a little behind his friend and contemporary William Robertson at Gladsmuir.

10 Carlyle, *Autobiography*, p.3.

On the very western edge of Prestonpans, across the little Red Burn, lies the small village of Cuthill or Cuttle. This collection of fishermen's dwellings is considerably cheered by the presence of two noteworthy watering holes, The Whale and Lucky Vint's. It was whilst visiting the latter with Lord Grange that Simon Fraser had been entertained by Lord Drummore's piper Geordy in 1741. Despite not appreciating the music's quality, Lovat was induced to dance a reel nonetheless. It may have been the fine claret, but it was more likely the bashful dark eyes of the landlord's daughter, Kate Vint. Certainly it was not the plain fare that got Lovat dancing: there was animated discussion over whether the fish was whiting or haddock! Young Kate must indeed have been charming, as even young Carlyle assessed her as 'alluring', despite her country manners.[11] Drummore had also noted Kate's appeal: she became his mistress and bore him two sons. Young Miss Vint would eventually become Mrs Merry after marrying an army officer, but she surely never forgot dancing that reel in 1741 with the notorious Fraser of Lovat.

Beyond Cuthill lies the great estate of Prestongrange which, as its name attests, began its days as a monastic grange belonging to the Cistercians of Newbattle Abbey in Dalkeith. The monks were granted these lands in the early twelfth century by the de Quincys, who had also given over the land for the hospital at St Germains. Prestongrange subsequently developed into a thriving hub of agricultural and proto-industrial activity. The monks and their agents spent the centuries exploiting the area's coal resources and establishing salt pans, as well as making the most of the agricultural potential of the land. By 1526 they had gained permission to build their own harbour north of the grange. Ostensibly this was required to offer safe haven for nearby fishing vessels if they should be caught out on the Forth in severe weather, but the monks were canny estate managers and would have been far more interested in the potential to export coal and salt from their own harbour facility.

This harbour, initially known as Newhaven, took the name of Acheson's Haven after the monks leased it over to a man of that name in the 1540s. After the Duke of Somerset had used Acheson's Haven to supply an invading army in 1547, a stone fort was built to protect the harbour. Only fragments of the fort remain by 1745, certainly not in a viable defensive condition. There are also two tidal mills at the harbour, grinding corn at present but later in the century at least one of them would begin grinding flint for the nearby potteries. Domestic and international trade had boomed during the seventeenth century and into the early eighteenth, with timber, tobacco, and luxury goods coming in whilst coal, salt, pottery, and oysters went out. The harbour originally opened out to the east, but less than ten years after the Battle of Prestonpans it would enjoy a major refurbishment and by the end of the century it had settled into a new form with its mouth facing westwards. In 1745 the harbour is most commonly known as Morison's Haven, but its

---

11 Carlyle, *Autobiography*, p.59.

trade was enduring a temporary slump like so many on the east coast in the wake of the Union.

Prestongrange had been transferred from the Newbattle monks into a secular barony during the Reformation, with Abbot Mark Ker showing a talent for survival by becoming the first lord of the old order's estates. The Kers undoubtedly had to invest heavily in turning the old monastic grange into a stately tower house, not least because the ravages of the Rough Wooings are unlikely to have been kind to Prestongrange. In the refurbishments which followed, a magnificent painted ceiling was installed at Prestongrange in the 1580s, reflective of the family's status. But less than thirty years later the family was obliged to sell up to John Morison, a baillie of Edinburgh. The Morisons would then hold the barony for almost a century and a half, extending Prestongrange House yet again. The land at Cowthrople came under their wing too, precipitating the sudden decline of the new house at Dolphinston. It was William Morison of Prestongrange who gave his name to the old Acheson's Haven after refurbishing it in 1700.

William would be the last of the Morisons to hold Prestongrange, however. He was a considerable figure, sitting in both the last Scottish Parliament and the first of the new British ones. He spent much of his time in either Edinburgh or London therefore, and despite the prosperity of his Prestongrange estates he was facing serious financial difficulties by the 1730s. His debts were enormous, especially those he owed to the notorious gambler Colonel Charteris who had a property at Haddington. Nor could the situation have been helped by the flooding problems which beset his coastal mining interests and further contributed to a slump in trade at his harbour, compounded by the new taxes which came in the wake of Union. Morison was fined twice for trying to evade the salt duty, but the truth was that he needed every pound to stave off the creditors. He died overseas in 1739, leaving his affairs in extraordinary disorder and his estates crippled by debts of scandalous proportion. Alexander Carlyle considered him a simple fellow, the word underlined for emphasis in his memoir, but that is hard to reconcile with a political career which spanned many turbulent decades. He was certainly eccentric, and sufficiently so to believe that the mysterious caves uncovered at Morison's Haven whilst a new water mill was being installed had once been inhabited by St John. A Masonic lodge met at the harbour each St John's Day, and Carlyle suggests this is what put the idea 'into his head'.[12] Morison's dramatic fall from grace was surely the talk of Prestonpans society for some time as his executors struggled to sort out the mess in the early 1740s, and his employees and dependents waited to see what the fall out would be.

It was only in May 1745 that a new owner took up the reins at Prestongrange: William Grant. At forty-four, Grant is a very well-connected former solicitor-general with immaculate Whig credentials. He has long enjoyed the sponsorship

---

12 Carlyle, *Autobiography*, p.7.

and friendship of Archibald Campbell, Duke of Argyll and one of the most powerful forces in Scottish politics, and Grant is as deeply involved in kirk matters as he is in the law courts. Now he is also the senior landowner in the area around Prestonpans, paying £160,000 for the Barony of Prestongrange and Dolphinston.[13] In Grant's time as baron and that of his Grant-Suttie successors, the estate will be pulled back onto its feet and the slump in economic activity reversed. Prestongrange House will evolve too, and the Kers' painted ceiling will be covered over by more fashionable contemporary plasterwork. In the wake of the coming uprising, William Grant of Prestongrange will become Lord Advocate and oversee the application of the Act of Prohibition, but all that lies in the future. The western edge of his estate is marked by the road across which lies Lord Drummore's land, which brings our circular exploration back to where it began.

In all there are probably around 1,500 people living in the parish of Prestonpans and in 1745, and perhaps another 2,500 in that of Tranent (which includes Seton and Cockenzie).[14] These are busy and interconnected communities: the harbours facilitating a thriving export trade as well as supporting the fishing fleets; the inland coal fuelling the coastal salt production; and the good farmland enclosed into great estates with forward-thinking landlords. There have been major social upheavals recently, with first the Setons and then the Morisons falling from grace, but those storms have been weathered and for most residents there is still plenty of work. The area is at the cutting edge of Scotland's agricultural and industrial revolutions, receiving ongoing investment and housing a busy and active population and influential and well-connected gentry. After all, the capital of Scotland, the hub of the Enlightenment, is less than ten miles away.

It is an unlikely setting for a battle.

---

13 Hopkins, B., *A Pride of Panners* (Prestonpans: Prestoungrange University Press, 2004), p.21.
14 These figures are approximate, based on the numbers cited for 1755 in the Statistical Accounts of Scotland 1791-99. They may be marginally too high. See under 'Parish of Prestonpans' in *The Statistical Accounts of Scotland 1791-1845*, at http://stat-acc-scot.edina.ac.uk/link/1791-99/Haddington/Prestonpans/ (accessed 4 November 2016).

2

'The King's Friends in the North'

King George II had probably never given Prestonpans a thought. This bustling little community was a long way from the focus of his attentions until the name suddenly burst into his thoughts in September 1745, and in that he was not unlike most of his predecessors. James VI and Charles I had both briefly visited, the latter being hosted at Seton Palace on the way to his belated Scottish coronation in 1633, but since then there had been no demonstrable royal interest in the area. In fact George II had shown little interest in Scotland at all, although he was certainly aware of its capacity to produce both talented loyalists as well as energetic dissenters.

The king had been born in Hanover, Germany, and until his father's accession on the death of Queen Anne he had never set foot in his future kingdom. The family were newcomers, catapulted to the throne past rival candidates with better claims but lacking in their impeccable Protestant credentials. As the second Hanoverian king, George II did at least enjoy advantages which his father had lacked: he had the inherited legitimacy of descent from a crowned predecessor who had eventually been accepted by the majority of his people. He also had more time to accustom himself to the country and ingratiate himself into its society, and George II was far better with the English language than his father had been. In fact he made serious effort to promote himself as being English in spirit if not in birth, efforts which were not entirely in vain. George had quarrelled seriously with his father and become a focus of parliamentary opposition, just as his own son Frederick would do with him, but he had probably felt his throne was pretty secure when he acceded in 1727.

Nevertheless, he had agents in Rome keeping a close eye on the exiled Stuarts, especially the two young princes who had given fresh hope to an old cause. But there had been no serious Jacobite Rising to mark the beginning of George's reign, as the failures of 1715 and 1719 had asserted the military superiority of the ruling regime. There had, however, still been plots in both the 1720s and the 1730s, many, it must be said, driven by English Jacobites, and the Stuarts remained a potential asset to Britain's overseas enemies as well as to internal malcontents.

In 1745 George II's domains were locked in a costly and large-scale continental war. The king himself was an eager proponent of British military involvement in Europe, being naturally determined to protect Hanover's interests as well as Britain's. George II was personally enthusiastic about military affairs and – a serious problem for Stuart ambitions – had gained considerable popularity amongst the Army and its officer corps. In 1743 the king had led the allied army in person at the Battle of Dettingen, becoming the last reigning British monarch to personally lead an army in the field. Sharing in his victory that day were William Augustus, Duke of Cumberland, the king's favourite son;[1] Charles Hay, the Member of Parliament for Haddingtonshire; and Sir John Cope, who would soon become head of the king's forces in Scotland. Both Cumberland and Cope were promoted to lieutenant general for their parts in the battle.

But as the War of the Austrian Succession dragged on, voices began to mutter that British coin and British lives were being spent on the preservation of Hanover, and that the price was perhaps not worth paying. The government was destabilised and John Carteret resigned as Secretary of State in 1744. The war was in deadlock and France was in discussions with the Stuarts about a potential invasion of Britain. By the summer of 1745 the king himself was in Hanover and his son Cumberland had been soundly beaten by the French at Fontenoy. Britain's eyes were firmly fixed on the Germany and the Low Countries.

In Scotland meanwhile it appeared to be business as usual. A few suspected Jacobite conspirators were arrested but there were no real signs of exceptional trouble. That certainly seems to have been the view of the Secretary of State for Scotland, John Hay, fourth Marquess of Tweeddale and brother of the East Lothian Member of Parliament praised for his valour at Dettingen. Tweeddale was close to John Carteret, Earl Granville, the minister who had been forced to resign as Secretary of State for the Northern Department at the end of 1744, under pressure from the more anti-war Prime Minister Henry Pelham. Carteret had been with the king at Dettingen too and was closely associated with the king's zeal for defending his continental interests, an increasingly unpopular position. Sir John Cope, who had served in parliament as well as in the army, considered that Carteret's resignation cast the government onto 'a stormy sea'.[2] Secretary Tweeddale was also governor of the Bank of Scotland, which did not help his rivalry with the Duke of Argyll who ran the newer Royal Bank of Scotland. If problems did arise in Scotland it would be Tweeddale's job to oversee their settlement, and in the turbulent political climate at Westminster he could not afford many slip-ups.

The Secretary of State administered Scotland from London, so the government's key representatives on the ground itself were the heads of the judiciary and the military commander. George II was blessed in enjoying the services of the

---

1 Van der Kiste, J., *King George II and Queen Caroline* (Stroud: Sutton Publishing, 1998), p.111.
2 Warrand, D. (ed.), *The Culloden Papers* (Inverness: Carruthers & Sons, 1927), Vol.III, p.214.

energetic Highlander Duncan Forbes of Culloden, Lord President of the Court of Session, a highly influential personality who divided his time between Edinburgh and his fine estate near Inverness. Forbes was well-connected and made it his business to know that of others. It was particularly valuable that Forbes had such strong links to the Highlands, understanding not only the mood of the clans but also the balances of power, loyalty and rivalry amongst their chiefs. Such knowledge was alien to most of George II's representatives and would prove critical in the coming crisis. The king's other chief legal officer in Scotland was the Lord Advocate, who in 1745 was Robert Craigie. He was a close friend of Tweeddale's and was considered by the king to be a trustworthy and reliable Whig.[3] But as an associate of Tweeddale and therefore of Carteret, Craigie's position was also vulnerable whilst the administration was dominated by Pelham and his brother, the Duke of Newcastle. Both the foreign and domestic political situations were far from stable in 1745.

These were the men who made and enforced Britain's laws; it fell to others to defend them.

King George II's military forces in Scotland were commanded by Lieutenant General Sir John Cope, a career soldier who was considered to be a safe pair of hands for such a position. Although his role in the events of 1745 has been much scrutinised – sometimes lampooned and at other times vindicated – it is less common to find serious analysis of his career, let alone his character. Cope has become a two-dimensional figure, which is as unfair as it is unhelpful. The reality is that he was an experienced and competent officer with a long and distinguished service record, who can hardly have imagined when he came into his Scottish posting that it would forever destroy his reputation.

Jonathan Cope was born in 1690 in Icomb in Gloucestershire. He had already been disinherited by his grandfather William to mark his disapproval at his son's marriage to Dorothy Walker, the widow of an excise man. The reason of such extreme disapproval is unclear, but William had himself married the daughter of an earl so perhaps he considered his son's match to be beneath them. Henry had been a soldier just as his two sons would be: he joined the Coldstream Guards as an ensign in 1670 and rose to become a captain.[4] He then resigned his commission for unknown reasons, but since it occurred in that momentous year of 1688 there may have been a political motivation. Henry seems to have resigned in April, six months prior to the landing of William of Orange, so it is unlikely to have been triggered by a refusal to accept the new regime. Perhaps it was a revolt against King James' Declarations of Indulgence suspending penal laws against religious non-conformity, which were issued around that time. The Copes had connections

---

3   Ramsay, J. *Scotland and Scotsmen in the Eighteenth Century* (Edinburgh: William Blackwood and Sons, 1888), Vol.I, p.110.
4   MacKinnon, D. *Origins and Services of the Coldstream Guards* (London: R. Bentley, 1833), p.453.

Sir John Cope, by Kate Hunter. (Reproduced with permission of the Battle of Prestonpans 1745 Heritage Trust)

to Ireland which may have influenced their opinions regarding the king's pro-Catholic leanings. Alternatively, of course, there could have been some totally unknown personal motivations.

Young Jonathan appears not to have been unduly disadvantaged by either his grandfather's will or his father's resignation from the Army: he attended Westminster School in the same year as John Carteret and just a few years ahead of future Prime Minister, Henry Pelham. Cope later travelled to Berlin as a page to Queen Anne's ambassador there, Thomas Wentworth, Lord Raby (later Earl of Strafford). Raby proved to be a useful patron, securing Cope a commission as cornet in the Royal Regiment of Dragoons, of which he was then colonel. Diplomatic duties kept Raby in Berlin away from his regiment, but Cope immediately travelled to Spain in 1707 in order to take up his new post. The War of the Spanish Succession brought plenty of opportunities for action, and Cope made a good impression. His commander reported back to Raby that, 'Mr Cope will make a very good officer if I am not mistaken, and I do not see he is given to any manner of vice.'[5] He was offered a staff post by General Stanhope, a sure way to come to the notice of his superiors, and took part in the successful Minorca expedition of 1708. The following year Cope was able to borrow enough money to purchase a captaincy in Wade's Regiment of Foot (later the 33rd Foot) for £350, although that commission lasted but briefly before a more profitable cavalry troop came his way.

Now a captain of Lord Peterborough's Regiment of Dragoons, Cope returned to action in Spain. He was amongst the 46,000 men who fought at the Battle of Almenar in July 1710. Typically of a young officer, however, John Cope was restless and eager to secure advancement. A few months after the battle he was offered a commission in the 3rd Regiment of Foot Guards, a highly attractive opportunity since Guards commissions carried a higher weight than those of line regiments. Such commissions required royal assent however, and Cope accordingly travelled to England to press for its confirmation. He must have cut a dashing figure in so doing: barely twenty years old and already a veteran with a fine record and recommendations. Cope had married his first wife Jane, daughter of the wealthy MP Anthony Duncombe, who soon gave birth to their son James. Socially as well as professionally, he was showing great promise. Captain Cope was also lucky. Whilst he was in England pressing for confirmation of his new commission, Stanhope's army in Spain suffered a major reverse at the Battle of Brihuega. The General was a prisoner, as were most of Peterborough's Dragoons. The British troops had fought valiantly but in vain, and most now faced a year in captivity. Cope was fortunate to avoid sharing their fate, although the disaster meant that nobody now wanted to buy his commission in Peterborough's.

Cope's career was able to continue in the ascendant however, as Lord Raby now recommended him to the new commander in the Spanish theatre, the Duke of Argyll, who would later battle with the Earl of Mar at Sheriffmuir. A wounded officer looking for an honourable way out of the frontline was happily found, a man content to accept the otherwise unattractive dragoons post. Cope was able to transfer into Macartney's Foot as lieutenant colonel in April 1712 (the weight of his Guards commission giving him a lift). The very next day, however, Cope moved to Wynne's Regiment of Foot as a means of resolving an internal friction between its colonel and another officer seeking advancement. The other officer swapped commissions with Cope to avoid future tensions with his superior. Cope joined his new regiment at Antwerp and in 1713 was brevetted to colonel. Crucially the rank was back-dated by more than a year, giving Cope a considerable jump in the army lists. That year also marked the end of the war, however, and the pace of his progress would now slow.

5   Letter from Colonel James St Pierre to Lord Raby, 6 January 1708, quoted in Burton, I & Newman, A., 'Sir John Cope: Promotion in the Eighteenth Century Army', *The English Historical Review*, 78: 309 (October 1963), pp. 659.

Colonel John Cope was nevertheless in a strong career position, gaining another Guards commission in 1715 as the Jacobite threat erupted once more, but the 1720s were relatively peaceful and so he was able to turn his hand to politics. Cope served for five years as the Member of Parliament for Queenborough in Kent, and from 1727 until 1734 for Liskeard in Cornwall, where a constituency of fewer than fifty elected two members. A rare contest saw him fail to secure Orford in Suffolk in 1734, but he took the seat four years later and held it until 1741. During that time he supported Robert Walpole, which put him at odds with his former patron Lord Raby, now the Earl of Strafford. Strafford was a Tory and the Hanoverian succession did him few favours: for his part in the Congress of Utrecht in 1715 he was impeached, Walpole himself reading aloud from Strafford's private papers. He retired to his fine new mansion at Wentworth Castle in Yorkshire, where the magnificent plasterwork there still speaks of his true sentiments: designs based on oak leaves were associated with the Royal Stuarts. Strafford was soon in direct communication not only with Jacobites but event with the King across the water himself.[6] He was a key player in the Atterbury Plot, which collapsed in 1722 just as John Cope was entering Parliament.

During this period Cope's older brother Henry had travelled a rather different path. He had resigned his Army commission in 1715 and crossed the ocean to set up business in the American colonies. His interests took him to New England, Nova Scotia, and Newfoundland, but Henry would re-join the colours when war broke out with Spain in 1739. He became lieutenant colonel of the American Regiment of Foot, but campaigning in the Indies proved fatal to his health and he died of fever in Jamaica in 1742, just as his younger brother was returning to the main theatre of war in Europe.

Benefitting from his seniority on the lists, John Cope had become a brigadier general in 1735 and a major general four years later, whilst possessing the colonelcies of the 39th Foot, the 5th Foot, the 9th Dragoons and then the 7th Dragoons. It was with the latter that Cope returned to Europe in 1742. The following year he led the second line of the British cavalry at the Battle of Dettingen, for which he was promoted to lieutenant general and invested as a Knight of the Bath. Sir John Cope was fifty-three years old, his son James had entered the diplomatic service, and he could look back on an active career and an unblemished record. His greatest independent command followed, when the king appointed him as commander-in-chief of the army in Scotland.

It is not easy to gain a clear vision of what sort of person Sir John Cope really was. As a young officer he earned the praise of senior commanders, and he rose through the ranks with considerable speed. In his restless ambition Cope was no different to most other officers in his position, although he clearly possessed an aptitude for exploiting the opportunities presented by purchase and patronage as

---

6　Cruickshanks, E. & Erskine-Hill, H. *The Atterbury Plot* (London: Palgrave Macmillan, 2004).

well as merit. He was a veteran of numerous major engagements, campaigning often in rough and unfamiliar terrain, had served with both foot and horse, and had experience commanding large formations in action. There is little from the surviving narrative of Cope's career which inclines us to criticism, but few clues to his nature. His demand for an inquiry in 1746 would show he was protective of his reputation, understandably enough, but not too proud to stand before his peers to defend his actions. Cope's correspondence during the Prestonpans campaign suggests that he was meticulous and clear-headed, not averse to taking action but certainly not impetuous. He was also cautious and perhaps fussy. One complaint is recorded shortly after his arrival in Scotland, of his intention to promote a 'favourite' over the head of another officer who had been raising funds for the same commission, but that is probably no more than an example of Cope exercising the same sort of patronage which had been shown to him.[7] One little hint of a more private vice also creeps into view: Cope enjoyed the company of the ladies, fathering two illegitimate children.

Lieutenant General Sir John Cope took up his post in Scotland on 18 February 1744, exchanging Piccadilly for the ancient city of Edinburgh. In October that year he wrote to Forbes of Culloden that he had 'great reason to speak of Scotland with satisfaction and gratitude,' and that his welcome had been warm.[8] He purchased a fine new home at 26, St James' Place in London. It backed on to Green Park, providing splendid views from its windows, and was just a few minutes' walk from the royal palace in one direction and the Prime Minister's house in the other. It was a location which suggests status and a proximity to power, and an expectation that Scotland need not consume all of his time and attention.[9] Sir John Cope had little reason to suspect that his career would soon come to such a dramatic and damaging climax.

On his arrival in Edinburgh, Cope left the frontline behind him and began a new phase of his career in command of a peaceful home garrison. That did not mean that he was idle or without important work. The continental war was a hungry beast and it needed feeding with large numbers of men. Whilst this meant that the best of the existing army was engaged far from home and that the attention of both king and parliament was focussed on Europe, it also meant that recruitment was a pressing priority at home. Scotland was no exception, and across the country the recruiting officers were placing shillings on the drum and luring both the eager and the idle toward the Colours. The small home garrison which Cope commanded was therefore swelling steadily as fresh forces were raised ready to be sent off to fight King George's war. How little the politics of the Austrian Succession mattered to these men can be readily imagined. General Cope's priorities in Scotland were

---

7   Warrand, (ed.), *Culloden Papers*, (Inverness: Carruthers & Sons, 1927) Vol.III, p.211.
8   Warrand, (ed.), *Culloden Papers*, Vol.III, p.212.
9   Cope does not appear to have purchased any property in Edinburgh.

therefore two-fold: maintaining the peace of the kingdom; and mobilising sufficient numbers of men to satisfy the manpower needs of the warfront. To put those numbers in perspective, John Cope had been one of around 35,000 soldiers in the allied army at the Battle of Dettingen, and at Fontenoy in May 1745 the allied death toll was equivalent to the total number of soldiers available to Cope across the whole of Scotland. Now he was tasked with feeding more men into that system, and in both the Highlands and Lowlands new companies were being formed. To Cope's angst however, he was not the only person recruiting on his patch: he reported to London that French recruiting agents were also operating in Scotland, continuing a long tradition of bringing Scottish soldiers into overseas service.

In the context of a major European war it is hardly surprising that the administration was eager to continue the policy of making the Scots police themselves, or, rather, each other. It had been twenty-six years since the last Jacobite uprising in Scotland in 1719, an inglorious enterprise which had failed to rekindle the fire of the far more serious threat which had been faced down only four years before. But time had not diminished the threat entirely, as 1720 had brought the birth of healthy Stuart prince; the cause of the exiles had passed to a new generation, raised on the stories of Killiecrankie, Sheriffmuir, and Glenshiel. Government agents in Rome watched the young prince closely, and despite attempts to pretend the contrary, Charles Edward Stuart was growing up to be a fit and engaging potential enemy. By early 1744 he was on the north coast of France planning to accompany a French invasion of Britain, and now appeared in no hurry to return to his father in Italy. He had to be taken seriously as a threat. But King George knew that Sir John Cope was a veteran officer with immaculate credentials, and some of the Jacobite ardour in Scotland had already been dampened by several arrests. Vigilance was key. Loyal Highlanders were recruited into Independent Companies, usually led by men they knew and respected socially as well as militarily, and to these fell the task of policing the glens.

Independent Companies of loyal clansmen had been used in previous periods of civil conflict, but they were re-established in the 1720s as a means both of improving order in the Highlands and deterring further Jacobite activity. Legislation had been introduced in the wake of the '15 to disarm the clansmen, but of course the loyal were more likely to obey than the disaffected. When George Wade had taken command in Scotland in 1725 he had further tightened enforcement (the law was tightened too) and the Independent Companies were established to ensure that the loyal were not left vulnerable. Raiding and feuding would now be controlled by Highland soldiers enjoying the authority and pay of official peacetime recognition. In 1739 ten such companies were merged to form the 43rd Highlanders. Their role in watching over the glens and the darkness of their issued tartan are said to be the source of their more popular and lasting name, the Black Watch. Becoming a regiment of the line brought new risks for its soldiers however: they were ordered to the frontline. Although some mutinied at the prospect, the regiment went on to fight with great distinction at Fontenoy. All that remained in Scotland were

'THE KING'S FRIENDS IN THE NORTH'   47

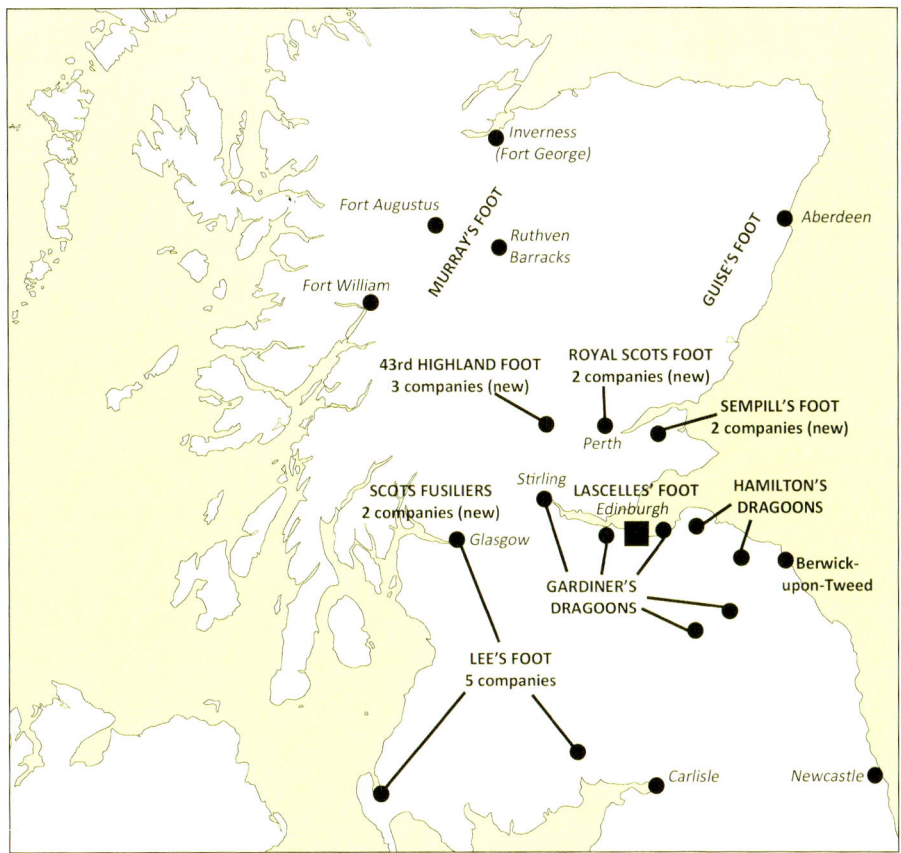

Map 2 The distribution of the British army in Scotland immediately before the Rising.

three companies based at Crieff, although Cope tells us these were 'pretty near complete'.[10] The colonel of the regiment was Lord John Murray, half-brother of the Duke of Atholl and of the Jacobite Lord George Murray.

John Murray's immediate predecessor at the Black Watch had been Hugh Sempill, who had only handed over the colonelcy in April 1745. Another Scotsman, Lord Sempill moved to command of an established regiment which had been formed to defend Edinburgh against the Jacobites back in 1689. It would later become the King's Own Scottish Borderers, but for now Sempill's Regiment was busy bearing

---

10 Robins, B. (ed), *Report of the Proceedings and Opinion of the Board of General Officers on their Examination into the Conduct, Behaviour and Proceedings of Lieutenant-General Sir John Cope, Colonel Peregrine Lascelles and Brigadier-General Thomas Fowke* (London: Faulkner, 1749), p.5. For clarity, evidence from this inquiry will hereafter be referenced as *Inquiry*.

its new colonel's name to glory in the Low Countries. It too fought at Fontenoy, and so only two companies remained in Scotland. They were based at Cupar in Fife, but since draughts were being sent overseas quicker than they could be replaced, these two companies barely mustered fifty men between them. The same was true of the two new companies of Royal Scots based in the important town of Perth. This was the senior regiment of foot on the establishment and was commanded by James St Clair. Another Scottish regiment, the Scots Fusiliers, or Royal North British Fusilier Regiment, had fought under Sir Andrew Agnew of Lochnaw at Dettingen, but once again only two small companies remained behind at Glasgow by the summer of 1745, 'all new rais'd men'.[11] Sir John Cope was therefore unable to call upon the strength of some Scotland's finest soldiers when the storm broke.

He did however have Lascelles' Regiment, which had been formed in Scotland four years previously under the colonelcy of the Englishman Sir John Mordaunt. This white-faced regiment was now commanded by Colonel Peregrine Lascelles, a career soldier from Whitby. Its ten companies were based around Edinburgh and its harbour town of Leith, and so Lascelles' was the most immediate formation available to the general at the Scottish capital.

If Lascelles' was a Scottish regiment with an English colonel, Murray's Regiment was the reverse. Thomas Murray was seventh son of the Earl of Dunmore and commanded the main body of regular forces stationed in the north-west of Scotland. Murray's men (not to be confused with the Black Watch, whose colonel bore that same surname) were quartered in the forts and barracks of the Highlands. Despite its later association with Devon and Cornwall, the regiment had been formed at Newcastle-upon-Tyne in 1741. Its soldiers were mainly English recruits and they wore green facings on their uniforms, which was appropriate enough since they were yet to face action.

Lieutenant Colonel Peter Halkett was, in the temporary absence of his colonel, responsible for the command of Sir John Lee's Regiment of Foot. Halkett had been raised in the splendid surroundings of Pitfirrane Castle at Crossford in Fife, which is now the clubhouse of Dunfermline Golf Club, and he would succeed to the baronetcy there on his father's death in 1746. He was elected as Member of Parliament for Stirling Burghs in 1734, the same year Sir John Cope failed to secure election for Orford. Since Halkett did not stand a second time they may not have known one another personally at Westminster, although they could probably talk of common acquaintances as well as experiences. Five companies of Lee's Regiment, which wore white facings like Lascelles', were stationed across a wide area in the south-west of Scotland, with bases at Glasgow, Stranraer and Dumfries. The rest were garrisoned in the border stronghold of Berwick-upon-Tweed.

Unlike all the other foot regiments in Scotland, Sir John Guise's Regiment was a battle-hardened unit with a reputation to maintain. Like Cope, the regiment

---

11   Cope's evidence, Robins (ed.), *Inquiry*, p.5.

had fought in Spain at the Battle of Almenar in 1710. It was then part of the heroic force which had been defeated at Brihuega whilst Cope was in Britain arranging his commission in the Foot Guards. Now based out of Aberdeen, Guise's was responsible for the north-east coast, an important and productive region which also happened to contain large numbers of people with Episcopalian leanings and Jacobite sympathies, as well as significant harbours through which the French might wish to communicate and supply. From here the regiment should also be able to support Murray's further west and the small garrisons of the Highland interior should trouble break out. Guise's men wore yellow-faced uniforms.

Spread as they were across the length and breadth of Scotland, these men needed good communications and even better roads in order to operate effectively in Scotland. This necessity had been understood by George Wade, who had commanded in Scotland in the 1720s and '30s. Wade's famous military roads were designed to facilitate easier penetration of the hinterland by royal armies should the problems of 1715 and 1719 recur. They traversed mountains and bridged waterways, and thus opened up the Highlands like never before. Many routes can still be traced today. Wade's roads connected a series of forts and barracks designed to protect the loyal and cow the mischievous. Some were rebuilds of old stations, but others were new and costly constructions. There were garrisoned barracks at Kiliwhimen on Loch Ness, Bernera (Glenelg) overlooking the Skye crossing, Inversnaid by Loch Lomond, and Ruthven in Badenoch. The latter commanded the main route north to Inverness or south to Perth.

The three main forts, however, were those that formed a chain along the Great Glen, the natural scar cutting diagonally across the Highlands. At the southwestern end stood Fort William, the oldest of the forts and named after King William. It was surrounded on three sides by water, making it both defensible and possible to resupply by boat. Combining the strengths of stone and earth, Fort William was stout and well-sited. Further up the glen, at the base of Loch Ness, was Fort Augustus, which had been completed only a few years before Cope's appointment. It was named after the Duke of Cumberland, the king's favourite soldier-son. Despite years of effort and cost in its construction, the buildings of Fort Augustus were roofed in straw. It was nevertheless a considerable improvement on the adjacent Kiliwhimen Barracks which it was designed to replace. A further twenty-eight miles up the Ness stood the fort at Inverness, the chief town of the Highlands. This fort was named after George II himself, but it was a rather more improvised affair than the more famous successor which would be built after the rising at nearby Ardersier. Rather than a cutting-edge defensive masterpiece, the original Fort George was merely a modernisation work around the old medieval castle of Inverness, sited on a raised bluff overlooking the river. The result was a less than perfect compromise. The ruined earthworks of the old Cromwellian fort lay on the other side of the river.

Fort George was not the only medieval pile which had been adapted to meet the requirements of modern warfare. In the west was Dumbarton Castle, sited on its ancient rock and now boasting a fine governors' mansion and modern artillery works. This strategic location had a long and important history, and since Dumbarton controlled access in and out of the Clyde its importance had not diminished with the passing of time. It also provided a convenient staging point for expeditions striking into the western Highlands and islands by both land and sea. Over on the opposite side of Scotland was Blackness Castle, jutting out into the Firth of Forth between Edinburgh and Stirling.

The castles of Edinburgh and Stirling were the most formidable defensive sites in the land. Both had once been renaissance royal palaces and were perched on high rocky crags dominating the towns below them. Both had benefitted from the addition of fore-works and artillery positions which protected their main entry points and gave the citadels considerable defensive firepower. But for all their similarities, they held different strategic significance. Stirling was still the guardian of the famous bridge across the Forth, where Andrew Moray and William Wallace had scored such success in 1297. For centuries this bridge was the only good dry crossing of the Forth, and so Stirling had the power to control the north-south passage of armies. Upstream the river looped through the flat and frequently flooded country, and it was bounded on the north by the bogs of the Flanders Moss.

There was a passable ford at Frew, but the track leading there was barely a road at all, utterly unsuitable for wheeled traffic such as a modern army would require. The Marquess of Montrose had taken this passage in 1645 with his hardy little band, but it was a risky route. Five years later, David Leslie's defence of Stirling was so successful that his opponents were obliged to bypass him with a risky river crossing at Inverkeithing. They succeeded, but left the road to England open and the Scots army rushed south unopposed until it reached Worcester. In 1715, government control of Stirling had checked the territorial gains made by the Jacobites and led to a stalemate which starved the Earl of Mar of momentum. He too sent forces across the Forth by sea, but with a fleet in the estuary it was a dangerous mission and only a relatively small taskforce was able to break out. Stirling Castle had again proven its worth. It was a highly significant strategic asset, and when news of trouble in the north broke Stirling would be placed in the capable hands of a septuagenarian Irishman, Major General William Blakeney.

Edinburgh Castle's importance rested primarily on its role as keeper of the capital; it was also the country's principal military garrison and arsenal. No longer a royal residence, the former great hall had been transformed into a barrack block by the insertion of wooden floors which made it capable of housing more than three hundred soldiers. The bristling half-moon battery and a projecting ravelin commanded the dead ground between the castle gate and the city itself, and although it had been battered into submission in the 1570s, the capture of Edinburgh Castle could only be achieved with considerable time, energy, and resources. The cannons of the castle were under the command of the master gunner, Major Eaglesfield Griffith, just as they had been for the last three decades.

Since the great Jacobite Rising of 1715 the castle had been commanded by Lieutenant General George Preston, who was old enough to have accompanied William of Orange on his expedition to overthrow the last Stuart king. In 1706 he had been badly wounded at Ramillies, as was the same James Gardiner who would later purchase Bankton House in Prestonpans. Preston was a formidable old Scots soldier, but he was in his mid-eighties by the time Cope arrived in the capital. When the crisis came in 1745 he was replaced by a younger man, Lieutenant General Joshua Guest– younger by just a single year! Born in the Restoration year, Guest's long career included fighting at the Battle of Almanza in Spain, where that eager young officer John Cope had also served. Drafted up from retirement, Guest was to be responsible for holding Scotland's greatest fortress. The castle garrison included two companies of Lascelles' Regiment as well as the usual Invalids. In the event both Guest and Preston would spend the opening campaign of 1745 trapped in the citadel together, two octogenarians looking down on the last gamble of a cause that had spanned their whole lives.

Also based around Edinburgh was one of Cope's two regiments of dragoons. Gardiner's 13th Dragoons were dispersed over a wide area which included Stirling, Linlithgow and Edinburgh, Musselburgh to the east, and Kelso and Coldstream down in the Borders. The other regiment, Hamilton's 14th Dragoons, was based at Haddington in East Lothian and Duns in the Borders. Both regiments had a similar history. They had been formed in England in 1715 during the crisis of the Earl of Mar's rising, and both had seen action at Preston Fight that November. Since then they had both been based primarily in Ireland, where they probably picked up most of their men in the intervening period before their return to England in 1742. Certainly the 13th had adopted a rather Irish character by this time, circumventing the regulations which prevented it recruiting in Ireland by sending candidates over to Scotland. On their swift return across the water they could be entered in the books as if they were Scotsmen. As they would in Scotland, the dragoons spent their time in Ireland distributed in small numbers across large areas, regularly rotated but rarely concentrated. Archibald Hamilton had become colonel of his lemon-faced dragoons in 1737, whilst James Gardiner had only taken over his in 1743. By then his green-faced regiment had already been transferred to Scotland. The dragoons were equipped with long-arms as well as pistols and broadswords, reflecting their flexible role as mounted infantry. In theory they could fight equally well on foot – as they had at Preston in 1715 – as on horseback. Combining firepower and mobility, the dragoons should have been a battle-winning asset against untrained irregular opponents. Together, Hamilton's and Gardiner's Dragoons mustered around 600 men in the summer of 1745.

Two years older than Sir John Cope, Colonel James Gardiner of the 13th Dragoons came from a military family. He was born in 1688 and grew up at Burnfoot House on the banks of the Firth of Forth at Carriden, west of Edinburgh. Today the ruins of his family home are hidden amongst the trees and undergrowth, but it is nevertheless possible to locate the gate through which he passed so many times, and some of the windows through which his young eyes had once gazed across the water to Fife. A worn stone plaque on the gate pillar commemorates him, and a more recent copy is mounted in the nearby churchyard. A scrappy lad, gaining his first duelling scars whilst still a pup, Gardiner was destined for the Army. He was only seven years old when his older brother Robert was killed on his sixteenth birthday at the Siege of Namur. His uncle, Colonel Robert Hodge, was already dead, slain at Steenkirk in 1692. Gardiner's father, Captain Patrick Gardiner, was himself killed fighting under Marlborough at Blenheim in 1704. Two years later the young James Gardiner was carrying the flag of Scotland aloft at Ramillies, where the French were doggedly defending the churchyard, when he was shot through the mouth. It seemed the Gardiner family was cursed to suffer death upon the battlefield.

But James Gardiner survived. Unsure of his nationality, French soldiers moved his body to a nearby convent after the battle and he was nursed back to health. His new scar added to his martial bearing, a strapping tall frame giving him a suitably heroic look when he returned to service. Gardiner was attached to the Earl of Stair and his embassy in Paris, where he was much in favour with the ladies. As a captain in 1715 he also fought at Preston, being commended for his actions in setting alight a Jacobite barricade. Eight of the twelve soldiers he took with him on this enterprise were shot down.[12] The future would again show how dangerous it was for such small bands to stand with Gardiner in action. Amongst those looking on at Preston were the men of the 13th Dragoons, the regiment which he would help make infamous in 1745.

It was whilst Gardiner was in Paris, awaiting a nocturnal rendezvous, that he had his famous religious experience. Killing the time, he flicked open a copy of *The Christian Soldier, or Heaven Taken by Storm*, by Thomas Watson. This 1669 essay sets out the case for the importance of demonstrating vigorous (metaphorical) violence in the pursuit of God's glory. This reader found nothing in its lines to change his life, but for James Gardiner it triggered a remarkable transformation. Alexander Carlyle and Philip Dodderidge, both friends of Gardiner who heard the tale from his own mouth, differ in some of their details but it is the outcome not the trigger that is important. Whether or not God's voice truly boomed in Gardiner's head, and whether or not the image of the crucifixion materialised before him, the young officer set about reinventing himself. No longer would he be known as happy rake; instead he would become the model of the Christian soldier.

The change was made somewhat easier by the long peace which now settled, stagnating military careers, but, unlike Sir John Cope, Gardiner did not go into politics. Instead he took pleasure in the company of clergymen like Phillip Dodderidge of Northampton. He married Frances Erskine, a daughter of the Earl

---

12   Dodderidge, P. *Some Remarkable Passages in the Life of the Honourable Colonel J. Gardiner* (Derby: H Mozley, 1822), p.85.

Edinburgh Castle from the south, showing the half-moon battery. (Author's collection)

of Buchan, and they set up home in that fine Dutch-gabled house in East Lothian, Olivestob (Bankton). Gardiner then set off for war once more at the outbreak of the War of the Austrian Succession, but he lacked a regiment of his own and so for some time accompanied the army in a sort of limbo. It was from a village near Frankfurt in May 1743 that he finally wrote home to Lady Frances that he had been offered command of the 13th Dragoons.[13] Had its colonel held onto his life a few days more then a vacancy would have arisen in a foot regiment which might well have been offered to Gardiner instead, but the 13th was a more attractive prospect as it was 'quartered at his own door' in the south of Scotland. So James Gardiner returned to his homeland, stopping to meet the Prince of Wales on his way, a year before Cope took up command in Scotland. Cope and Gardiner had not served together before, but it seems likely that they would have met during the course of their last foreign campaign prior to each of them travelling to Scotland.

These, then, were the forces available to Lieutenant General Sir John Cope in the summer of 1745. Most of Cope's paperwork was lost at Prestonpans and so even he struggled to recall the figures with certainty, but it is possible to piece the picture together to a reasonable degree. The British Army in Scotland appears to have had a total strength of around 2,725 foot and 600 dragoons, not including

13 Dodderidge, *Gardiner*, p.126.

garrison companies of Invalids or the brand new recruits fresh to the colours.[14] On paper this does not look like a large army with which to hold a potentially volatile country, nor was it. There was also a total lack of proper field artillery crews, although no shortage of actual cannons. But perhaps the biggest flaw in Cope's army was its lack of battlefield training. Each company would have been effectively drilled and trained in its marching and firing disciplines, and the infantry's performance in the campaign shows that it was not without ability. But the complexities of platoon firing and co-ordinated manoeuvre in a large formation are simply not something in which they would have been regularly exercised. Such training would normally occur as an army assembled for campaign, and performance would increase with experience as operations got underway. With his men dispersed across the country Cope simply had not enjoyed the luxury of ever being able to concentrate his regiments together for massed drills, nor did the emergent crisis of the late summer in 1745 provide much time to remedy this failing. His regiments of horse were at grass, and the training of the mounts may have been as deficient as that of the riders.

However, we must not be tempted to allow the benefits of hindsight to warp our perception of Cope's forces. Yes, most of the foot regiments were relatively young, but they had existed for years rather than months and were more than capable of fulfilling their functions. Yes, some of their training was reliant on theoretical knowledge rather than practical experience, but all were aware of the basic tasks required of them and how they would be expected to behave. There were young officers amongst the army who had talent and potential, and others who were older and experienced. The soldiers were properly equipped with their standard arms, including Long Land Pattern Brown Bess muskets with socket bayonets, and apart from the lack of trained gun crews there were few obvious deficiencies in the capacity of the army to campaign. Most importantly of all, it was led by an experienced officer who had the confidence of his superiors and the support of the civil and military officers of the state. Sir John Cope and his little army should have been capable of containing or defeating anything short of a major French invasion. But in the wake of France's triumph at Fontenoy, there seemed little reason for the French to risk such a gamble. Any trouble in Scotland would surely be homegrown, and even with a small army that 'could be crush'd in the bud'.[15]

On the morning of 2 July 1745, Duncan Forbes of Culloden visited Lieutenant General Sir John Cope in Edinburgh and passed on a 'groundless report' that the Pretender's eldest son might make a landing in Scotland. Cope immediately informed the Secretary of State in London, in case the French 'take a fancy to fling away some money, and a few men'.[16] Cope was already watching potential Jacobite

---

14   Jarvis, R. *Collected Papers on the Jacobite Risings* (Manchester: Manchester University Press, 1972), p.44.
15   Forbes' evidence, Robins (ed.), *Inquiry*, p.5.
16   Cope to Tweeddale, Edinburgh, 2 July 1745, Robins (ed.), *Inquiry*, Appendix, p.1.

activists with a wary eye: Hector Maclean had been arrested in June, and it had not escaped the general's notice that the Duke of Perth 'has not been at his own house for some time.'[17] Whether he believed the rumours of an imminent landing or not, Cope was suspicious that something might be stirring and he requested muskets for distribution to the Highland forts. The Disarming Acts, as he well knew, had been more effective at emasculating loyal clans than weakening potentially hostile ones. An agent was sent to chase up a late delivery of firelocks for the Black Watch, and the dragoons in the Lowlands were told to stand ready to bring their horses in from grass. An order ought to be placed in the *Gazette*, Cope suggested, calling in officers from their leave. James Gardiner headed home from Scarborough on 2 August.

Tweeddale was rather less excited by these rumours than Sir John. He instructed the latter not to proceed in bringing the horses in from grass or taking any other measures which might alarm the public unnecessarily. On the same day as Charles Edward Stuart landed on the mainland of Scotland, the Secretary of State for Scotland was conceding that officers should indeed be recalled from leave but in a suitably discreet manner. The rumours would not go away, however, and an attempt by Captain Duncan Campbell of Inverawe to dupe the Duke of Perth into custody had failed, driving him to ground. By 1 August it was confirmed that Prince Charles was indeed 'somewhere in Scotland,' news which prompted the government to offer a staggering reward of £30,000 for his capture.[18] At last the horses were brought in from grass and, a full month since the first rumour broke, an additional quantity of arms was dispatched to Scotland. There was still much uncertainty, and on 3 August Cope was still expressing doubts as to whether Charles had actually arrived in person, since so many of the King's friends in the north were supposedly keeping their eyes peeled.

But already Cope was thinking ahead and assessing his capacity to hold Scotland in the event of an invasion or insurrection: 'if I come to want to make use of any field-train or artillery at all, we have not any gunners for that purpose,' he wrote.[19] He began calling in isolated work parties, such as a road-building detachment working near Dumbarton. The sloop *Happy Janet* was redirected from its patrols of the Firth of Forth in order to take arms to Inverness for potential distribution amongst the loyal clans, whilst other weaponry was sent for the use of the Duke of Argyll. So much correspondence was flying between Edinburgh and London that letters were outdated before they were even despatched, and updates were being hurried sent in their wake.

Sir John had only a small number of strategic options available to him, all of which presented problems. One course was to concentrate his forces on protecting

---

17 Cope to Tweeddale, Edinburgh, 2 July 1745, Robins (ed.), *Inquiry*, Appendix, p.1.
18 Tweeddale to Cope, Whitehall, 1 August 1745, Robins (ed.), *Inquiry*, Appendix, p. 6.
19 Cope to Tweeddale, Edinburgh, 3 August 1745, Robins (ed.), *Inquiry*, Appendix, p.7.

Edinburgh, the centre of Scotland's commercial and political life and the necessary target of any meaningful attempt to seize the crown. As he himself put it, Edinburgh was 'the metropolis of this country, from whence all credit flows, and all business is transacted'.[20] Cope had correctly identified the military, economic, and political importance of the capital but his attempt to suggest a defensive strategy centred on the city was half-hearted. He knew that whilst it bought him time to reinforce himself, it surrendered the initiative and abandoned the loyal clans to the rebels. A better alternative was a strategy of containment. By arming the Duke of Argyll's loyal Campbells in the west, the roads south towards Glasgow could be controlled. Well-affected clans in the north could be supplied out of Inverness under the well-informed advice of Lord President Forbes, whilst the forts and barracks provided bastions in the hinterland. In the centre of a line of containment would be the crucial Atholl territories, controlled by the well-affected Duke who could be supported as needed by the field army, which could be held back as a strike force centred on Stirling or Perth. Thus the Jacobites could be denied territory, although it placed the immediate burden of war on the loyal clans. It also gave the insurgents the opportunity to choose where they would strike, and Cope's resources would be stretched pretty thin to cover all possible avenues.

The final option was to destroy the threat at source, taking the field army into the Highlands as quickly as possible. This would not only deny the Jacobites room to make decisions of their own, but would also act as a show of strength to encourage the loyal and deter the wavering. Crucially it would allow Cope to bring his small army into action before the enemy could grow too strong for him to oppose alone. This option bore the most promise for a quick result, nipping the fledgling rising in the bud; the other options could easily allow it to bloom into a crisis comparable to 1715. As early as 3 August, Tweeddale and Cope had accepted this line of thought. The general assured the secretary he would seek a swift resolution: 'I shall march with what force I can get together'.[21] One week later Cope had been furnished with full details of Charles Edward Stuart's voyage, of the sea-battle off the Lizard point, the Prince's landings on Eriskay and then on the mainland, who he had brought with him and with whom he was now speaking. In his need for support Charles Edward had inevitably made contact with enemies as well as friends. Now Sir John Cope was coming for him.

---

20 Cope to Tweeddale, Edinburgh, 3 August 1745, Robins (ed.), *Inquiry*, Appendix, p.7.
21 Cope to Tweeddale, Edinburgh, 3 August 1745, Robins (ed.), *Inquiry*, Appendix, p.7.

3

'Very Troublesome Neighbours'

To the Jacobites, James Francis Edward Stuart was the man who should be king. Cutting through to the nub, there was no denying that this was the rightful claimant to the British crown: his father, uncle, grandfather and great-grandfather had all been kings before him, and the long succession of Stuart monarchs in Scotland ran right back to their kinship with the Bruces. It was an unrivalled pedigree if not a happy one. Despite their remarkable talent for dynastic survival, the Royal Stuarts had suffered fraught minorities, assassinations, deaths on the battlefield, two royal executions, and now their second period of protracted exile. Some of this simply reflects the ups and downs of medieval and renaissance kingship. Some Stuarts were ineffective, some unlucky; others were canny, skilled, and dynamic. They were hard to predict.

James VI of Scotland, James Francis' great-grandfather, had inherited the throne of England in 1603 and moved the royal court to London. He was succeeded by his son Charles I, the last of the family to be born in Scotland, who possessed many praiseworthy virtues but failed to appreciate the differences in character between his kingdoms to such an extent that war broke out between them over his religious policy. When he called on England's parliament to fund his defence against the Scots Covenanters, its members turned on their king after finding more common cause with the enemy. After an increasingly bitter civil war and fruitless negotiations following his defeat, Charles was beheaded in 1649. The young and charming Charles II, a warmer character by far than his more saintly father, made a dash for Scotland the following year and made an accommodation with the same Scots who had initially triggered the crisis more than ten years before. Many Covenanters felt betrayed by their former allies and accepted Charles' rule, on their own terms, but their strength was soon broken by Oliver Cromwell at the Battle of Dunbar. The king seized what remained of the Scots army and dashed for Worcester, where he in turn was beaten exactly one year later. The Stuarts did not lack courage or audacity. But it would be 1660 before Charles II would finally enter into his own again, brought back from exile after the great republican experiment had floundered in the wake of Cromwell's death.

In Scotland, the ancestral home of the Stuarts, the Restoration had brought little comfort for some. The Covenanters had particular reason to wince: they had both brought about the downfall of Charles I and then had the audacity to bargain with his son over the terms on which they would accept him. The latter might have mattered less if they had not then failed to secure his restoration themselves. A decade on, Charles II had little cause to love them and much reason to hate. The authority of the king over church and state was restored along with the king's person, and the Covenanters were driven out of the churches and onto the hillsides. Those who did not mend their ways were punished, and thus began the so-called 'Killing Times'. The level of repression has been over-stated subsequently and some of those killed were militant extremists who could simply never have been accommodated politically, but the Merry Monarch is not well remembered in parts of south-west Scotland. He did, however, revitalise the royal residence at Holyroodhouse, transforming it into a modern palace fit for a king of his stature. But the memory of the sermons he endured in 1650 was clearly too strong as he never came north to see the finished project. Nevertheless, Charles II still gazes across Parliament Square today in the very heart of Edinburgh, in bronze.

If Charles II did not return to Scotland in person, he did at least send the next best thing: his heir. The king had no legitimate son to succeed him, which created a succession crisis which threatened to seriously destabilise the restored monarchy. He did not lack illegitimate sons of course, the most prominent of them being James Scott, Duke of Monmouth, who commanded the king's forces in Scotland during the defeat of the Covenanters at Bothwell Brig in 1679. The following year, Charles' younger brother arrived in Scotland as Lord High Commissioner. This was James, Duke of York, whose excellent service to the king had been critically undermined by his conversion to Catholicism. York was nevertheless the heir to the throne, and although he had no son of his own yet he did have a daughter, Mary, who had married William of Orange several years before York arrived at Holyrood. When Charles II died in 1685, the Duke of York became King James II of England and King James VII of Scotland.

The last Stuart king to reign, James' rule was not destined to last long. Coordinated rebellions in his coronation year came from his nephew the Duke of Monmouth and from the Earl of Argyll, a veteran of Dunbar and Worcester. Monmouth led a West Country rising which sought to mobilise Protestant opposition to the Catholic king, but it failed to win over significant support amongst the gentry or nobility and defeat at Sedgemoor paved the way to the scaffold for the hapless Duke. In Scotland the cause had fared even less well, and Argyll's head had fallen from the 'maiden' – an early form of guillotine, now on display in the National Museum of Scotland – even before Monmouth's last battle had begun. But James earned the suspicion of his subjects through his determination to expand and improve the standing army and his push for religious toleration. James sought to neutralise the penal laws which repressed his Catholic subjects, whilst remaining wary of the Covenanters. In some respects he was far ahead of his time, declaring that it was just as unreasonable to fall out over religion as it was over the colour of one's skin, but there was no appetite for a Catholic resurgence and in 1688 a group of conspirators invited William of Orange to invade England.

The tragedy of the Williamite invasion, benignly branded as the Glorious Revolution, is that James was both a competent and experienced commander and the patron of a highly capable army. But in 1688, unable to tell friend from foe and unsure where to turn, the king's nerve broke and he failed to fight it out. Even his escape was haphazard, but eventually James reached France. The immediate trigger for the plot had been the birth, at last, of a male heir to the Stuart throne. The thought of a Catholic succession was the final straw for the Protestants in Parliament, and the crown was offered instead to the king's daughter and her Dutch husband. In Edinburgh an anti-Catholic mob celebrated the king's overthrow by smashing into Holyroodhouse and desecrating the royal chapel. James recovered his wits and invaded Ireland in an attempt to recover his fortunes, whilst John Graham of Claverhouse, Viscount Dundee, raised a Highland army in Scotland. The Highlanders won a victory at Killiecrankie in 1689, but the price had been the loss of their leader and after a brutal rebuff at Dunkeld the first Jacobite rising stuttered out of life. In Ireland the king himself was beaten at the Boyne the following year, showing none of his previous energy and skill in command. He lived in exile at the Chateau de Saint-Germain-en-Laye near Paris until his death in 1702.

James II & VII had lived long enough to see another of his daughters ascend to his throne. Mary had died in 1694 leaving her husband to rule alone until 1701. Then the throne passed to her younger sister Anne, who had chosen not to support her father during the invasion crisis. Although she had spent almost a year at Holyrood with James during his time as Commissioner, Queen Anne did not visit Scotland during her reign. She did however oversee the Union of the Parliaments in 1707, which occurred amidst stiff popular opposition in Scotland. None of Anne's many pregnancies resulted in an heir who survived childhood, and her death in 1714 opened the door for her half-brother James Francis Edward to return the throne to its natural line.

Except that Parliament had already moved to prevent that happening. Anne had taken the crown in the full knowledge that her father's line would be bypassed if she had no heirs of her own: the Act of Settlement had made it law that Catholics were barred from the throne, which would pass to the heirs of Sophia of Hanover. Sophia, who ruled the small German state from which her son's dynasty would take its name, was a grand-daughter of James I and VI through the maternal line. The claim was slender according to the laws of primogeniture, but Sophia was Protestant and that was all that really mattered to her advocates in Britain. As she predeceased Queen Anne by just two months, it was her German-speaking son George who became King of Great Britain. Anne was the last of the reigning Stuarts.

Not surprisingly, this was a time of immense activity and opportunity for the supporters of James Francis, whose birth in 1688 had unwittingly triggered his father's deposition. Raised at Saint-Germain, James Francis enjoyed the recognition of France, Spain, and the Papacy for his right to rule as James III & VIII. It was to Scotland that he turned for active aid however, and in 1708 he made his first attempt to reach his supporters there in the wake of the Act of Union. Undermined first by measles and then the Royal Navy, compounded by a French reluctance to hazard so great a resource as a king in exile, the attempt failed. Like his father, James then spent some of his exile gaining military experience in French service, but whilst keeping the court close to Paris had its advantages such close links to the court of King Louis did not help his cause at home. The Treaty of Utrecht, which brought to an end the War of the Spanish Succession, also ended James' convenient proximity to the centre of French politics: its terms demanded his removal. James was relocated to the Duchy of Lorraine, where it was harder for him to influence the course of events just as Queen Anne's health began to fail. James, showing the unfortunate Stuart capacity for stubbornness, advised correspondents from Britain that he was unwilling to convert to Protestantism in order to secure the throne. It was for others to bend, not kings. So the crown went to Hanover.

James was on the brink of losing his best opportunity to recover what his father had lost. The declaration he published in October 1715 explains that he had expected Anne to renege on the Act of Settlement 'by securing to us at last the enjoyment of that inheritance, out of which we had been so long kept, which her conscience must inform her was our due'. That hope, and the relative peace of the home countries, were the only things that had alleviated the trials of his exile, he said. And no doubt whilst the throne was held by another Stuart it still felt within reach. The accession of George I changed all that: 'we have beheld a foreign family, aliens to our country, distant in blood, and strangers even to our language, ascend the throne'.[1] If James did not act now then a new dynasty would take hold in Great Britain.

And yet it was not James who acted in 1715, it was the Earl of Mar. John Erskine had served in Queen Anne's administration and had offered to continue in office under the new king. George of Hanover had snubbed him, however, tipping Bobbing John back to the cause of the Stuarts. Mar rushed to Scotland and prepared for a general uprising in the name of King James. Over the water, the king was left to react to this unexpected initiative, issuing his declaration and retrospectively authorising Mar's actions. But by the time he finally made landfall in Scotland it was all virtually over. Mar was no general, as he himself would not have denied, and thus he had squandered the momentum he had gained at the outset until his enemy was able to concentrate sufficient strength to resist. In both Scotland and England the Jacobites had been beaten back even before James'

---

1   Declaration of King James VIII, Commercy, 25 October 1715, printed in Struthers, J., *The History of Scotland from the Union to the Abolition of the Heritable Jurisdictions*, (Glasgow: Blackie, Fullarton & Co, 1827), p. 392.

landing at Peterhead in December. At Sheriffmuir the opposition had been led by John Campbell, Duke of Argyll, the grandson of the Earl who had lost his head for rebelling against James II & VII. How the tables had turned. On 5 February 1716 the king returned to exile, moving his court to Papal territory first at Avignon and then Rome.

Although James was still young, time was very much against him. His removal from the suburbs of Paris not only denied him direct influence at the French court but also made it harder to seize any sudden opportunities to cross to Britain. Time and geography, not to mention James' steadfast devotion to the Roman Church, meant that a Stuart restoration now seemed further away than ever before. But James did not give up and travelled to Spain when war with Britain opened up a new opportunity. A plan was hatched to land a diversionary force of Spaniards in the Western Highlands, supported by local Jacobites and commanded by George Keith, the Earl Marischal. This would distract attention from the main invasion of England. This new armada sailed in the spring of 1719 but was driven back by storms; unfortunately Keith's expedition was already underway and so the intended feint became the main affair. The Highland clans were reluctant to move without assurances as to what was happening further south, and so the Jacobite muster was little more than a thousand men by the time the British army moved against them at Glenshiel. Amongst the Jacobite leaders were Mackintosh of Borlum, survivor of Preston Fight, William Murray, Marquis of Tullibardine, and the latter's younger brother Lord George, who was wounded as his men were dislodged by mortar fire. The famous Rob Roy Macgregor shared a similar fate, and after three hours the whole Jacobite force was either dispersing or retreating up the mountainside. The Spanish regulars surrendered as prisoners of war, an option not available to their allies. The Murray brothers eventually made their way into exile, as did the expedition's commander George Keith.

The '19 was a measly affair compared to the events of 1715, but it showed the Jacobites were still a viable threat both at home and abroad. Imagine then the horror of George I when he heard that the Stuart had been betrothed to one of the wealthiest princesses in Europe, the beautiful Maria Clementina Sobieska. Not only did she bring the King across the water fresh resources, but also some much needed glamour. Hardworking and well-meaning, James lacked something in the way of dash and fire. Something inspiring was needed to boost and renew the residual loyalty of his name in his subjects' minds, and a royal marriage might do just that – especially if it led to the birth of an heir. The grandfather of the queen-to-be was none other than John III of Poland, the warrior king who had smashed the Turks at the Battle of Vienna in 1683. Hanover was so alarmed at the prospect of this marriage that attempts were made to stop it. The Emperor Charles VI apprehended Maria Clementina's party, but they made their escape from Innsbruck and reached Italy. There a proxy wedding was held to prevent further interference, and when James returned from Spain they were able to hold a more personal ceremony in September 1719. The event was immortalised by the artist Masucci, whose grand painting now hangs in the Scottish National Portrait Gallery. A Papal guard escorted the royal couple to their palazzo in Rome, and in 1720 the queen in exile gave birth to a healthy boy whilst a hurricane blew over Hanover.

By the time Charles Edward Stuart was born, his father was far from a spent force but the best opportunities for decisive action seemed to have passed him by. The prince grew up in a court populated by exiles from the three kingdoms, in an artificially British environment that was as alien to his father's real experience as to his mother's. No amount of roast beef could disguise the fact that this was a court in exile, a long way from home and from the imminent prospect of a restoration. James himself had never known anything other than such a court, and as the years went by he seemed to be becoming increasingly comfortable in this unreal world. Another son, Henry Benedict, was born in 1725 and so the baton would soon pass to a new generation. Hanoverian agents kept a close eye on the Stuarts, but much of their news was domestic gossip rather than political intrigue. The marriage had turned sour, the queen's piety making the king look positively indifferent, and there were fraught and unhappy scenes. Neither party was truly to blame, but Maria Clementina became paranoid and depressive whilst her husband prioritised affairs of state, maintaining visibility amongst his remaining supporters through constant correspondence. It was hard for the king to find a winning position: the more pious the queen appeared the more support she gained in Catholic circles and the more James lost with potential supporters. Ultimately, Maria Clementina's piety would prove her undoing as her fasting undermined her health. She died, aged just 32, in January 1735.

Charles Edward was much affected by his mother. He shared some of her temperament and volatility, the depression and sense of isolation. Much of this would be most manifest in his later life, but there were periods in 1745 when such traits were apparent too. Where Charles differed from her most was in his attitude to religion, and that was likely down to the fact that he had seen the toll that devoted faith had taken on his mother. Never did Charles Edward show any great attachment to the Church, seeing it primarily as a political force. That is not to say he was not religious, no more than anyone else in the mid-eighteenth century, but rather that his faith was personal rather than institutional. Here was a young man who, unlike his father or grandfather, accepted that London might well be worth neglecting a Mass. The instability of his parents' relationship did not mean that Charles' childhood was unhappy, and both his parents cared for him sincerely, but little Carluccio spent far more time with his father.

Much has been said and written about the childhood of Charles Edward Stuart and it is not our purpose here to explore it in detail, but it is worth addressing some important points. Most importantly, Charles grew to be a fit, athletic young man with a constitution suited to adventure. The outdoors suited his health as action suited his temperament. Charles may not have been as bookish and orderly as his younger brother, but he was far from a fool. His spelling was no more erratic than

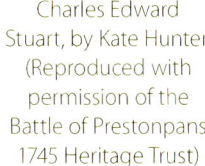

Charles Edward Stuart, by Kate Hunter. (Reproduced with permission of the Battle of Prestonpans 1745 Heritage Trust)

his contemporaries, and his letters show he had a good grasp of history. Musically accomplished and linguistically capable, Charles Edward might not have been a brilliant scholar but nor was he unintelligent. In 1734 he earned admiration for his coolness under fire at the Siege of Gaeta near Naples; by the age of seventeen he was turning heads at the courts of Italy; and in 1741 he made a public appearance in Highland dress. Charles knew how to win a crowd, and here he was stating his intent. He would not live out his days in idle exile; he wanted action. James Drummond, 3rd Duke of Perth, sent a silver-mounted targe and broadsword to the young Prince of Wales: Charles longed to put them to use.[2]

2 Various, *The Swords and the Sorrows*, (Edinburgh: National Trust for Scotland, 1996), p.56. The Prince's targe and sword are in the collection of the National Museum of Scotland in Edinburgh.

This was the man, young and inexperienced but charismatic and energetic, to whom the French turned at the beginning of 1744. As David Wemyss, the young Lord Elcho, put it, 'the weary years of waiting, or espionage, of eavesdropping and intrigue were at last to give place to action'.[3] The court of Louis XV was not unequivocal in its support for the Stuarts, but for the moment the king was inclined to favour opening an ambitious new front against the old enemy. Charles slipped out of Rome under cover of a hunting expedition, fooling even his brother Henry, before taking ship from Genoa to Antibes and riding on to Paris. Initially his incognito held whilst the serious planning got underway. George Keith, Earl Marischal, was called upon to reprise his role from 1719 and command the supporting expedition of 3,000 men due to land in Scotland. Keith was also a veteran of the 1715 Rising and the wars of Marlborough; he was a more than capable commander and his name carried much weight in Scotland.

Lord Elcho also joined the Prince in Paris at this time. Just a year younger than Charles, the two had met during Elcho's visit to Rome several years before during which they are said to have stood back-to-back whilst the proud king in exile compared the teenagers' heights. As the Winchester-educated heir to the Earl of Wemyss, Elcho was well connected and well financed, and a potentially valuable ally for the Prince; he also had much to lose if he backed the wrong horse. Elcho was told to be ready to sail home to help mobilise Jacobite sympathy. Charles and the Earl Marischal moved up to Gravelines and the French invasion force of 15,000 men began to concentrate.

Across the sea, Jacobite agents were becoming anxious. Despite an earlier flurry of correspondence, information had dried up. John Murray and the Duke of Perth were 'in the utmost dilemma, not knowing what to think or how to move'.[4] Murray, two years older than the Prince, was a Scots Borders gentleman who had followed the feet of many young Scots to be educated at Leiden in the Netherlands. For several years he had been involved in the passage of information between the homeland sympathisers and the exiles abroad. The thirty-year-old Duke of Perth had also been educated overseas, at Douay and Paris, but he was now back in Scotland and was the most senior of the Jacobite aristocrats. Perth's support was therefore important, but he was also openly Catholic. His interests also seemed rather more rustic than martial. Such men were risking all in 1744: if they moved too fast they risked exposure and arrest; if too slow, they risked being unprepared for the coming trials. Some were reluctant to commit: the Earl of Traquair hardly stirred, and Simon Fraser of Lovat, who had danced the reel with Kate Vint in

---

3 Lord Elcho, D. 'Memoir of David, Lord Elcho', in *A Short Account of the Affairs of Scotland in the Years 1744-46, with a Memoir and Annotations* (Edinburgh: David Douglas, 1907) p.48.
4 Murray of Broughton, J., *Memorials of John Murray of Broughton*, (Edinburgh: Edinburgh University Press, 1898), p.61.

Prestonpans, became conveniently ill. The Prince's presence on the French coast now filled the newspapers, and the British government was on high alert.

The great expedition ultimately came to nothing. A February storm battered the French fleet as the troops began to embark, the Royal Navy hovered close at hand, and 'the French gave up'.[5] King Louis' enthusiasm waned as costs and casualties were counted even before the invasion had begun, and the initiative passed. Charles was left to fume, proposing to Keith that they hire a boat and go it alone instead. The earl rejected the plan as foolhardy, but a seed had been sown in the Prince's mind which would take firm root. He returned to Paris. Maurice de Saxe, instead of leading a highly risky invasion of England, focussed his attentions back on the main front. George II had survived the invasion threat and now, like the French, the British concentrated their military resources on the deepening continental conflict.

But the French had misjudged Charles Edward Stuart, and not for the last time either. They had invited him over to act as a figurehead, to give their planned invasion a veneer of respectability in Britain. They had offered him no true role in the expedition's planning and had cast him loose when it was postponed. Louis does not seem to have realised, or at least to have cared, that he had unleashed a young man who was driven forwards by a sense of his own destiny and driven mad by delay and prevarication. Charles knew time was not on his side and that the French were not really either. Such a man needed careful nurturing, needed to be kept busy or sent home, but the French did neither. Instead the Stuart Prince was permitted to linger close enough to the seat of power to stay connected but far enough out to feel cut out of society, 'not much frequented by the French people of fashion, but much by the Irish and Scots'.[6] John Murray of Broughton was amongst those who visited, crossing the sea at considerable risk to consult with the Prince directly once the abandonment of the French designs had at last been confirmed. In August 1744, behind the stables at the Louvre, Murray heard the Prince's single-mindedness straight from the horse's mouth. Perhaps he tried to dissuade him, as he later claimed, from undertaking anything rash. Perhaps he was swept away by his master's infectious confidence.

There were plenty of Scots and Irish exiles in and around Paris to keep Charles Edward in company, many of whom had built themselves useful new lives. Charles, now more than ever convinced that he might have to act independently of the French court, sought out the sort of men he thought he needed, like Aeneas Macdonald the banker and the Irish cavalry officer Sir John Macdonald. Some would prove more useful than others, but none would become so close to the Prince as John William O'Sullivan. Born in County Kerry around 1700, O'Sullivan had left Ireland as a boy to train as a priest in Paris. After his father's death he returned

---

5   Elcho, *Affairs*, p.232.
6   Elcho, *Affairs*, p.232

home, but as a Catholic he was not permitted to run the family estates himself and he chose to sell up and return to the Continent. Now of age, O'Sullivan also decided it was the sword rather than the cross which called him. He found a useful patron in the Marquis de Maillebois whose children he had been tutoring, and so he secured a commission and a post as aide-de-camp. Maillebois was an experienced commander who had fought in the wars of the Spanish and Polish Successions. In 1739 he landed in Corsica, where O'Sullivan gained experience campaigning in mountainous terrain, before moving along with the army to the Rhine the following year. These were just the sorts of adventures Charles Edward would enjoy talking about, and gave O'Sullivan the sort of recent practical experience of operations which the Prince needed to have at hand. The two had previously met in Rome, and before the end of 1744 Charles had brought O'Sullivan into his service. He came well recommended: with Charles' former tutor Sir Thomas Sheridan reporting his 'general good character', and King James calling him a 'very proper person'.[7]

O'Sullivan's initial duties were restricted to the organisation of Charles Edward's household. By now, as that momentous year of 1745 dawned, it was becoming clear that the Prince had little intention of returning to Rome empty handed. He had tasted independence, and was now far closer than his father to both the centre of European politics and to Stuart supporters back in Britain. Both at home and abroad, a new generation was assuming the Jacobite mantle. But it was not at the court of King Louis that the Prince of Wales now found his opportunity. It was amongst the Irish and the Bretons. Charles O'Brien, Viscount Clare, was a distinguished officer of France's Irish Brigade and a veteran of Dettingen, where he and his regiment had fought against George II (and Sir John Cope). Clare now aided Charles by introducing him to Walter Rutledge, an Irish merchant based out of Dunkirk. Rutledge had possession of a warship, *L'Elisabeth* of 64 guns, which had been captured from the Royal Navy forty years past.[8] What she lacked in youth she made up for in size and firepower, and Rutledge had official letters of marque to make what use of her he could as a privateer. Clare also used his leverage to fill *L'Elisabeth* with seven hundred Irish volunteers from his regiment, whilst Rutledge now introduced Charles Edward Stuart to Antoine Walsh.

Walsh was a prominent and wealthy member of the Irish community at Nantes in Britany, a privateer and slaver with considerable connections and influence. His father, Philip, had sailed Charles' grandfather King James II & VII out of Ireland in 1690 after his defeat at the Boyne. As naval advisor to the Prince's little court there could be few better. Walsh added his 18-gun *Du Teillay* to the modest armada and agreed to mastermind the naval operation. Charles Edward's plans

---

7   Taylor, A. & H., *1745 and After*, (Edinburgh: Thomas Nelson, 1938), pp.14-15.
8   Gibson, J.S., *Ships of The '45: The Rescue of the Young Pretender* (London: Hutchinson & Company, 1967), p.9.

were coming together quickly now, and O'Sullivan had to be 'let into the plan' in order to use his organisational skills for the purchase of arms and stores for the coming campaign.[9] In three weeks and with limited spending power, he managed to find 1,800 swords, several cases of pistols, and all that the Prince might need along the march. Charles travelled first to Navarre, then on to Nantes and thence to Saint-Nazaire. Disguised as a clerical student and growing a ruddy stubble, Charles descended onto the pretty beach at Bonne Anse on 22 June 1745 and was rowed out to the *Du Teillay* at 7pm. After a rendezvous at Belle-Isle, this tiny invasion set sail for Scotland.

Charles carried with him a commission of regency from his father, prepared ahead of the 1744 invasion which would have seen him nominally at the head of thousands of regular troops. Instead Charles was throwing himself on the mercy of his Scottish supporters, all of whom were totally unaware of his intentions. So too his father the King, who had been kept in the dark by a Prince who knew all too well the gamble he was taking. The French government had turned a blind eye, but henceforth it would be watching with increasing interest. But none of it could have happened without the Irish: the only Scotsmen aboard were Aeneas Macdonald the banker and William Murray, the Marquis of Tullibardine.

William Murray ought to have been the Duke of Atholl, enjoying life as one of Scotland's senior peers, but he had sacrificed this inheritance for the Stuart cause. In 1715 he had led the Athollmen out under the Earl of Mar, although his own father had refused to stir. His regiment had been broken at Sheriffmuir and when the Rising collapsed he was forced to live on his wits until he managed to escape. Tullibardine had returned to arms in 1719 and, along with his younger brother Lord George Murray, had taken the Athollmen to Glenshiel. There, perhaps having fallen out over command with the Earl Marischal, he was again defeated and this time severely wounded. Again forced out into exile, Tullibardine had lost all hope of a pardon and when his father died in 1724 only the Jacobite court acknowledged his title. He had remained in exile ever since and now, aged fifty-six, he was at last sailing homeward. Tullibardine's brothers had not shared his fate thus far: James Murray, having stayed out of the uprising, had inherited the Duchy of Atholl; Lord George was pardoned in 1725 and returned to Perthshire. Their step-brother Lord John Murray had become colonel of the 43rd Highland Regiment (Black Watch). Theirs was very much a family divided.

Tullibardine's fortunes would only now turn if Charles Edward was successful, but there were plenty amongst the Athollmen who shared the attachment of the older brother to the house of Stuart. Theirs was a productive and fairly prosperous country, straddling the uncertain border between Highland and Lowland, centred on the splendid seat of Blair Castle. If the Prince could get Tullibardine home to Blair, perhaps the Athollmen could help carry Charles to Holyrood. But to get

---

9   O'Sullivan, quoted in Taylor, *1745 and After*, p.47.

to this land-locked Perthshire heartland, the expedition must first pass through the more mountainous regions of the western Highlands. This was a region of mountain and glen, steep-sided lochs slicing through the land and encouraging a sense of localism amongst the inhabitants. Wade's new roads had opened the landscape up a little, but many Highlanders made more frequent use of traditional trackways and water transport was often quicker and easier than travelling by land. The sea lochs could offer access into the hinterland, or easy escape out of it, whilst the wildness of the untamed landscapes offered plenty of opportunity for the raider or fugitive to simply disappear. These were important considerations for the Prince as he sat aboard the *Du Teillay*, hoping to land amongst sympathetic subjects who could keep him safe in their remoteness until he was ready to sally forth in strength.

There was no guarantee that the Highlanders would rise for Prince Charlie if he landed, nor that they would prove suitable for his purposes if they did. Highland hosts had frequently proven themselves to be difficult instruments: for all their potential capability in the shock of battle, they could lack discipline and staying power. Victory on the field could be counter-productive, as large portions of a triumphant army dispersed home with its loot. Campaigns reliant on Highlanders could achieve great things, defying geography and nature, but they needed to be fast and targeted as the warriors would often return home to attend to their domestic needs when the necessity or opportunity arose. There was also the complex and delicate issue of inter-clan rivalry, which could mean a clan's support was dependent on their being given the chance to strike against a long-term enemy or avenge a grievance. This had the potential to divert strength away from other more strategically important objectives, and once their own priorities were satisfied the clansmen might well lose interest in campaigning further. Nor were clansmen, hardy though they were, necessarily suited to fighting in the manner that Charles might need them to. Hit and run raids were their speciality; toe-to-toe firefights were not. Applying them to siege work or assaults on entrenched positions was a thankless exercise. All these truths had been proven by the campaigns of the great Montrose a hundred years before, in Dundee's rising of 1689, and in the subsequent Jacobite campaigns of 1715 and 1719.

But if a leader were able, as Dundee had done, to command sufficient respect amongst the Highlanders he had assembled that he might both inspire them to follow and instil in them some discipline and regularisation, then the potential was considerable. The Highlanders were smart fighters who knew how to seek and maximise advantage, they were courageous in the fray and they were tough and hardy on the march. Well-led, they were a formidable enemy. But they needed that leadership which could stand above the local politics, which could command, mediate, and unify. To keep a Highland force in the field for a season, and to keep them from plunder or desertion, they would have to be provided the type of commissariat and staff work which they might not be experienced in supplying for themselves. They also needed a clear and decisive strategic direction which could keep them moving and keep them aggressive. All this was a considerable challenge for a young, militarily inexperienced Prince who had never set foot in the Highlands before. The Highlanders also needed weapons: the disarming of the Highlands had been a key objective of the British authorities in the wake of the earlier risings, and although their efforts had not been totally effective it would be wrong to imagine every Highlander had access to a panoply of weapons. Unaware of Charles' imminent arrival, little was being done internally to concentrate what resources there were.

Most of this was not unknown to the Prince. It was precisely why he had filled the holds of his ships with muskets, swords, pistols, and coin. Sufficiently armed, the Highlanders would be a considerable asset, and 700 French volunteers would more than compensate for any deficiencies they might have in a set-piece battle. But by the end of 9 July, Charles no longer had access to either his soldiers or the bulk of his supplies. The little armada was intercepted by HMS *Lion*, some distance off the Lizard Point. The *Lion* was a good match for *L'Elisabeth*, and Captain Piercy Brett would not decline the chance to deter a French warship venturing so close to Great Britain. The ships engaged in a furious exchange of shot, but eventually the ageing *L'Elisabeth* proved too slow in corresponding her movements and Captain Brett saw his chance. A blistering broadside raked the French ship 'from stem to stern' as the *Du Teillay*'s log reports, killing many and devastating the ship. The smaller ship, to the chagrin of Prince Charles, was helpless in aiding her companion as *Lion*'s big guns could have blown the little privateer out of the water before she herself was within range to reply. Instead she hovered close about in the hope of gaining an opportunity to intervene, whilst the captain sternly obliged the Prince to stay out of harm's way. By 10pm both the British and French ship had done such damage to one another that neither could continue. Captain D'O was dying of his wounds, as were many of *L'Elisabeth*'s crew. The warship had suffered so badly she could barely be handled into Brest, taking with Charles' Franco-Irish soldiers, much needed military supplies, and even the Royal Standard. The Prince at least was unscathed, although the *Du Teillay*'s sails had been peppered with grape-shot holes.

Charles pressed on alone, now lacking the items most likely to endear him to his friends in the Highlands and most essential to his chances of success. He was fortunate in being able to consult with so connected a banker as Aeneas MacDonald who, as a brother of MacDonald of Kinlochmoidart, intimately knew the region to which they were headed. Macdonald was an invaluable source of information and advice, especially in regard to who the Prince might be able to call upon when he landed. Charles was not sailing entirely into the dark, but he must have known that his project would look considerably less appealing to his supporters without an immediate injection of resources and military capacity. Even before the loss of *L'Elisabeth* his chances of bringing some clans to his side had been slender.

The Highlands of Scotland were not a harmonious and isolated ancient feudal idyll, brimming with martial honour and unquestioningly loyal to the House of Stuart. The area was not cut off from outside ideas and influences any more in its politics than it was in its fashions. So alongside a rich and vibrant Gaelic culture and language there were also modernising influences which were already starting to undermine the traditional purity of the clan system. Chieftains were becoming land-lords like their lowland counterparts, in some cases faster and more consciously than others. Traditional bonds of service still held true, but few self-respecting Highland leaders intended to get left behind as the rest of Scotland sought a share of the benefits of the modern world. Some were therefore closely tied into the Hanoverian system; others had sensed the opportunities opened up by the emergence of Glasgow and, through its port, access to the empire. Even for those not feeling any benefit from Union with England, there was no guarantee of loyalty to the Stuart. Hard livings in hard lands meant the risks of leaving home were considerable and the benefits of such a gamble dubious. Besides, there were the garrisons to consider; often not too far away and sometimes providing a welcome market for local goods. Such people would need persuading, or coercing.

Charles Edward Stuart stepped ashore on the little island of Eriskay on 23 July 1745. He is said to have dropped some seeds as he came ashore, the pink and white flowers still blooming on the Prince's Strand today. Still bearded and disguised, he walked upon the soft white sands of the beautiful beach and sensed that his moment was dawning. But the mood was not yet contagious. Sir Thomas Sheridan, Charles' former tutor, was well into his seventies and present only out of his affection for the Prince, and along with Tullibardine he was advising Charles now to turn back before it was too late. As they crouched together in a hut beside the beach, roasting flounders over the coals, it must indeed have seemed a forlorn episode. But Charles was insistent and messengers were sent out with the first discreet news that the Prince of Wales had come out of exile. The next day Alexander Macdonald of Boisdale came over from South Uist and offered his unequivocal assessment. He told Charles to go home. 'I am come home, sir', replied the Prince, 'and I will entertain no notion at all of returning to that place from whence I came, for that I am persuaded that my faithful Highlanders will stand with me'.[10] The next day he sailed on to the mainland.

In the crucial weeks that followed, the Prince's greatest ally was the relative remoteness of his location in Borrodale. Even if they did not intend to support an uprising, the clansmen in the immediate vicinity would not see a prince of the blood harmed or betrayed whilst he was a guest on their land. The MacDonalds of Clanranald therefore mobilised a small bodyguard to protect Charles whilst his messengers carried invitations to audience across the region in the hope of assembling enough support. The least they could do was preserve the royal person until it was clear whether he was determined to stay, which of course he was. On

---

[10] MacDonald, N.H., *The Clan Ranald of Garmoran: a History of the MacDonalds of Clanranald*, (Edinburgh: Forrest Hepburn and McDonald, 2008) p.345.

5 August he moved permanently ashore into Borrodale House; 1,500 muskets and 1,800 broadswords had already been unloaded from the *Du Teillay*, along with the powder supplies and the ship's swivel guns. A few days later the Prince said his farewells to Antoine Walsh, and the ship's departure sent a clear signal that Charles Edward Stuart meant business. Walsh had performed invaluable service to the Stuarts, like his father before him, and it had not gone unnoticed. Charles promised, 'you may be quite sure that if I ever come to the throne to which my birth summons me, you will have as good reason to be satisfied with me as I am now with you'. Before the ship departed, the crewmen indulged their curiosity and made sure to 'have a look at the Highlanders'.[11]

The Prince was now firmly ashore and able to equip almost two thousand men if they could be found. A rendezvous had been set for the 19 August at the head of Loch Shiel, a convenient location at the confluence of several glens and waterways if not of decent roads. Thus it was accessible enough to the Highlanders even though the garrison of Fort William sat barely a dozen miles to the east. There, at Glenfinnan, Charles would discover what support he had gathered and how convincing his appeals had been. Above all, he needed to know if he had turned Donald Cameron of Lochiel. They had met aboard ship on 30 July, when Lochiel had attempted to add his influential voice to those urging Charles to reconsider. His audience with the Prince had left him rather less certain of his own mind, softened by appeals to his honour and a little emotional blackmail. Lochiel was a crucial ally if Charles could persuade him to come out: his grandfather had fought with Dundee and his father with Mar at Sheriffmuir. But the latter, now in his eighties, was living out his last years in exile for his part in the '15, leaving his son to act as chief in his stead. He knew the risks.

The forty-five year old Lochiel was something of a model clan leader for his time: upright and honourable, attentive to the status and needs of his clansmen, well educated, and comfortable in both Highland and Lowland culture. His opinion carried weight beyond his own clan, which may not have been affluent but was populous and maintained a readiness for action. Unlike his near neighbour Argyll, he had not severed the bonds of kinship between chief and tacksmen – the tier of Highland gentlemen lying between the laird and his tenants – and that gave him cadre of loyal officers in time of war, who were also close enough to the clansmen to ensure they too fulfilled their feudal duties. Lochiel was not insensitive of the risks he could be exposing his dependents to, but nor did he expect that they would do anything but abide by his decision. Would their ever be a better opportunity than this to oust the intrusive garrison at Fort William and extend Cameron authority at the expense of the Campbells to the south? Or was the risk

---

11   From the Captain's Log of the *Du Teillay*, presented in Robertson, J. L., 'Log of the "Dutillet'" *Transactions of the Gaelic Society of Inverness*, Vol XXVI, (Inverness: Gaelic Society of Inverness, 1910) p.31ff.

of losing everything too great, with the lessons of 1715 and 1719 large in the mind? Charles could only wait and see.

In the meantime, Charles was on the move. With only a small entourage he travelled by boat to Kinlochmoidart house, where he was entertained by the brother of Aeneas MacDonald. The Clanranald men, humping the crates of weapons and barrels of powder, took the less direct overland route. For once the Prince enjoyed a succession of positive developments. First came a large quantity of barley and oatmeal, sent as a parting gift from the *Du Teillay*, which had succeeded in capturing three cargos of meal and another of timber and iron before sailing off with a passing salute to the soldiers at Bernera Barracks. A condition of these ships' ransom was their delivery of their cargo to the Prince, who purchased what he could, no doubt at good prices, and sent them on their way. Even more welcome was the arrival of John Murray of Broughton, who had rushed north on receiving word this the Prince had landed. He had arranged with James Mor Macgregor, son of the famous Rob Roy, that the Macgregor would make a pretence of loyalty to King George by informing Sir John Cope he had certain intelligence that the Prince was in fact secretly at St Omer, and that the Highland enterprise was merely a ruse. Broughton was a familiar and welcome face and Charles immediately found him important duties. He would serve from here on as Secretary of State.

From Kinlochmoidart House the small retinue now moved overland to Dalilea on the northern shore of Loch Shiel. Here the Prince met the renowned bard Alexander MacDonald (Alasdair Mac Mhaighstir Alasdair), a local poet and schoolmaster in his late forties. It seems that he and Charles instantly connected, not least because the teacher did not initially know whose company he was keeping and so remained convivially at ease during their meeting. Thus the Bard of Clanranald became Gaelic tutor to the Jacobite Prince of Wales. There were few better choices, as MacDonald was the author of a Gaelic-English lexicon as well as a number of poems which are said to have been read to Charles in exile to massage his affection for the Highlands. If the Prince had indeed heard verses such as those in *Oran Nam Fineachan Gaidhealach* (The Song of Clans), then he came to the Highlands believing in his destiny, that his moment had come, and that the Gaels yearned for his coming with a devoted longing. In the hearts of men like the Bard that might well have been true, but how much more pragmatic everything must now have seemed to this young messiah. But things were at least moving forward: the rendezvous was just a day away. With about fifty Clanranald men as his guard, the Prince's party boarded a flotilla of galley boats and set off towards their final stop ahead of Glenfinnan. But when the Prince entered Glenaladale House he found someone quite unexpected: a British officer.

4

The Race to the Capital

Back in Edinburgh, unaware of the countdown to the rallying of the clans at Glenfinnan, Lieutenant General Sir John Cope was doing everything in his power to prepare his army for a march northwards to nip the rebellion in the bud. His own forces were concentrating at Stirling whilst he saw to the final arrangements at the capital. Frustrated by delays, including a long wait for funds to be released on credit, there was nevertheless plenty of activity with which to fill the time. The general was fortunate in the presence of Colonel John Campbell, Earl of Loudoun, who had that very month been authorised to raise a new twelve-company Highland regiment on the model of the Black Watch. It had barely got off the ground, however, and its first few companies of recruits were quickly ordered into the safety of Fort George at Inverness. There Duncan Forbes could determine what to do with them if needed, as he could with the one thousand muskets sent up on the *Happy Janet*. Loudoun himself was therefore at a loose end and able to join Cope's staff as Adjutant-General, a role befitting of his rank as Cope was able to confer with him on all matters. Meanwhile, 'the ovens of Leith, Stirling and Perth were kept at work day and night, Sunday not excepted', to provide sufficient bread and biscuit for twenty-one days of campaigning.[1]

Cope's plan, as agreed with the officers of state, was still to march north and confront the rising directly before it got out of hand, raising as many loyal Highlanders as possible along the way. On 13 August the Secretary of State confirmed unanimous approval of the plan by his colleagues in Whitehall: 'a little vigour, shown in the beginning, might prevent their coming to a head'.[2] Two companies of Lascelles' Regiment and two weeks' supply of bread were given to the two generals in Edinburgh Castle, and Hamilton's Dragoons were posted to the Canongait and Holyrood areas of the capital. The two raw companies of Scots Fusiliers were left in Glasgow, two similarly weak companies of recruits were added to the garrison at Stirling, and a company of the Black Watch was posted to

---

1 Cope's evidence, Robins (ed.), *Inquiry*, p.8.
2 Tweeddale to Cope, Whitehall, 13 August 1745, in Robins (ed.), *Inquiry*, Appendix, p.13.

Glenfinnan, where the Jacobites raised their Standard on 19 August. (Author's collection)

Inverary to support the Duke of Argyll in his efforts to prevent any Jacobite breakout towards Glasgow. They would also seize all the available water transport on the west coast to restrict the potential for enemy movement between the Western Isles.

The rest of Cope's strength was to assemble in the parkland beneath Stirling Castle or else on the road from Perth to meet him en route. Gardiner's Dragoons had also concentrated at Stirling but were to remain there whilst the army advanced in order to cover that critical crossing point. Cavalry were of limited value in the Western Highlands, after all. When Cope left Edinburgh on the evening of 19 August, it was therefore to take command of five companies of Lee's, eight of Lascelles', and two of John Murray's Highland Regiment (the Black Watch). Guise's more experienced soldiers had been moved from the east coast into the Highlands in order to support Murray's Regiment. Three companies went to Fort William, three to Fort Augustus, two companies to Inverness, one to Bernera Barracks at Glenelg and one to Ruthven in Badenoch. There were also eighteen men and an officer on Mull, from where their contribution to the campaign would likely be limited. Finally, the two raw companies of Royal Scots at Perth were despatched as a further reinforcement for Fort William.

It was this last motion which triggered the first land action of the Rising, and the immediate cause of it was the anxiety of Lieutenant-Governor Alexander Campbell at Fort William. This officer had written to Cope that he had information which suggested two thousand Frenchmen had landed in Moidart on a dozen transports. Campbell had heard this from an informant who had himself heard it from a relation, making it fairly dubious intelligence. But if it were true it would be Campbell's post which would take the brunt of the invasion, and at this point he had only 130 men to resist it. Far from posing a threat to the assembling Highlanders, Fort William was on the defensive from the outset: 'unhappy for us in this place, if we are attacked!'[3] The fort itself was in need of urgent repair too, as the inner gate had been pulled down some time before. Campbell pointed this out to add further urgency to his letter. Cope could not ignore this short but sensational letter from the deputy-governor. If he did not act and the fort fell prematurely, then the fault might well be perceived as his. Accordingly, those fresh-faced Royal Scots were dispatched to Fort William in addition to the two companies of Guise's Regiment that were already on their way.

Ahead of them went Captain John Sweetenham, an engineer from Guise's Regiment, who was sent on from Ruthven to take over the party which was busily repairing that gate. Sweetenham stopped at an inn at the side of Wade's military road to take some refreshment when he was suddenly surprised and arrested by four clansmen under the command of Donald MacDonnell of Tirnadris. His sword was taken and in due course he was handed over to old Gordon of Glenbucket. This Jacobite veteran had been out in all the previous risings, and despite his age and infirmity was hurrying off with a party of his men to join with the Prince. He took Sweetenham off Tirnadris' hands, and it was this British officer who found himself facing Charles Edward Stuart at Glenaladale. No doubt the captain was all too aware that, however well he had been treated, his seizure on 14 August had signalled the official commencement of hostilities. Scotland was in a state of civil war.

Unfortunately, nobody had told Captain John Scott of Scotstarvet. With about eighty-five men of the Royal Scots he was obediently following in Sweetenham's wake along the military road. Tirnadris was now ready for him too. Wade's road crossed the deep gorge of the River Spean over a stunningly impressive stone bridge. These days the arches are ruined and only the great stone pillars remain, but the location remains evocative. In its time it must have been a marvel. From the bridge, the road ran straight to Fort William past Ben Nevis. There were just a few miles left to march, therefore, when Scott's men stepped out onto the bridge on 16 August 1745. Trapped in this bottleneck, they suddenly found themselves under fire. Pipes struck up behind the trees, and muskets cracked from the foliage. To these unseasoned redcoats there seemed to be Highlanders lurking behind every rock and branch, calling out to one another and rushing from cover to cover for a better chance at spilling blood. Highbridge was a death trap; Scott and his men fell back along the road towards Fort Augustus, but the Highlanders now filled the

---

3   Campbell to Cope, Fort William, 11 August 1745, quoted Robins (ed.), *Inquiry*, Appendix, p.15.

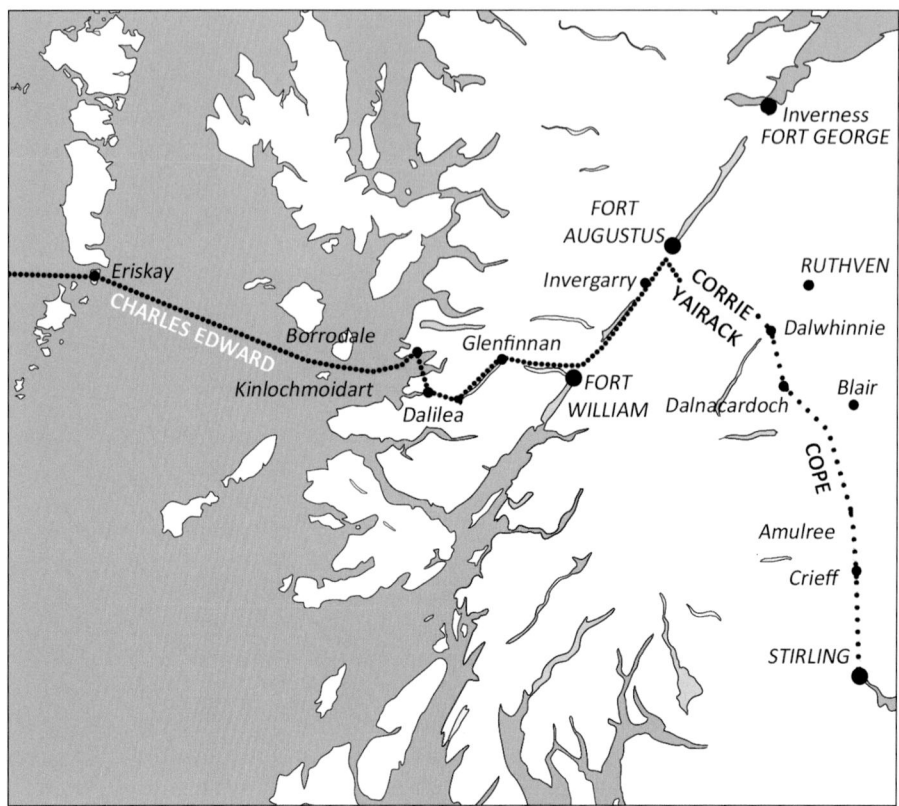

Map 3 Phase One of the northern campaign: the race to the Corrieyairack Pass.

landscape all around them. Men were dead, men were wounded. Eventually Scott was able to form a hollow square, surrounded on all sides now, but he himself was injured and his men had no stomach for a last stand. Both companies surrendered.

The skirmish at High Bridge must have been a shocking and terrifying experience for Scott's men, whose training had done nothing to prepare them for it. In fact they had been initially opposed only by Tirnadris, his piper, and a dozen vocal and cunning clansmen. They had successfully duped their opponents and driven them down the road before it could become clear how few they were. The initial flight had been hopelessly disordered, but eventually Scott's men had recovered sufficiently to make a fighting retreat of it, exchanging fire before finally giving up after a large body of Jacobite reinforcements arrived under Alexander MacDonald of Keppoch. Another veteran of the '15, Keppoch had served his exile in the French army and now had valuable military experience in his hand. Now the MacDonalds had struck the first blow for Prince Charlie, and had prisoners aplenty to show for it. Two hundred and seventy-one years after the skirmish at Highbridge, one of the lead balls fired that day would be found on the valley-side by swordsmith Paul Macdonald, who now lives in Prestonpans.

The scene at Glenfinnan on 19 August 1745 has since been immortalised in art and film. It is one of the most stirring tableaux in Scotland's history. Initially finding the meeting point empty, Charles Edward Stuart fretted in a small hut beside the loch where the Clanranald men could not witness his anxiety. But in due course more clansmen began to trickle in and, at last, Cameron of Lochiel came up with around 600 well-armed warriors. Keppoch brought several hundred more, and the sight of the clansmen descending the mountain tracks behind their pipes and banners was, as the Irishman John Macdonald rather understatedly put it, 'quaintly pleasing'.[4] By the end of the day something close to 1,200 men had gathered, the Royal Standard had been raised and the Prince's Commission of Regency read. The Rising was now formally underway: Charles Stuart had come home, to win the throne of his ancestors or to perish in the attempt. Captain John Sweetenham was brought along to witness the jubilant scenes, before being given an honourable parole and sent on his way to inform General Cope.

Charles now had an army, and arms were distributed according to need to ensure that it was ready to fight. But even in the first hours and days of its existence there were problems. The army lacked a train, and there were insufficient horses and waggons to transport the spare weaponry and supplies. Most of the meal purchased at Kinlochmoidart from the prize-ships never made it out of the immediate vicinity since there was no way of transporting it. Swivel guns from the decks of the *Du Teillay*, brought ashore with no little effort and then carried by hand down to Glenfinnan, had to be buried in a bog less than a mile away. And although he now had the semblance an army, and from Highbridge proof of its potential, Prince Charles had none of the time he needed to strengthen and train its soldiers. The clans formed their own regiments under their own officers, often with disproportionate numbers of the latter for their strength; Charles simply had to trust that they could be relied upon. The Prince was the only thing that held this army together, and the only person who could drive it.

For the moment the tables had turned: now it was Charles Edward who was kept static whilst his supplies were concentrated and his army made ready for campaign. In contrast, Sir John Cope was on the move. He arrived in Stirling as soon as he had the released the cash he needed to pay his way on the road, and with the exhortations of Tweeddale ringing in his ears he delayed no longer. The supplies could follow on with eight companies of Lascelles' Regiment as a guard; the rest of the army had to move. Nor was Cope the only British officer on the road: William Blakeney was heading to Scotland to take up command of the Stirling garrison. King George II himself was preparing to return to Britain from the continent, a statement of the seriousness with which events were at least

4 Taylor, *1745 and After*, p.60.

perhaps being treated. The Duke of Argyll hoped his return would inject some vigour into the government.

Meanwhile the Duke of Atholl, whose attainted older brother was helping Charles Edward to raise his Standard, had appointed his other brother Lord George Murray as Sheriff Deputy with responsibility for assisting the passage of His Majesty's forces through Perthshire. To Cope's disappointment, however, this support did not go so far as the raising of additional manpower. This was a worrying sign, as Atholl himself was loyal and his lands were far from any immediate threat of intimidation from the Jacobites. If Atholl could not get his men to march with Cope, how likely was it that others could? The raising of fresh loyal companies was a central pillar in Cope's strategy, making up for his deficiencies in manpower with a surplus of weaponry. Even before the army had entered the Highlands Cope was expressing doubts to General Guest back in Edinburgh, reporting that nothing short of the positive orders he had received from the government would incline him to push forwards in these circumstances. But now he was committed.

Cope had other concerns too. The cartloads of supplies which had caused him such delays continued to slow his march: some even had to be left behind. An anonymous letter to the Prime Minister would later joke about the length of the baggage train which accompanied such a small army. Its author would also state that it was discovered at Crieff that there was a shortage of black powder, which deficiency Cope attempted to cover up by repeatedly requesting more arms and ammunition, ostensibly for distribution to the well-affected. This sounds suspiciously like a retrospective smear, making play upon the fact that Cope had more firelocks than recruits to bear them. The same source, claiming to have been a volunteer on the march, recalls that many of the musket balls issued were too large for the barrels of the guns, obliging the soldiers to chew the lead until they fitted. If true this would have been a major scandal, but no mention of it can be found elsewhere and the form of this letter, which the author clearly considers to be the height of wit, suggests that its objective is more to do with fingering Cope for subsequent failures than with providing a fair assessment of events. Whether or not he believed them, Henry Pelham wrote himself a neat summary of the author's accusations.[5]

Speed was of the essence for Cope's army if it was to engage whilst it still had the advantage. Just as Charles was discovering, the want of decent horses was a major problem. The abandonment of the bread was on account of this, as was the decision to send 700 muskets back to Stirling after the conference with Atholl and Lord George left Cope and Loudoun convinced that they would not find a use for them. Lord Glenorchy asked for the arms to be sent out to him, but Cope was unconvinced of the value of doing so and he anyway lacked the transport to affect

---

5   Nottingham University, Newcastle (Clumber) Collection, Papers of Henry Pelham, Ne C 1707: Some Reflexions on General Cope's Behaviour in Scotland.

it, so instead he instructed Glenorchy's men to come and receive them in person. They never appeared. What baggage horses Cope did have proved hard to keep a hold of, as there was 'no such thing as Inclosures to keep them in'.[6] As a result the horses could not be kept together and guarded at night; they disappeared in large numbers. The later inquiry specifically asked what measures were taken to prevent this, but it seems that, regardless of the posting of guards, the losses could not be stopped. Cope was obliged to abandon yet more supplies for this want of horses, but he did at least try to make arrangements for them to catch up. As the army headed to Dalnacardoch, it fell to the sheriff deputy Lord George Murray to arrange for the supplies to be forwarded when sufficient horses could be rounded up. Only a fraction of the bread was sent.

To unencumber his men a little on the march, Cope had instructed the soldiers to leave their side-hangers at Stirling. These clumsy short swords were more use in camp than in battle, and nothing in the British Army's training instructed in their use; they were jettisoned as a possible hindrance. For the most part the men were doing well on the march, despite their inexperience of the urgency of a campaign. Cope was all too aware of how green some his men were: 'as all the troops in this country are raw, and unused to taking the field, it makes it very difficult for me to put them in motion in the manner I could wish'.[7] Further evidence of the shortcomings of the men at Cope's disposal came at Dalnacardoch, where the general learned from Captain Sweetenham of the surrender at Highbridge. He also heard the captain's account from Glenfinnan, which must have been sobering. But Cope had come too far to turn back now, and as he repeatedly reminded the Board of Inquiry in 1746, his instructions from Tweeddale were unequivocal. The advance would continue.

Across the mountains, the Jacobites knew he was coming. Charles moved first to Fassfern, where he is said to have plucked a white rose for his hat, before leaving Loch Eil behind and entering the mountains. This way took him by Achnacarry, seat of the Camerons, and on to Moy. The move allowed the army to bypass the guns of Fort William, no doubt to the relief of Alexander Campbell who did nothing to interfere. The only downside was that this route put them on the north side of the River Lochy, which then had to be crossed in order to take advantage of the military road. This done, with O'Sullivan supervising the passage of the baggage and supplies by boat, the Prince surged forwards over the Highbridge and up Wade's road towards Invergarry Castle. This sudden burst of speed had been triggered by reports that Cope was drawing near. Charles sent orders back to O'Sullivan that the baggage must not hold up the army, and even if only a few barrels of powder got up with them then that was more important than anything else. He even ordered most of his own baggage to be left at the back, so that nobody could

---

6   Cope's evidence, Robins (ed.), *Inquiry*, p.17.
7   Cope to Tweeddale, Edinburgh, 13 August 1745, Robins (ed.), *Inquiry*, Appendix, p.17.

General Wade's road, at the western end of the Corrieyairack Pass near Fort Augustus. (Author's collection)

complain if their belongings had to be abandoned to facilitate a rapid advance to battle. At Invergarry, where the weather turned suddenly foul, the little army was considerably strengthened by the appearance of the Stewarts of Appin, led by the famous swordsman Charles Stewart of Ardsheal, by MacDonalds from Invergarry and Glencoe, by Grants of Glenmoriston, and by other assorted small bands from elsewhere. On 27 August the Prince pushed the army on further, marching on foot amongst his men and sharing in their excitement. They came within sight of Fort Augustus, bypassed it, and ascended the military road into the Corrieyairack Pass. The Highland forts, 'after all the boastings of Marshal Wade,' had failed to contain the threat.[8]

The British army arrived at Dalwhinnie on 26 August, whilst Charles was at Invergarry. A short distance north of the village Wade's military road divided: one

---

8   Nottinham University, Newcastle (Clumber) Collection, Papers of Henry Pelham, Ne C 1640: Letter from the Duke of Argyll to Henry Pelham, Edinburgh, 17 August 1745.

branch headed north past the barracks at Ruthven towards Fort George; the other headed to Laggan and Garvamore, beyond which it headed into the Corrieyairack towards Fort Augustus. General Cope was therefore at a literal as well as figurative crossroads. The road he had intended to take would lead him along the bottom of the Spey valley to the way-station or 'King's House' at Garvamore, a long recently-built structure which served as the last place of comfort for travellers using the King's road over the pass. It was frequently used by the military of course, which is probably why it is still sometimes referred to as a barracks. From here the army would have crossed another of Wade's famous bridges at Garva, beyond which the road continued on the north side of the river until it turned north-west into a short glen beneath the shadow of the Corrieyairack Hill. Turning sharply west at the glen's end, the road then mounted the steep hillside in an improbably tight zig-zag, before running across the exposed terrain until it was forced into another ziz-zag as it approached the bridge over the Tarff at Snugborough. The crossing, about twenty-five miles from Dalwhinnie, is overlooked on all sides by high ground and flanked by trees. The road then continues onwards in a rather straighter course before eventually making a windy descent towards Fort Augustus and the glistening waters of Loch Ness, which after this arduous and bleak approach look like nothing short of paradise. From the camp at Dalwhinnie the route to Fort Augustus is about thirty miles, and few of them are easy.

From a military perspective the Corrieyairack was a nightmare. The road was narrow and easily blocked and there were no alternatives, especially for wheeled vehicles. Major Griffith, brought out of Edinburgh Castle to run Cope's artillery train, had four galloper guns and four Ceohorn mortars to transport, the ammunition and supplies for these alone requiring ten covered waggons.[9] Even Cope's small army, just shy of 2,000 at this point, would take time to successfully cross the pass, especially after the recent rain, and if the Jacobites had only done so little as to break a bridge the redcoats would be forced to halt and left vulnerable. Worse, if the enemy had actually occupied the road then passage would be bloody at best, impossible at worse. A few men and guns could command this road against a force far larger, since there was little room for deployment and few places from which to return artillery fire. The zig-zag ascents were the most dangerous places, although the bridge at Snugborough was also fraught with risks as the narrow ravine was overlooked and invited ambush. Even if the first ascent was successfully forced by the redcoats, Snugborough provided the enemy with a second line on which to fall back. Even a beaten force of Highlanders was capable of breaking the bridge as it departed, and the British army would then be as vulnerable in victory as in defeat. Casualties would have had a long way to go for aid, and there were few means of transporting them. If – and it was a big if – the Prince had got men up into the Corrieyairack in numbers then the coming confrontation would be deadly and one-sided.

---

9   Cope's evidence, Robins (ed.), *Inquiry*, p.20.

There was an alternative possibility of course. If Cope and his army got over the Corrieyairack before the Jacobites, then it would be the Highlanders who would be trapped. With the garrisons at Fort Augustus and Fort William on their flank or rear, the fledgling Jacobite army might find itself forced to attack the enemy on the hills above. Such an assault would scarce have been plausible in the face of such a disparity in firepower, and the clans might well have been forced to disperse into the hills even if there was no pitched contest. As it stood on 26 August, Charles Edward was roughly five miles from the western entrance to the pass by Fort Augustus, ten miles from the bridge at Snugborough, and fifteen from the zigzagging eastern descent. In contrast, General Cope was about twenty miles from the eastern entrance, twenty-five from Snugborough, and thirty from western descent. The Jacobites had the edge.

Sir John Cope knew just about everything he needed to know at this juncture except the exact whereabouts of the Highland army. He had the benefit of an eye-witness report from the Jacobite muster at Glenfinnan, as Captain John Sweetenham had joined him at Dalnacardoch on 25 August. Sweehenham had been released four days earlier, before the new arrivals had joined Charles at Invergarry, and so he had informed Cope that the Prince had at least 1,400 men at the moment of his departure, armed with an assortment of firelocks, broadswords, pistols and French cutlasses. The captain had seen several bodies of Highlanders in motion since his release, taking the total perhaps to around 1,800. He also faithfully reported the presence of twenty-one swivel guns off the *Du Teillay*, which would have been fatal opponents if the pass had to be forced. He was unaware, of course, that the Jacobites had already abandoned most of these. Other rumours about the Jacobite numbers went as high as 4,000 but when Duncan Forbes sent what he had learned on to Cope he had pitched for the more realistic suggestion of around 1,800-1,900. These were realistic figures.

This intelligence was sent with reports that the enemy intended to hold the pass at Snugborough whilst flanking parties worked round the glens to the west to descend on Cope's rear once battle had been joined.[10] That was a disturbing proposition, although the surviving Jacobite narratives do not suggest that a detailed plan had in fact been decided upon other than simply getting up there first. Cope received his letter from Forbes on the road to Dalwhinnie, but the Lord President's unsubtle hints as to the dangers of the Corrieyairack were not needed: Major William Caulfield, Quartermaster-General to Cope's army, was also the Inspector of Roads. As Wade's successor, Caulfield knew every inch of the military road network and certainly understood the risks ahead. With such information at his disposal it is not difficult to understand how Cope came to the conclusion that to press forwards into the pass was to 'expose the troops to certain destruction'.[11]

---

10   Forbes' evidence, Robins (ed.), *Inquiry*, p.20.
11   Cope's evidence, Robins (ed.), *Inquiry*, p.26.

A council of war was called in Cope's tent 'very early in the morning' of the following day, 27 August, and the general's ten most senior officers put their signatures to a unanimous agreement that entering the Corrieyairack would lead to the army being 'cut to pieces, or reduced to the necessity of surrendering'.[12] They were shown Tweeddale's exhortations to advance and seek battle, and they had heard the latest information from Forbes and Sweetenham. Their decision was based, as is made clear by the statement the officers signed, on the belief that the enemy already held the pass. They also unanimously accepted that the general, and by extension they themselves, had done everything possible to reach the pass in time to prevent that.

The decision not to enter the pass was most probably the right one, in light both of what the British officers believed and of the reality on the ground. Charles Edward would not begin his climb until dawn on 28 August, twenty-four hours after Cope's council of war at Dalwhinnie, so assuming Cope could have marched the fifteen miles to Garvamore and camped on the 27th, the two armies would have been entering the Corrieyairack from opposite ends at exactly the same time. That would have made it impossible for the Jacobites to stop Cope on the famous zig-zag ascent, but they would easily have reached Snugborough before him and could have dug themselves in for a fight.[13] Deep inside what must now be considered hostile territory for them, the only British army in Scotland might well have been annihilated. Both well-informed and inclined to caution, Cope had avoided such a catastrophe for the time being. But having decided not to continue the march towards the enemy, Cope was acting against the consistent orders of his superiors in London and this was why he needed the written support of his officers. Having got it, he now needed them to agree to a new strategy. Having already ruled out the advance to Fort Augustus, Cope's options were either to stay put and wait for the rebels to come down from the pass; to withdraw the way the army had come towards Stirling; or to take the other road north, to Inverness.

Each of these choices had drawbacks of course. The first was the most risky, as there were passes through the mountains which, whilst utterly unsuitable for a regular army with an artillery and waggon train, were perfectly viable for Highlanders marching light. That meant Cope's position could be circumvented or even surrounded, especially if the clans continued to rally around the Stuart prince at the same pace they apparently had since Glenfinnan. At Dalwhinnie the British army was therefore vulnerable. The second option, withdrawal to Stirling, was equally unappealing. Those alternative roads meant the Highlanders could potentially even reach Stirling faster than Cope, who was also less than keen to

---

12 Their written agreement is quoted in full in Robins (ed.), *Inquiry*, p.26.
13 Snugborough or Snugboro appears on General Roy's military map but it does not seem to warrant a mention on many modern ones. How different that might have been if the bloody Battle of Snugborough Bridge had taken place on 28 August 1745!

return through Atholl. Although the Duke remained openly loyal, none of his vassals had turned out and his brother Lord George, as sheriff deputy, was either incompetent or a saboteur. This was especially concerning as there were barely three days' worth of rations left. Considering the original allowance had been for twenty-one days, that means the army must have consumed or discarded eighteen days' worth of food in a week. If the Athollmen proved hostile even only so far as to not cooperate over supplies, the march home would be difficult. If they went so far as to break bridges and block roads, the army might find itself obstructed, hungry, and pursued. There were eighty long miles back to Stirling, along which anything might happen. Gardiner's Dragoons would be waiting there in support, but such a retreat without making contact with the enemy could finish Cope's career. It would also abandon the loyal clans to the mercy of their enemies and irreparably damage the King's prestige in the north.

The remaining option therefore was the one which initially seems to make the least sense: the march to Inverness. This was a shorter journey than Stirling, being only sixty miles, and it took the army past Ruthven and on to Fort George, both of which could add to Cope's manpower and supplies. At Inverness the general could consult with Lord President Forbes, arrange the arming of the loyal clans, and deny at least part of the Highlands to Charles Edward's remarkable recruitment drive. The risk was that the march north left the road to the Lowlands open behind them, but there was no guarantee that the Jacobites yet felt strong enough to strike south. Even if they did, they might well find themselves caught between a hammer and an anvil: the two regiments of dragoons at Edinburgh and Stirling amounted to nearly 600 men and were easily capable of containing and harassing a Highland force without cavalry of its own. Stirling and Edinburgh were both highly defensible against an enemy armed only with swivel guns, and the main British army would be hot on their heels and stronger than ever. And whilst the campaign moved south, the war would still continue in the Highlands as Cope planned to order the loyal companies he raised at Inverness to enter 'the country of the rebels, to drive their cattle, to distress their families, and thereby force them to return home'.[14]

The decision was duly taken, and, after advancing a short distance towards Garvamore, the army changed direction and re-joined the King's Road to Inverness. The garrison at Ruthven, a company of Guise's Regiment, was carried along with the army, leaving just 'a sergeant and 12 men, and some invalids' behind.[15] The march can hardly have been a happy one as now the initiative of the campaign had passed to the enemy. Although it could not yet have been predicted, Cope would never regain it. The road northwards must have seemed threatening, flanked in places by woodland and shadowed by the mountains. These had to be

---

14 Cope's evidence, Robins (ed.), *Inquiry*, p.28.
15 Cope's evidence, Robins (ed.), *Inquiry*, p.31.

crossed first above Aviemore and then at the Slochd Pass, a more dangerous prospect altogether. Cope had sent an appeal for the well-affected clans to secure the pass before his arrival, fearful that the Jacobites might try to seize this road too; but although they failed to fulfil their promise the crossing was made unopposed. The road then passed close to Moy Hall, home of Angus Mackintosh who was one of Cope's officers and a signatory of the agreement not to enter the Corrieyairack. His wife, Lady Anne, would soon be raising their tenants for the Prince's service.[16] If he had been able to see into the future, the Earl of Loudoun would discovered that in six months' time he would be leading a raid against Moy Hall to capture Charles Edward Stuart, only for his forces to be routed by Mackintosh's son with two retainers and a blacksmith in the so-called Rout of Moy on 16 February 1746. A few miles on and the army skirted the western extremity of Culloden Muir and arrived in the reassuring sanctuary of Inverness.

Early in the morning of 28 August, the Jacobites passed within sight of the Fort Augustus garrison before taking a shortcut from Aberchalder to Snugborough via Glen Buck. They marched in two columns, 'like lightning, but in good order', according to O'Sullivan.[17] Charles had surged ahead on foot, wearing through his shoes in his eagerness to secure the Corrieyairack. The Prince then had the leisure to pause at the site of the proposed battle, swallowing his irritation that the scouts sent up the previous night had failed to bring in any sensible reports and sending Secretary Murray and MacDonnell of Lochgarry to scout the road ahead. The rains of the march to Invergarry were long gone and the day promised to be hot and fine. Whilst the army was readying for battle behind them, Broughton and Lochgarry were amazed to discover that from the summit of the pass 'not a creature was to be seen'.[18] They approached a cluster of idlers and found them to deserters from Cope's own force of Highlanders, about forty of whom had slipped off when the army had turned away from the enemy. The Prince told his men that the enemy's behaviour was a sure 'presage of their future success', but the Jacobite Highlanders did not know whether to be overjoyed or outraged at the loss of the opportunity to show their worth.[19] Most clansmen could not have realised, as Charles Edward surely did, that they had won a critical strategic victory. After a long march without shelter under a hot sun, the Jacobite army reached the King's House at Garvamore by 2pm and cattle were slaughtered to prepare a meal.[20] These beasts were easier to transport than sacks of meal, and rather more satisfying.

---

16 Anne Mackintosh, a Jacobite heroine, is named on a plaque in Leith old cemetery where she was buried, although her grave has been lost.
17 Taylor, *1745 and After*, p.63.
18 Murray of Broughton, *Memorials*, p.177.
19 Murray of Broughton, *Memorials*, p.177.
20 The King's House, otherwise known as Garvamore Barracks, still survives but is disused and considered a building at risk.

Dinner had to be delayed however, as the men were crying out instead for action. They wanted to march on and cut off the redcoats at Slochd. Charles obligingly called for a council of war and 'made the map be laid before him', by which means the impossibility of getting the army to the pass ahead of Cope was demonstrated.[21] An alternative proposal was to send 500 of the hardiest men over the mountains to secure Slochd whilst the rest of the army followed the military road via Ruthven to come in Cope's rear. Again the risks were shown to be too great, as Cope had too much of a head start. Besides, the Jacobites had just completed a long and gruelling march, and so even if their advanced guard secured the pass it was unlikely the army could be expected to catch up in time to rescue them from an overwhelming disadvantage in numbers and firepower. Charles was aware that leaving an enemy in his rear presented disadvantages, not least in restricting the movements of potential supporters, but a greater opportunity now lay before them. He acted decisively: since General Cope had opened the road to the Lowlands for him, that road should be taken. Charles wanted Edinburgh.

The Jacobite council of war at Garvamore, which perhaps took place inside the King's House, is as important to understanding the campaign as Cope's council at Dalwhinnie. On 28 August we see Charles Edward at his soldierly best: leading the men by example on the march; adapting to the changing tactical situation; addressing the troops with encouragement when they are unsure how to react; and calling a council in response to their entreaties. At the council itself the Prince is seen to be firmly in control, hearing out the alternatives but demonstrating the strengths of his own thinking. Consult he will, but he alone commands the army and determines its course according to his own strategic instincts. And he was almost certainly correct in so doing. More to the point, the Highlanders accepted it without demur, however disappointed they might first have been. This would not always be the case in the future, regardless of how right Charles might yet be.

Charles did however make one concession: an attempt would be made to seize Ruthven Barracks. Thus far the army had steered its way around the government's forts and barracks, showing contempt for their garrisons and avoiding the risks and delays of an attack or siege. It was a wise strategy, but it was believed that Ruthven had been virtually abandoned. Indeed, only Sergeant Terrence Molloy and twelve men had been left there and it was indeed vulnerable. But, despite the protestations that the attack was being proposed in order to liberate the surrounding countryside, deny shelter to the enemy, or seize valuable stores, the main reason for proposing it was to satisfy the desire amongst the clansmen for some action. It appears the idea came from old Glenbucket, and whilst the Prince gave it his permission he seems to have been rather disinterested in a potentially foolhardy operation. Had he thought the mission significant or worthwhile, he would likely

---

21 Murray of Broughton, *Memorials*, p177.

Ruthven Barracks, Badenoch, which successfully defended against the first Jacobite attempt. (With thanks to David Beards)

have gone himself. Instead, perhaps to ensure that lives were not needlessly wasted in a futile gesture, he bade O'Sullivan command the operation.

Ruthven Barracks was comprised of two large barrack buildings, three stories high, linked together by a high barmkin wall pierced with loopholes. Two corners had the additional protection of projecting bastions. Adjacent to this main arrangement was a detached stable building, which created something of a blind spot on one approach, but the whole complex sat on a high motte providing commanding views over the plain around it. O'Sullivan called it 'two buldings upon a sugre loaf', and correctly assessed that its two small entrances made it a formidable nut to crack.[22] Sergeant Molloy professed he was too old a soldier to surrender so strong a fort 'without bloody noses', so the Highlanders were obliged to attack. From the cover of the stables they gave a covering fire to some stout-hearted volunteers who attempted to set fire to the gate, but the tiny garrison was able to concentrate its fire on the sappers whilst others poured down sufficient water to douse the flames. Two Highlanders were killed and several others wounded, whilst a careless redcoat poking his head over the parapet was also slain.[23] O'Sullivan was permitted to collect his casualties and he had the wisdom to fall back, 'very

22 Taylor, *1745 and After*, p.65.
23 Molloy to Cope, Ruthven Barracks, 30 August 1745, quoted Robins (ed.), *Inquiry*, p.43.

sorry to have attempted it'. The Jacobite army would return to Ruthven six months later, when the threat of their cannon would oblige Molloy at last to surrender. He received a commission as lieutenant, on Cope's recommendation, in recognition of his defence. After defeat at Culloden the remnants of the Jacobite army would assemble at Ruthven, only to discover the Prince was cut off from them and that the Rising was over. The burning of the barracks would be their final act of defiance before they dispersed. All that lay in the future.

Needless to say, Charles Edward Stuart was unsurprised by the failure of the Ruthven raid, and although it was technically the army's first setback he did not much feel the sting. It neither weakened his position nor strengthened his enemy. It was a pointless loss of two lives however, and for that the Prince expressed regret. He was rather more interested in arranging the main army's descent into Atholl, which followed the route of Cope's earlier march as far as Dalnacardoch, from where he turned off towards Blair. Here Charles was able to fulfil at least one of his objectives: he had brought Tullibardine home. The marquess, although not as old in years as he is sometimes assumed to have been, was rather gouty and well past the best of his campaigning years. Now he could assume his rightful place as Duke of Atholl and work the Prince's service by raising his tenants for King James. His brother, the officially recognised Duke, had fled at their approach. One wonders how much of Cope's bread and how many of his horses now started to reappear. The famed soldier-poet John Roy Stuart now joined the Prince after rushing back from the Continent, arriving in time to accompany him on the march through the Pass of Killiecrankie and on to Dunkeld. The Jacobite march was now on a different route to that which Cope had taken north, as the important town of Perth represented a significant prize and was well worth the diversion. On 4 September 1745, the Prince rode into Perth on Captain Sweetenham's horse. That same day, 120 miles to the north, the British army was preparing to depart from Inverness.

On his arrival in Inverness, Sir John Cope had written to 'every body that we could recollect' in order to raise the local clans in defence of King George's throne. These latest overtures proved as successful as all the previous ones, and Simon Fraser of Lovat used the expected 'ambiguous expressions' to excuse himself. Others promised much but delivered little. The only meaningful addition to strength was the addition of three companies of Loudoun's new regiment. Loudoun continued to serve as one of Cope's principal advisors, as did the ever-informed Duncan Forbes, and agreed with the general that if sufficient Highlanders now joined them it might be possible to march back south to confront the rebels.[24] If not, then the best way to make his troops 'useful to Britain, was to march them to Aberdeen.' Since there was little faith now that the Highlanders would respond in strength, orders were sent by sea to General Guest in Edinburgh that all available transports be sent up to that harbour to facilitate an embarkation. Once again Cope set ovens

---

24 Cope's evidence, Robins (ed.), *Inquiry*, p32.

to fire as he ordered large quantities of bread for his troops, and the bulk of the supplies were transferred onto a ship which could accompany the army along the coast. Another company of Guise's Regiment, along with two more gallopers and two more mortars, were brought out of the garrison into the field army. Angus Mackintosh's company of the Black Watch and a company of Loudoun's were transferred to garrison Fort George, and the army prepared to march.

The British army now burst into action: with the supplies following by sea, the army achieved a rapid pace of nearly twenty miles a day, covering the 115 miles to Aberdeen by 11 September. There a letter was waiting from Tweeddale, responding to notification of the Dalwhinnie decision. Ominously the Secretary of State stressed that he had shown Cope's letter to the King, who had now returned from the Continent. Accepting that events were now beyond control from Whitehall, Tweeddale passed the baton to Cope: 'as you are on the spot, you must now be left to act as you will judge best for His Majesty's service'.[25] He also advised that Dutch forces were on their way towards Leith, and that Brigadier Thomas Fowke had been ordered to Scotland from Yorkshire. Cope's own letters had been showing signs of strain in recent days, becoming increasingly defensive over his actions since Dalwhinnie. He knew it had been a turning point. From Inverness he was explaining that he was always obliged to write in a hurry, and that he hoped no errors on his part were being inferred from any lack of detail or clarity. 'I have not found any body here yet,' he wrote on 3 August, 'either civil or military, who thought I could do otherwise than I have done, consistent with the repeated orders Your Lordship did me the honour to send'.[26] These sound suspiciously like the opening moves in a game of blame.

On Cope's first night in Aberdeen, Charles Edward Stuart was dining at Balhaldie House in Dunblane. The last week had been an important one for the Jacobite army. Whilst Cope's men were enduring the forced marches to Aberdeen, most of the Jacobite strength was camped on the North Inch at Perth learning its new trade. For the first time there was the opportunity for some rudimentary training and consolidation. Much-needed money was raised through contributions, and Clanranald and Keppoch had successfully seized two vessels laden with arms and ammunition at Dundee. The pause at Perth allowed fresh recruits to arrive, but none were more important than James Drummond, Duke of Perth, and Lord George Murray. Perth had been close to fleeing the country after his brush with capture, but had been informed of the Prince's landing in sufficient time to prevent his departure. He was a popular and genial personality, and his status as a duke made him an important addition to the army. Charles appointed him lieutenant general, second only to the Prince himself. The only drawbacks were that Perth was a Catholic and had no great skill or interest in military matters.

25 Tweeddale to Cope, Whitehall, 7 September 1745, Robins (ed.), *Inquiry*, Appendix, p.26.
26 Cope to Tweeddalte, Inverness, 3 September 1745, Robins (ed.), *Inquiry*, Appendix, p.69.

But the arrival of Lord George Murray complicated matters. It was preceded by warnings reported both by John William O'Sullivan and Sir John Macdonald that Murray's intentions were not honest. O'Sullivan thought 'his character was not of the best', and recalled him being intimidating even to his friends and family, although he admits that Murray's presence was deemed necessary if the Athollmen were to come out in numbers.[27] Notwithstanding the poor character reports, passed on by two Irishmen who had no reason to bear Murray any love either during or after the rising, Lord George did of course have a respectable Jacobite pedigree. He had served in their armies and taken his time in exile, and had lately hindered Cope's march north as subtly as he had dared to do in the circumstances. Yes, he had accepted a pardon and left his older brother behind in exile, but the plain truth is that there was no real reason to suspect him of active disloyalty. The problem with Murray therefore lay not in his politics but in his overbearing manner and his astonishing arrogance.

Murray himself recorded his first day with the army: 'As I had formerly known something of a Highland army, the first thing I did was advise the Prince to endeavour to get proper people for provisors and commissaries'.[28] This sentence alone gives some insight. Although he did indeed have experience of campaigning with Highlanders (mainly in defeat), he had no more than many others around the table. Nonetheless, immediately upon his arrival he felt not only qualified but entitled to advise them. His relationship with the Jacobite command began with him pointing out what the existing staff officers were not doing right, and this approach could only set him on a collision course with men like O'Sullivan. Whatever his talents as a regimental officer, Murray's forcefulness in giving counsel, and his difficulties in heeding any but his own, would make him a destabilising factor in the centre of the Jacobite command.

On this occasion Murray's observations were not wrong: the army did need to arrange a proper means of supply as the campaign went on. He therefore deserves, as he took, some credit for organising the distribution of knapsacks for personal provisions. According to O'Sullivan, Charles initially appointed Murray as major general but on hearing that this made him only third in command the newcomer demanded equal rank with the Duke of Perth. Thereafter the two were supposed to share the duties of the day on rotation, but Murray's heavy manner and the easy-going Perth's lack of military knowledge led to the latter receding into the background when decisions had to be made. Murray would later press for Perth to be excluded from council on account of his Catholicism. Charles Edward, as ever in the early months of the campaign, did his best to please the statuses and ambitions of all comers. But Murray mistook youth for

---

27 Taylor, *1745 and After*, p.67.
28 Murray, G. 'Marches of the Highand Army', in Chambers & Forbes, *Jacobite Memoirs of the Rebellion of 1745*, (Edinburgh: W. & R. Chambers, 1834) p.30.

THE RACE TO THE CAPITAL 91

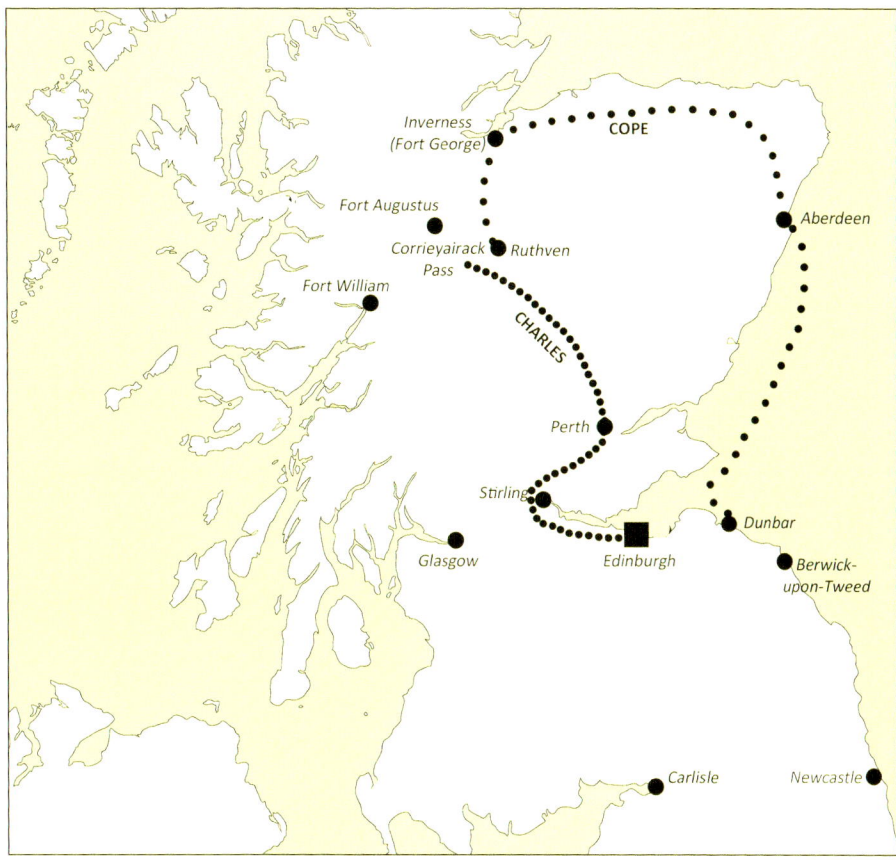

Map 4 Phase Two of the northern campaign: the race to Edinburgh.

incapacity and royalty for ignorance, and made no bones about expressing his views publicly. The relationship would not hold, but for now, at Perth, the Prince could hear only good news.

Leaving the restored Duke of Atholl behind to raise his tenants, Charles continued his advance. His men had been rested whilst his enemy had been force-marching along the Moray coast. From Dunblane, where more of the Duke of Perth's men joined, the army passed through the famous pistol-making village of Doune and headed towards Stirling. The castle there meant that there was no possibility of crossing the bridge where Wallace had once earned renown, and so the army moved instead towards the Fords of Frew in the footsteps of the great Montrose. Here, for the second time in just a few short weeks, Charles was astonished to find there was no opposition at an important strategic location. His army would be vulnerable as it waded into the water, and the south bank could easily have been held against them sufficiently to 'cost the Chevalier a good many men'.

Instead the Prince was left to ask what sort of 'officers they got in Britain, who were capable of abandoning so advantageous a post'.[29]

The officer who should have been facing Charles across the fords was Colonel James Gardiner of the 13th Dragoons. Based out of Stirling, where he had secured his wife and daughter in the care of Blakeney and the garrison, Gardiner had just shy of three hundred mounted troopers at his command. Hamilton's 14th Dragoons, with the same strength, were only thirty-five miles away in Edinburgh. The dragoons therefore had the capacity to make life very difficult for the Jacobite army, in theory at least. With the bridge at Stirling covered by the castle, and all shipping suitable for crossing the estuary already dispatched to Aberdeen, the Fords at Frew were the only realistic option for the Jacobites if they intended to march on Edinburgh. As Murray of Broughton recalled, 'had the two regiments of dragoons first cut the banks of the river, and then entrenched themselves with two or three piece of cannon, they would have made it very difficult'.[30] There do not appear to have been any positive orders for Gardiner to do so, but a vigorous officer could have been expected to act on his own initiative. It is also unclear whether Hamilton's had any lee-way in being able to move out of the capital to support to Gardiner, but as things stood there was little military risk in so doing. The dragoons should have been capable of dismounting to hold static positions without any disadvantage in a firefight, with the advantage of being able re-mount and disengage as the situation evolved. Even the 13th on its own had the potential to give the Jacobites a bloody nose if they obliged them to force the crossing under fire.

But instead Gardiner was falling back to Falkirk, where he visited the Earl of Kilmarnock at Callendar House before withdrawing again to Linlithgow. The dragoons, with their advantage of mobility, made no attempt to shadow or observe the Jacobites let alone oppose them. The Highlanders would have been vulnerable to harassment, especially at night when the operations of hostile horsemen could have denied them any security. Such operations might not have been decisive in and of themselves, but they could have slowed down the Prince's progress and unsettled morale. Instead Charles Edward passed Stirling, pausing at Bannockburn to rest and resupply the men, before pressing on to Falkirk himself. There Kilmarnock provided him with all the information he had gleaned from Colonel Gardiner, and although the earl had failed to raise the townsfolk for the cause he nevertheless agreed to join himself. In grave financial difficulty, Kilmarnock was willing to gamble everything on a Stuart victory. At about 1am on Sunday 15 September, Lord George Murray led the Jacobite vanguard to attack Gardiner's men at Linlithgow and secure the road to Edinburgh. Marching with commendable discipline and silence, the intention was to strike with the dawn.

---

29 Murray of Broughton, *Memorials*, p.191.
30 Murray of Broughton, *Memorials*, p.191.

Such a move showed confidence, but it was an anti-climax: 'we found the dragoons had gone off the night before', reported Murray.[31] Gardiner was already retreating to Edinburgh.

Thus the Jacobite army had crossed the Forth, resupplied itself out of Stirling in defiance of the garrison, and secured Falkirk, Linlithgow and the main road to the Scottish capital. The only sign of opposition had been a token salvo from the guns of Stirling Castle which did nothing to hinder the army's progress. The critical question, one left noticeably unasked at the subsequent inquiry, was why the dragoons had failed so spectacularly. After all this was Gardiner's home turf – he had been born and raised in Carriden near Bo'ness – and the regiment had been based in this area prior to the Rising. Gardiner himself must bear some of the blame. He was not well, that much is clear, and when the Prince landed the colonel had been taking the waters in Scarborough in the hope of improving his health. So perhaps he was not driving his men with the spirit which might have been expected from such a veteran. The horses had also been at grass when the storm broke and were probably as green as the men, most of whom had not seen battle before as the 13th's last engagement was Preston in 1716. But that could equally be said of their opponents.

Whilst it is understandable in part that Gardiner would be reluctant to give his troopers their first experience of being under fire when he had little by way of support, it was also an opportunity missed for them to gain a little confidence through controlled aggression. At the very least they should have been able to shadow and observe the enemy, or to break bridges and block roads to delay them. Unlike most of Cope's forces, the dragoon regiments had the benefit of almost a month to drill together as a unit and prepare for engagement. The enemy lacked cavalry of their own, giving Gardiner the free run of the land. That the dragoons failed to delay the Jacobites would have fatal consequences. Not only had a critical opportunity been missed to buy Cope time – time which might have enabled him to save Edinburgh – the retreat was undermining the morale of the dragoons themselves whilst allowing the Highlander to grow in their minds into a bogeyman.

Meanwhile, General Cope had embarked his men at Aberdeen, successfully getting the whole army aboard on a single tide. But the weather was against him and it was not until the following day that the transport fleet was able to sail. It was 15 September, the same day that Charles Edward Stuart visited the ancestral Stuart palace at Linlithgow. It was also the day that Thomas Fowke arrived in Edinburgh and took command of Hamilton's Dragoons. He found General Guest and the city's Lord Provost Archibald Stewart locked in discussions with other civil and legal officers about how they might defend the capital. Hamilton's Dragoons had been posted forwards at Corstorphine to cover the main approach to the city, and these had by now been joined by Gardiner's weary and jittery regiment. Gardiner

---

31   Murray, 'Marches', p.36.

withdrew the combined force a short distance to Coltbridge, near modern Murrayfield, leaving only a picket at Corstorphine village. The dragoons had been joined briefly by the 120 infantry of the Edinburgh City Guard, and a company of enthusiastic civilian volunteers had been ordered out to join them too. This latter body included young Alexander Carlyle, son of the minister at Prestonpans, along with several of his friends since many of the volunteers were students. But at the last moment the authorities lost their nerve, unwilling to risk the pride of the city's youth, and the volunteers were forbidden to leave the gates. The City Guard was then also recalled, leaving the dragoons without any infantry support at all.

By the morning of 16 September the Jacobites were edging cautiously towards their goal whilst Brigadier Fowke rode out to review his command. He was accompanied by Francis Scott, Lord Napier, and William, Earl of Home, a cavalry officer who happened to be home in Scotland on leave and was eager to volunteer his services. What Fowke found at Coltbridge was hardly inspiring:

> I found many of the horses' backs not fit to receive the riders; many of the men's and some of the officers' legs so swelled that they could not wear boots; and those who really were to be depended upon, in a manner overcome for want of sleep.[32]

Gardiner's Dragoons had only been under threat for three days; Hamilton's had even less excuse than that. As the Jacobites approached Corstorphine, according to the British narrative, the pickets fell back to Coltbridge and Fowke ordered the regiments to 'retire slowly and without confusion' towards Leith. The reality was rather messier. John Home reports that in the early afternoon the Jacobites sent forward a number of mounted young scouts, who rode enthusiastically close to the pickets and fired their pistols. At this, the dragoons 'without returning one shot, wheeled about and rode off, carrying their fears to the main body'.[33] Regardless of Fowke's repeated orders, the withdrawal to Leith degenerated into an unseemly scramble, all of which was witnessed by the anxious citizens of Edinburgh and the castle garrison above. The so-called Canter of Coltbridge therefore somewhat lessened the ardour of the capital for continued resistance. On arriving in Leith the dragoons discovered that their baggage and supplies had not been sent out to them from Edinburgh as expected, and so Colonel Gardiner advocated a further withdrawal to Musselburgh.

Cope's transports were by now entering the Firth of Forth, but Charles Edward was already establishing camp just east of the capital at Slateford. The confused and dispirited authorities in Edinburgh knew not what to do, whilst General Guest busily collected in the cannon which had been mounted on the old town walls in

---

32 Fowke's evidence, Robins (ed.), *Inquiry*, p.70.
33 Home, J., *The History of the Rebellion in 1745* (Edinburgh: Peter Brown, 1822), p.63.

expectation of a defence, along with the muskets of the Volunteers. False rumours flooded the city, especially when the fire-bell was rung to call a public meeting to debate the crisis, triggering a general panic. The Prince however knew that he was up against the clock, lacking both the time and the firepower to force entry into Edinburgh. Bluffing, he sent a threatening summons for the city to surrender, adding to the tinderbox atmosphere inside the walls. Could such a letter even be read out, or was that in itself treason? The Highlanders could not be expected to show mercy if the citizens resisted but failed. But if the city could hold the Highlanders off even for a few more hours, General Cope might yet be able to save them. If they let the Jacobites in, what retribution would King George demand? And yet that was to measure a threat in the future against a threat at the door, and the will to continue resisting was fading with the daylight.

The race to the capital was over, but it had been a photo-finish. Only the collective will of the people of Edinburgh and the winds of the Firth of Forth could decide the outcome.

5

The Road to Prestonpans

Monday, 16 September 1745

By the evening of Monday 16 September, events were clearly building towards a crescendo. General Cope was hovering with his fleet between the Isle of May and the Dunbar coast, denied entry into the Firth of Forth by contrary winds. Had they been blowing in his favour, Cope's achievement in saving Edinburgh just in the nick of time would have been given the appearance of a masterstroke. Instead his army's long and fruitless march around Scotland gave the whole campaign the look of a blunder. Even if Cope had successfully made it into Leith that night he might have found his landing opposed by the Jacobites who were gathering around the capital, a risk he would not have been wise in taking. Instead, still aboard his ship, the general wrote to the Secretary of State at 7.00pm that he intended to put the army ashore at Dunbar, less than thirty miles from the capital. But Edinburgh was not yet lost, and it was all still to fight for.

Cope also fired off a letter to Brigadier Fowke, advising him of his proximity. It reached the dragoons at Musselburgh, through which they were retreating after abandoning Leith only in marginally better order than they had departed Coltbridge. The brigadier knew this was a critical moment and that the outcome of the campaign was hanging in the balance. Accordingly he halted the dragoons for an hour and half, withdrawing into a private house, possibly Hugh Forbes' house at Loretto,[1] to write out a message for Provost Archibald Stewart in Edinburgh. The royal army was at hand, he wrote, and if the provost required it there was still time for Fowke to send at least a part of his cavalry back to the city. Walter Grosset, the customs officer of Alloa, was despatched with all haste to bring this vital news to the dithering Edinburgh authorities. Had Fowke sent his troopers as well, the resolve of the populace might yet have been stiffened. Instead the dragoons lingered with increasing anxiety, caught between the enemy

---

1   Oliphant, J., *John Forbes: Scotland, Flanders and the Seven Years' War 1707-1759* (London: Bloomsbury, 2015), p.11.

The Royal Palace of Holyroodhouse, where Charles Edward held court and council from 17 September until 1 November. (Author's collection)

forces gathering about the capital and the apparent safety of Cope's approaching army. There is little doubt as to which direction they would rather be riding. The general had also written to Guest, calling his eagerly awaited artillery crews out of Edinburgh Castle to Dunbar, where Cope was already making the preparations to disembark.

If Edinburgh chose to resist the Prince's summons, its gates might yet hold for long enough for the army to come up in relief. But the departure of the dragoons had sapped what remained of the will to seriously resist; most of the loyal volunteers had been disarmed, their muskets handed in to General Guest and the castle garrison. The City Guard was once again the only armed body in the capital, barely enough to man the gates let alone defend the walls. At about 8.30pm the Netherbow Port was opened, allowing Alexander Carlyle and a number of other volunteers to slip out of the city. At the gate they passed the baggage carts of the two dragoon regiments, which had not moved as fast as their owners and had not been sent out to join them. If these civilian amateurs were able to sense the direction of events in time to get out of time and join up with Cope at Dunbar, there is no reason why those much-needed artillerymen could not have done so as well. Why they did not remains a mystery.

Receiving no answer from Collector Grosset's mission to the provost, Fowke ordered the dragoons to continue their eastward withdrawal. From Musselburgh it was but a short ride to Prestonpans, where Colonel Gardiner had offered to select a suitable camp site. The location for the stopover was a field lying between Prestongrange, Dolphinston, and Gardiner's own estate at Bankton. Stopping here would allow Gardiner to rest in his own bed. Fowke knew his subordinate was 'very ill, and extremely weak', and the troopers themselves were in no great spirit either.[2] Gardiner reached Bankton at around 8pm and locked himself in for the night with no intention of being disturbed. Fowke ordered an appropriate screen of sentries to be set about the camp. The tents and baggage were still in Edinburgh so there was to be no shelter for the men, but many of the officers made their way to Lucky Vint's tavern where they dined with Lord Drummore.

There, between 10pm and 11pm, they were infected with a sudden panic at the rumour of an enemy advance; Carlyle arriving just in time to witness a scene of 'the utmost alarm and confusion – the officers of the dragoons calling for their horses in the greatest hurry'.[3] Drummore, who of course knew Carlyle, urgently sought out what he news he brought from Edinburgh. In vain did the pair then attempt to persuade the officers that the Jacobites could not yet have taken the capital, let alone sallied forth to attack. Highlanders, Carlyle quipped, had 'neither horses nor wings, nor were invisible'. Nevertheless the officers rushed to the field in which their troopers lay and soon set them in motion, most of them pouring down Prestonpans High Street along the coast road through to Cockenzie and on to Aberlady. Those who dithered were left to find their own way east in small groups. Carlyle recalls that Gardiner was left behind in his bed only to discover what had happened on waking the following morning and rushing off in pursuit. But Adjutant Kerr gave evidence that he had taken a sergeant and six men to fetch his colonel from Bankton, returning in time to find the regiment mounted for departure outside Preston village. The detail has the ring of truth.

The 1746 board of inquiry spent some time examining witnesses about this incident. Obviously Carlyle's experience of events, although written down much later, was similar to that described by others. Carlyle and Home both offer the same explanation for this extraordinary panic: the misfortune of a single dragoon stumbling about the fields in the dark. Searching for fodder, this unhappy fellow had fallen into a flooded old coal pit and created such a confusion of noise that his fellows mistook it for an ambush. Given the performance of the dragoons thus far, it is hard not to credit this story with plausibility. Fowke initially kept his description of the event suspiciously simple: 'after halting there [near Preston] for some time, we proceeded on our march to North Berwick'.[4] But he was asked by the

---

2   Fowke's evidence, Robins (ed.), *Inquiry*, p.71.
3   Carlyle, *Autobiography*, p.126.
4   Fowke's evidence, Robins (ed.), *Inquiry*, p.71.

board if he could prove that it was done in good order. The brigadier duly called up junior officers to offer supporting evidence, but amongst their recollections it is just possible to spot further reason for doubt.

Captain Clarke of Hamilton's Dragoons confirms the withdrawal from Musselburgh was well ordered, but that a false alarm then threw them all into 'great confusion' and that their subsequent movements were affected by the darkness of the night.[5] Adjutants Cowse and Kerr both provide the same explanation for the alarm – a false rumour spread deliberately by locals to prevent their forage being requisitioned by the troopers – and insist that the retreat which followed was orderly and that a rear-guard was maintained throughout. The mischievous villager theory was apparently confirmed to Kerr by an interview with the gardener at Bankton House. Whether it is true or not, this evidence does prove that troopers were moving around the fields in the darkness looking for forage, the very circumstances in which one might fall into a collapsed bell pit. Several of the witnesses also confirm, perhaps a little hesitantly, that during the alarm some troopers had mounted up before any such orders had been given. Are these hints enough to confirm the civilian evidence of the chaotic flight, or is the evidence of the military professionals sufficiently convincing? It is hard not to conclude that these officers had long since agreed a narrative between them which put the best possible light on things for their commander and, by extension, themselves.

Lord Napier was absent on military service at the time of the inquiry but he wrote in defence of Fowke, that any accusation that the march from Preston to North Berwick had been 'too precipitate' was unfounded. His argument was simply that the dragoons could not have run off in flight because it took them eight or nine hours to reach North Berwick![6] Considering that he gives the distance as eleven miles or so – and in all fairness it is actually nearer fifteen – this journey could be accomplished in half that time on foot let alone on horseback. From this we are presumably to imagine a slow, deliberate withdrawal with a rear-guard always facing the illusory enemy, as attested by those other officers who were present. And yet it must have been clear to Fowke that the Jacobites, with no cavalry force of their own, could not possibly have mounted a serious threat to his position in East Lothian. As has been said before, with nearly six hundred dragoons roaming about the countryside it should have been the Highlanders who were sleeping uneasily. Nevertheless, Fowke apparently kept his men on the road for an unnecessarily long time, denying them any rest for the night, despite being aware since Coltbridge of the saddle-sore state of both mounts and troopers. Either that or he had no control over their movements and their pace.

A slow and tightly controlled rear-facing withdrawal might well have helped steady the nerves of jittery troopers, but it can only have further exhausted them

---

5   Clarke's evidence, Robins (ed.), *Inquiry*, p.76.
6   Letter from Napier to Fowke, Vigimont, 5 September 1746, Robins (ed.), *Inquiry*, p.81.

if Napier is right in saying they arrived in North Berwick at 7am or 8am. Nor is it even clear that all of the dragoons went to North Berwick at all. Carlyle specifically says that they took the coast road out of Prestonpans and through Cockenzie. The coast road continues on through Aberlady, past the grand ruins of Dirleton Castle, and on to the harbour settlement at North Berwick. Longer than the post road through Haddington, this route followed the hump of the county all the way around to Dunbar. Assuming it was a conscious choice, Fowke presumably chose this road in case Cope had changed his plans and put in at North Berwick rather than Dunbar.

But other participants say that the force was split into two parties, some taking the direct road to Dunbar via Haddington. Both Adjutant Kerr and Captain Clarke say so, the latter blaming the darkness, whilst Fowke makes no mention of such a division: unsurprisingly so, as it would have been hard to explain why he deliberately chose to divide his forces whilst they were in such a volatile state. But if we believe that the false alarm caused rather more panic than the officers would later admit, that at least some troopers mounted up on their own initiative and made a dash for it, and that it took Fowke and his officers a considerable time to locate their scattered men in the darkness and restore some order to them, then we start to get closer to a plausible picture. Those who say the force took two different roads do not say that they did so by regiment, an omission which by implication suggests it was not a deliberate partition. A reasoned conclusion is that after much riding about and gnashing of teeth, Fowke was able to take the larger body of men around to North Berwick whilst the remainder ended up taking the inland route towards Dunbar. Perhaps the affair was not so chaotically comic as Carlyle would lead us to believe, but nor was it as respectable a performance as the British officers claimed. It was disorderly, it was frustrating, it was yet another demonstration of the dragoons' weaknesses, and its only redeeming feature was probably that it happened overnight: at least that saved too many civilians from witnessing it.

At the same time as Fowke and his officers were trying to restore order amongst their men, the Lord Provost of Edinburgh had finally deigned to inform Walter Grosset that he would not be requiring the services of the dragoons in defence of the city. Since he had already sent a deputation to negotiate terms with the Prince, it was impossible for him now to call in the troops. However much we might criticise Stewart's tactics, he had probably been wise not to pin too much hope on the performance of two such shaky regiments – these 'poltrown sqwadrons' as Patrick Crichton called them.[7] After all, they had already abandoned the city once.

---

7   Crichton, P., *The Woodhouselee Manuscript* (Edinburgh: W & R Chambers, 1907), p.29.

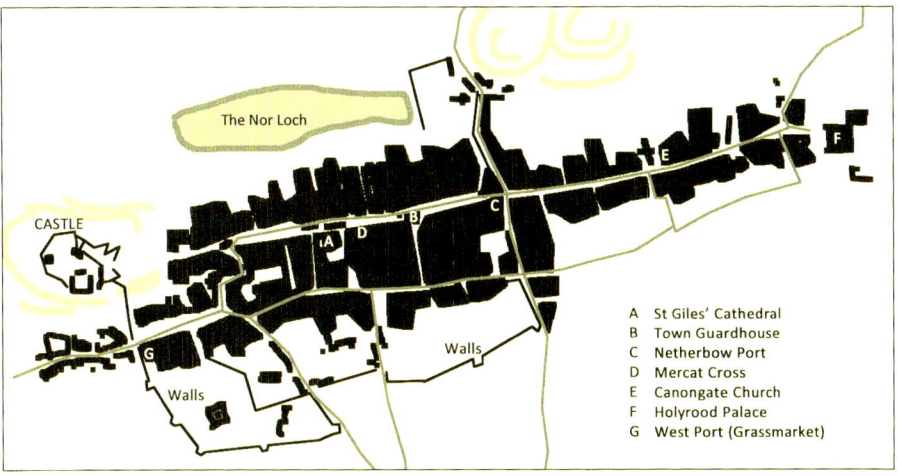

Map 5 Edinburgh in September 1745.

Tuesday, 17 September 1745

Alexander Carlyle, after a few hours' sleep, stepped outside the manse at Prestonpans around 6am. He saw that the dragoons had 'strewn the road eastward with accoutrements of every kind – pistols, swords, skullcaps'.[8] These he helped to collect into a covered cart which was sent on discretely to Dunbar. Whilst he breakfasted in Prestonpans, the Jacobites were busy securing the gates of Edinburgh. In the early hours of that morning the Netherbow Port had been opened to allow the passage of a carriage to its stables on the Canongate, and the Jacobite advance guard had simply run on in. Without noise or fuss and with commendable efficiency, they had then disarmed the City Guard and secured their arsenal, taken control of the town walls and gates, and demanded the keys to the old Parliament Hall. John William O'Sullivan was soon dictating the conditions which the city fathers were now obliged to accept. Few are likely to have been fooled by the pretence that the gates had genuinely been opened accidentally, although two attempts to prosecute Provost Stewart for complicity failed. In reality the 'accident' was probably the best outcome for all concerned as it prevented bloodshed whilst granting the citizens some cover from blame.

Edinburgh's residents awoke to discover their city had changed hands peacefully before the dawn, and that the terrifying Highland savages were in fact behaving with unexpected restraint. By 10am the initial buzz of excitement had swollen to create a huge and star-struck crowd, straining their necks to catch a glimpse of the Stuart prince taking possession of the palace of his ancestors. From

---

8 Carlyle, *Autobiography*, p.127.

the battlements of Edinburgh Castle, the two ancient generals Guest and Preston looked on impassively whilst the fickle crowd below cheered the proclamation of King James at the Mercat Cross. No doubt the generals' spyglasses were peering down the coast in search of Sir John. They were confident that they could hold out in the short term, and equally sure that this precocious prince would be swept away with ease once he faced an enemy on the open field. So the castle guns could afford to save their powder and bide their time.

Meanwhile Alexander Carlyle had become anxious as to the fate of his friends in Edinburgh. He walked out towards Drummore in the hope of finding news, successfully linking up with the young minister of Gladsmuir, William Robertson, from whom he learned of the city's fall. The companions returned to Prestonpans, no doubt spreading the news amongst their friends and neighbours before arranging for their dinner at the manse to be ready by 2pm. The meal was followed by a bowl of punch, after which they were sufficiently refreshed to set off eastwards so as to discover whether Cope had in fact landed, and whether they could be of use to him. Robertson needed to pick up some coin from his home at Gladsmuir first, anticipating the expense of meals and board when they reached the army as Volunteers were not eligible for tents in the lines. They therefore arranged to separate and rendezvous again at Maggie Johnstone's tavern at Bangley Brae, just north of Haddington and close to the post road. The following year this same hostelry is said to have been visited by none other than William Augustus, Duke of Cumberland, who complained about the price of his breakfast.[9] No wonder Robertson needed to fill his purse.

Events further east were moving somewhat faster than Carlyle and his companions. General Cope had stayed aboard ship on Monday night but had been busy all evening sending messages ashore ordering up horses and wagons to facilitate a march to the relief of Edinburgh. Bad news travels faster than bad dragoons however, for early on Tuesday morning a messenger rowed out from Dunbar harbour with the first report of the fall of Edinburgh. Cope wrote to Tweeddale expressing 'no small surprise and concern' that the capital had been taken so 'quietly' by the rebels. He also clearly identified that the city authorities had known by 7pm that his army was off Dunbar: there was no excuse for their premature capitulation.[10] Lieutenant Colonel Charles Whitefoord, an officer of marines on leave who had volunteered with Cope's artillery during the crisis, recalled that the news caused Cope 'the utmost pain' when it was brought to him.[11]

---

9   The tradition of Cumberland breakfasting at Bangley Brae is preserved in Miller's 1884 local history. Nothing survives of the inn, which stood on a branch of road which struck into the Garleton Hills to bypass Haddington on a more direct route eastwards. Miller, J., *The Lamp of Lothian, or The History of Haddington* (Edinburgh: James Allan, 1884), p.292.
10 Letter from Cope to Tweeddale, off Dunbar, 16 September 1745, Robins (ed.), *Inquiry*, Appendix, p.76.
11 Whitefoord's evidence, Robins (ed.), *Inquiry*, p.50.

Victory in the field was now an urgent and essential priority and Cope was wasting no time in providing for it: Dunbar harbour was bustling with activity from early on Tuesday morning. The Old or Cromwell Harbour was formed of a long stone pier extending up along the north-eastern end of the town, the entrance being around its northern tip into the shelter of the rocky little Lamer Island. The shallow rock-bed spread around the eastern flank of the harbour made the approach to Dunbar a potentially hazardous one, but it would be just short of a hundred years before a more benign western approach would be blasted through the crags where the famous castle once stood proud. The harbour was undefended, the castle having last seen action in the Rough Wooing and now standing ruinous, whilst the Lamer Island battery fort was still thirty-six years in the future. Today the original entrance into the haven is blocked up with rubble but still easily visible from both the pier and the later battery, and standing in the old harbour it remains perfectly possible to visualise the disembarkation of Cope's army.

The safe and efficient transfer of over two thousand men along with all their baggage, horses and equipment was no small exercise. The larger vessels, including the 20-gun sixth-rate frigate HMS *Fox*, stood out to sea whilst the cutters, launches, and jolly-boats plied their way back and forth. Some of the smaller transport vessels may have put into the harbour directly, but the narrow neck of the harbour would have created a bottleneck best avoided by the use of the ships' boats. The upper portion of a set of stones still project from the harbour wall today, known locally as Johnnie Cope's Steps, and atop these it is possible to imagine the frustrated general casting his eyes over the busy scene around him as he clambered ashore. It was a logistical challenge, but Cope had already successfully embarked

The Cromwell Harbour at Dunbar, where Cope landed the British army. (Author's collection)

this army with great efficiency at Aberdeen, so the exercise was not a totally new experience for his men. No doubt locals and their craft were set to work as well, and by late morning a considerable portion of the infantry were already ashore.

With no central rallying point in the town large enough to accommodate the army, the men probably marched straight up the hill from the harbour and past the splendidly sited and presumptuously named Dunbar House. This fine recent mansion stood at the north end of the town's broad high street, staring proudly down its entire length, and it had been built to reflect the dominant status of the Fall family. These prosperous merchant brothers effectively controlled Dunbar politics in the mid-eighteenth century, and even sent a member to Westminster in the county seat to further their interests yet further. They engineered such a corrupt election to get him there that it was satirised in rhyme. James Fall MP, recently deceased, had built his new house five years before Cope's red-coated companies came filing past its gates, and it is even possible that the general called in on the family. Before the end of the century the Falls' dominance would come to an end and Dunbar House would be sold to the Earl of Lauderdale, who then commissioned Robert Adam to add large new wings. It would go on to become a military barracks and would play an important role in Dunbar's future military history. Now known as Lauderdale House, it still dominates the High Street today. On 17 September 1745 there was another symbol of the Falls' importance within view: the sloop *Happy Janet* had once been the flagship of their trading empire, before showing promise as a privateer against the Spaniards. She was then leased to the Royal Navy and was now busily supporting Cope's transports as part of the naval taskforce attempting to starve the Jacobites of overseas aid.

After passing Dunbar House, the soldiers either quitted the town immediately along the back road westwards, or marched half way along the High Street before turning down the road known as the West Port. Both possible routes ran in parallel towards Belhaven, where the back road then joined the other. The road which ran out of the West Port was the senior of the two, but the lesser gave access to a large open area now known as Winterfield which is a good candidate as the site of the army's camp. About a mile west of the harbour and filling the space between Dunbar and Belhaven, this ground was large enough to accommodate the army and its train, and it would be a matter of moments before a column formed on the back road could join the main road west at Belhaven. This location therefore fulfils all the required criteria for Cope's camp, as well as correlating with the clues provided by Carlyle and others. An additional benefit would have been the old windmill tower on the mound at Knockenhair, which would have provided a vantage point for surveying the surrounding country. Cope himself gives us no further guide as to his camp's location beyond the bare fact that it was in a field west of Dunbar.[12]

---

12   The site is now occupied by Winterfield Golf Course, which at least means it remains open and that it is possible to visualise the camp. Bounded by cliffs on the north and Belhaven Bay to the west, it would

The private soldiers of King George's army were no doubt glad to be back on dry land after several days at sea in cramped and improvised quarters. The opportunity to settle down and await the rest of their baggage was likely accepted without complaint. Dunbar must have been good for their spirits too. In the north there had been a creeping sense that the army was marching through hostile territory; it was hard to know who to trust or where the danger lurked. But for the Lowland, English, and Irish soldiers in the army especially, things here in the south-east will have seemed more settled and familiar. The arrival of lords, dignitaries and 'gentlemen of high employments' in the town will have helped reinforce their sense of mission: these men were fighting for law and order, to protect the status quo from something unknown. Some might well have seen this concentration of dignitaries for what it really was, however: a symptom of the fall of the capital which left Cope as the sole focus of government authority and its principal hope. The British army's camp had effectively become the temporary capital of Hanoverian Scotland. But Cope was holding together well under the strain and felt revitalised now that he was in 'a country where I found a cheerfulness in everybody's countenance to forward the service.'[13]

Between 11am and noon, Gardiner's and Hamilton's Dragoons arrived safely at Dunbar. If Napier's timings are correct, the dragoons had covered the twelve or so miles from North Berwick in half the time that they had taken to travel that same distance earlier in the morning. The daylight clearly made a big difference, even apparently countering the effects of their increasing fatigue. For all the professional gloss at the inquiry, Cope saw them then as they really were: the arrival of the dragoons cheered him less than he had hoped. They were clearly in a sorry state, and his disappointment is clear in his letter to Tweeddale later that day reporting that the dragoons were 'extremely fatigued with the forced marches they made to arrive here.'[14] Lieutenant Colonel Whitefoord confirms that the dragoons arrived 'without their tents' and baggage, after a 'precipitate retreat'.[15] Obviously those who were not involved in that march felt less inclined to defend it later. With the horse in such a poor condition little could be expected of them in the short term, and so Cope was obliged to postpone any thoughts he might have entertained of a forced march westwards.

At the same time as the weary troopers were riding into Cope's camp at Dunbar, preparations were being made to proclaim King James at Edinburgh's Mercat Cross. In the shadow of the High Kirk of St Giles, whose bells rang for the occasion, the cross was draped with what finery could be found before the resplendent

have been a contained area for encampment conveniently close to both the road and the harbour. The windmill has been incorporated into a later house but is still clearly visible as a circular tower, and its prominent position is unmistakable.

13   Cope's evidence, Robins (ed.), *Inquiry*, p.35.
14   Letter from Cope to Tweeddale, Dunbar, 18 September 1745, Robins (ed.), *Inquiry*, Appendix, p.76.
15   Whitefoord's evidence, Robins (ed.), *Inquiry*, p.47.

heralds came forth at 1pm to the sounds of pipes and trumpets. Ross Herald, Roderick Chambers of Portlethen, solemnly read out the commission of regency granted by the exiled king to his son and heir, followed by the manifesto of the Prince himself. There was a great huzzah from the Highland men and the vast crowd around them, whilst the windows overlooking the High Street were 'full of ladies who threw up their handkerchiefs and clapped their hands and showed great loyalty to the Bonny Prince [sic]'.[16] Charles Edward himself was not present, having already shown himself to the multitudes in the King's Park before entering Holyroodhouse.

It was a long time since there had been a royal resident at Holyrood. The last had been Charles' grandfather, who had spent a short time governing Scotland for Charles II whilst Duke of York. A few years later, in 1688, the Edinburgh mob had rioted in favour of William and Mary and stormed the empty palace in an iconoclastic rampage. It seemed Holyrood's days of glory had gone with the last of the Stuart kings. But now they were back, and the palace was not ready. Charles was given the apartments of the hereditary keeper, the only ones fit and furnished for immediate accommodation. The Great Gallery, with its procession of portraits asserting the purity of Charles Edward's claim, became a buzzing hub of clerks and officers as Holyrood adapted to become both a seat of government and a military headquarters. Charles' proclamation had offered a free pardon to any who had served against his family's interests and issued a call to arms to the loyal. People were soon drawn to the palace as much by curiosity and self-interest as zeal for the cause. Few had really believed that the Prince would get this far; how many fewer believed he would prevail in the coming battle.

The main strength of the Jacobite army was initially concentrated around Hunter's Bog, a sheltered space between the volcanic eminence of Arthur's Seat and the Salisbury Crags. John Home called it 'the hollow between the hills'.[17] Here they were out of sight of the castle's garrison and removed from the temptations of the city. Murray of Broughton confirms that 'no more men were quartered in the town than were necessary for its preservation'.[18] Provisions were sent out to feed the hungry Highlanders, and John Home was able to observe them as they set about their meal. As they ate in their ranks he was able to make a fair count of their number, which he estimated with some skill at around 2,000.[19] His duty done, Home then slipped out of the city to carry what he had learned to the army at Dunbar.

As Charles Edward was settling in at Holyrood, his adversary was continuing the disembarkation of the British army. By the end of the day all the infantry were

---

16 Gibson, J S., *Edinburgh in The '45: Bonnie Prince Charlie at Holyrood* (Edinburgh: Saltire Society, 1995).
17 Home, *History of the Rebellion*, p.74.
18 Murray of Broughton, *Memorials*, p.198.
19 Home, *History of the Rebellion*, p.74.

Hunter's Bog, 'the hollow between the hills', where the Jacobite army camped on 17 September. (Author's collection)

ashore, as were most of the cannon and mortars. Having already decided he could not push his weary men any further that day, Cope wrote to Tweeddale confirming his landing and then no doubt sought some brief rest for himself. Men had been prioritised over baggage during the disembarkation, so the army's encampment lacked even the rudimentary soldiers' comforts, but the pickets were posted and security was tighter than it was amongst the Jacobites at Hunter's Bog: when Alexander Carlyle finally reached the lines he was refused entry. This was hardly surprising as it was well into the night by then. He would offer his services again in the morning, but in the meantime his priority was to find lodgings for himself and his companion. William Robertson had shown the greater foresight by refusing to go any further than East Linton, where he had secured a comfortable bed. Carlyle and another companion, Edinburgh university professor William Cleghorn, had pressed on only to find that Dunbar was so filled up with civic and military officers that there was not a place to found. With no tents of their own, the dragoons had been quick to secure lodgings.

Retracing their steps, Carlyle and his friend next tried the inn at Beltonford, which stood a short distance west of the camp. The little settlement here has now disappeared, but it stood on the north side of the modern Beltonford Roundabout on the A199 until the middle of the 20th century.[20] The inn here was also full,

---

20 There is a copse of trees beside the modern road where the hamlet used to stand. There was a smithy as well as the inn and several cottages. The inn seems not to have survived into the 20th century, but there

with lounging infantrymen filling even the kitchen space. Worse still, the tavern at Linton was now full too, so by 2am Carlyle was banging on the door of the local minister Matthew Reid. After an hour's delay, caused by Reid's understandable reluctance to open up the house in the dead of night with the army in town, the would-be warriors were finally able to lay down their heads. Robertson had already been asleep at the inn for five hours.

Wednesday, 18 September 1745

At the Palace of Holyroodhouse, Charles Edward Stuart awoke at his usual early hour and set to business consolidating his control of the capital. A general order, drafted by Secretary Murray, was issued to the citizens of Edinburgh requiring them to hand in 'the whole arms and ammunition in their custody and possession.' Unless you were joining the Jacobite army, you had no business possessing weapons and would be considered as 'disaffected to our interest, and treated as such.' This demand was probably not motivated by a want of arms, as the 'Town Arms' had been secured and distributed (probably the City Guard's arsenal from the guardhouse at the Tron).[21] O'Sullivan reports that around 1,200 stand of arms were secured, their quality 'good or indifferent'.[22] The short-lived Volunteer company had returned their arms to the castle of course, although James Johnstone believed many of the inhabitants had done the same, leaving 'very few arms at Edinburgh.'[23] Johnstone was the son of an Edinburgh merchant and should have been well placed to read events in the city, but he was also writing from memory some time after the event. John Murray of Broughton was more confident in the army's supplies than his comrades, reporting that they had more than enough muskets for their present need. As a senior member of the party he was certainly in a position to know. The order for the surrendering of private arms was, Broughton said, more a security measure than a military necessity. If the army suffered a setback, those who were once too timid to face them openly might find courage in their discomfort. Charles did not wish to march on General Cope with an armed populace at his back.

Twenty-five miles away in the east, the British commander was busy bringing the rest of his equipment ashore. Even for a relatively small army the operation was complex: cannon barrels, gun carriages, wheels and limbers, powder kegs and barrels of musket flints, food and fodder, tents, horses, the military treasury, and the personal baggage of the officers and staff. All had to be brought ashore,

---

was an old petrol station at Beltonford which is remembered locally. A tarmac path preserves the line of the original roadway.
21 Murray of Broughton, *Memorials*, p.198.
22 Taylor, *1745 and After*, p.74.
23 Johnstone, J., *A Memoir of the 'Forty-Five* (London: Folio Society, 1958), p.34.

inventoried, and either dispatched to where it was needed or loaded onto waggons ready for the march. Cope was also gathering important intelligence, not least from John Home. He had arrived in camp and was admitted to the general to share his appraisal of the enemy in Edinburgh. In his account of the Rising, Home refers to himself anonymously in the third person but tells us of the grateful thanks of the general. Home's information to Cope was detailed and accurate, giving not only raw numbers but sensible assessments of the Highlanders' appearance and equipment. Cope could not claim to have been uninformed as to his enemy, even if allowance would have to be made for fresh Jacobite recruits arriving since Home's departure. The question for the army's staff was how much faith could be placed in military intelligence gathered by enthusiastic civilians.

Alexander Carlyle had managed just three hours' sleep at the Prestonkirk manse at Linton before Robertson of Gladsmuir was knocking at the door with a gloating glimmer in his eye. After breakfast they made their way back along the road past Beltonford, through Belhaven and up to Cope's picket lines. They were presumably more cordially received than they had been in the darkness of the previous night, but with no more success in finding a role within the army. Instead Carlyle was left to enquire where Colonel Gardiner was lodged, and, on discovering his location, he paid a brief visit to his friend and was invited to return for dinner. The bustle of the disembarkation buzzed around them.

John Cope was eager to get his army in motion. Every day the Jacobites were left in Edinburgh increased their strength and credibility. Nevertheless, the situation was far from being a crisis and there was every reason to feel confident in the ultimate outcome. What he had seen of his infantry had given him 'all the Reason in the World' to trust in their courage and capability.[24] Cope called his officers to council. Marching directly against the rebels was not the only option available. To withdraw further, towards the safety of the Border and the garrisons at Berwick-upon-Tweed and Newcastle, was pretty much out of the question. It would effectively mean that all Scotland had been given up without a fight. The king's friends, abandoned, would soon reappraise their loyalties. There was a real possibility, however, that Cope might be reinforced if he waited just a little longer at Dunbar. Allied Dutchmen were already at sea, reportedly close at hand, and their numbers would tip the balance decisively in Cope's favour if he delayed long enough to effect a rendezvous. But that advantage might well be offset if Charles Edward's control of Edinburgh and the north meant that his ranks were swelling every day as his successes went unpunished. So Cope would not take that risk. His letters to Tweeddale from Dunbar all emphasised his intention to move quickly and decisively. Perhaps the general was questioning whether his initial delays in August had indeed given the Jacobites a critical head start. He would not make such an error a second time. Tweeddale replied that

24 Cope's evidence, Robins (ed.), *Inquiry*, p.35.

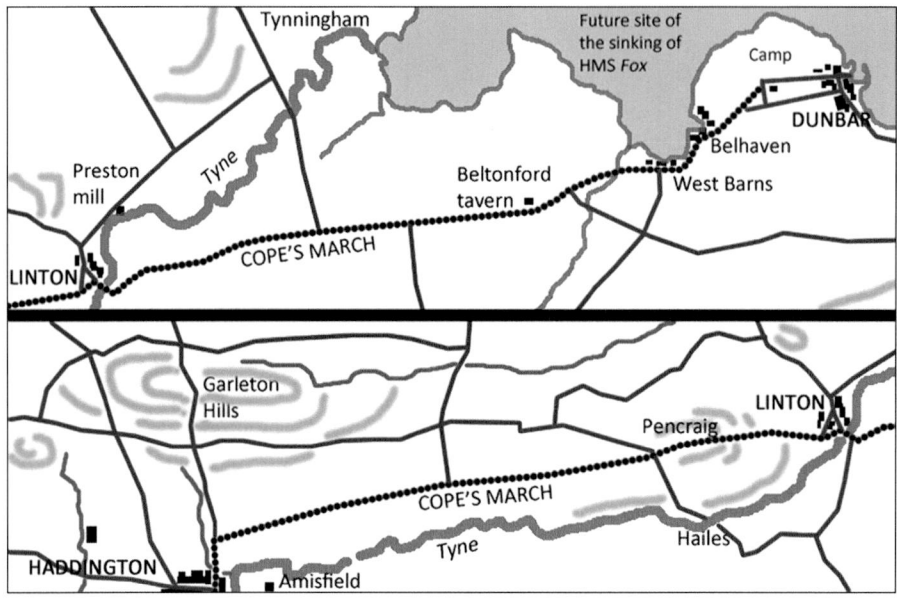

Map 6 The British army's march from Dunbar to Haddington.

when George II was shown Cope's letter from Dunbar he approved of the need for celerity. By the time that letter was written, however, the issue had already been decided.

Cope certainly did not lack sources of advice in Dunbar. He had been joined now by the Earl of Home as well as by a number of senior legal officers including the Lord Advocate and Lord Drummore. The result was that Cope was, as ever, equally aware of the political as well as military effects of his decisions. Ultimately the buck stopped with him now and he knew it. He determined to march out and face the enemy without further delay, and had the hour not already been advanced would have preferred to set out immediately the last waggon was ready.[25] The best course, therefore, was to allow the army one further afternoon of rest as preparations were made to march the following day. In case the Dutch had indeed made good progress towards them, Cope despatched the *Happy Janet* to seek them out. They were ordered to put in somewhere on the south coast of the Forth and move up in support of the main army; any harbour north of the Forth was to be considered as potentially occupied. An officer was also sent out in a cutter from the *Kinghorn,* carrying a duplicate set of orders as a double surety. In the event, Cope was wise not to wait for these reinforcements as they were not at all so near as Tweeddale had led him to believe.

---

25 As attested by Whitefoord: Robins (ed.), *Inquiry*, p4.7.

There was one further matter which required attention. Despite his appeals there was still no sign of the artillery crews that had been sent up for him. However much he hoped they might yet appear, it was now possible they were now trapped inside Edinburgh Castle. It was at this point that Cope called for the aid of Captain Edmund Beavor, RN. HMS *Fox* was a sixth-rate frigate mounting 20 9-pounder cannon. She had been launched on 1 May 1740, having cost £3,771 to build at Rotherhithe and £2,974 to fit out at Deptford. She was not a big ship – a little over 32m long and just 9m wide – but light frigates were designed to be fast predators and *Fox* had already taken a number of Spanish prizes in her short life. In April 1744 she was given to Edmund Beavor, an enthusiastic officer who found himself chasing French privateers in the North Sea the following year. *Fox* took another prize in May 1745 before receiving word a few months later that the Prince had landed on the west coast of Scotland. Beavor and his crew of 140 men were to cruise the east coast and trouble the Jacobite enterprise however they could. The east of Scotland naval taskforce would come under overall command of Rear Admiral John Byng, although in ordinary circumstances the Lord Provost of Edinburgh held the rank of Admiral of the Forth. Bigger than the *Happy Janet*, now sailing away from Dunbar to seek out the Dutch, *Fox* was perhaps the most powerful ship in Cope's improvised armada. That meant Captain Beavor possessed something that Cope lacked: trained gun crews.

A small number of sailors were accordingly loaned to the army for land service. How such men were selected is unclear, but from their performance it should be assumed that they were not the Navy's finest. It seems there were six of them (one witness says nine), so it seems likely they were intended to oversee a gun each, supported in the loading process by others. To hand, Cope had only three invalids from the Edinburgh garrison and 'one old man' who had once been an artilleryman in the old Scottish Army.[26] These men were able to help manoeuvre the guns with handspikes and serve as matrosses in the loading, but the actual science of gunnery was beyond them; hence the need for the sailors. Commanding this motley crew were Lieutenant Colonel Whitefoord of the marines and the veteran master gunner of Edinburgh Castle, Major Eaglesfield Griffith. In total that provided ten men and two officers to man six cannons, four Coehorn mortars and two heavier Royal mortars. No wonder the artillery train was a nagging concern. At least they were well supplied with ammunition, enough for forty rounds from each gun.[27]

The gunners Cope needed had not yet shifted from Edinburgh Castle, where the two octogenarian generals were awaiting events. They could not risk a sally from the gates as a rumour had spread that hundreds of Highlanders had been hidden

---

26 Griffith's evidence, Robins (ed.), *Inquiry*, p.54.
27 Griffith's evidence, Robins (ed.), *Inquiry*, p.96. This is stated in response to Richard Jack's accusation that some of the guns had only 10-15 rounds available for them at the battle.

in the closes and cellars ready to spring a trap. Beneath the ramparts, drums beat unchallenged calling out volunteers in the name of the Stuarts. A good number responded and signed up for the Duke of Perth's Regiment. Lord Nairne had arrived at the head of a considerable body of Athollmen, and there followed all the necessary activity of distributing arms and provisions. The Prince went out to review the Athollmen and was evidently satisfied with their fitness for service as they were immediately sent into Edinburgh to relieve the guard. A pattern for the garrisoning of the city had been implemented, with a hundred men being posted at Holyrood, fifty covering the Canongate area between the palace and the Netherbow, fifty more operating from the city guardhouse at the Tron, a further hundred around the weigh house and the top of the Lawnmarket to keep watch on the Castle, and a final detachment of twenty-five down on the Grassmarket.[28] There was also a reserve company quartered around Parliament Square: the Prince's hold on the capital was secure for the moment. Lord Elcho had spent the morning at Provost Stewart's house instructing the magistrates to provide a thousand tents, two thousand targes, six thousand pairs of shoes, and the same number of water canteens. The workshops if Edinburgh were set in motion, but it would take time to produce what the army needed. The Jacobites were showing their confidence, planning for the long game, and looking beyond the coming battle.

At 1.30pm, as the Duke of Perth's recruiting officers signed up their volunteers on the Royal Mile, Alexander Carlyle made his way to the house of Alexander Pyot, the minister of Dunbar's old parish church. The church itself, a venerable old structure with a pinnacled tower, sat on a mound just outside the town on its south side. The soldiers of Cromwell's army had burned its furniture for warmth before smashing an army fighting for another Charles Stuart ninety-five years before. The manse, however, was at the other end of town, on the back road which led west from Captain Fall's mansion. It was a convenient location for James Gardiner to lodge, just a few minutes away from the encampment. It was a commodious house with a fair garden, and he was probably more comfortable there than most of his troopers. Still without tents, they were either sleeping in the open or billeted around the town. The old manse still stands well today, although a large part of the gardens have sadly been given over for housing in the last few years.

When Carlyle arrived he found Gardiner looking 'pale and dejected,' and the two lamented the manner of the dragoons' flight from Prestonpans on Monday night. They walked together in the manse garden, the grand veteran with his tall frame and battle scars, in his scarlet coat with gold lace and touch of regimental green, fighting both sickness and melancholy, and the young ruddy-cheeked civilian adventurer, eager to be helpful yet longing for reassurance. Gardiner's words brought little comfort: 'I have not above ten men in my regiment whom

---

28 Elcho, *Affairs*, p.265.

I am certain will follow me'.[29] If this was a colonel's assessment of his own men, then we can only hope that he did not let it show outwardly. Such feelings can be infectious, and what the 13th Dragoons needed more than anything was inspiration. Perhaps Gardiner would have been better walking amongst his troopers, telling tales of his campaigns with Marlborough or his storming of the barricades at Preston. He had fought the Jacobites before and whipped them, he could have said. And the 13th had been there too, sharing in a glory that would shine so dim compared to the fame they were about to achieve! But, not unusually for the age, this was not Gardiner's style. He forbade any 'familiarities which might degrade the superior' and preferred to keep his men at a decorous distance.[30] They were soldiers, and they would do their duty or be damned. Gardiner would at least set them an example: 'I have one life to sacrifice for my country's safety, and I shall not spare it'.[31]

After this melancholy promenade in the minister's garden, the two men were called in to dine. They were joined by Reverend Pyot – whose arrival in Dunbar some years before had originally been vigorously opposed by the congregation – his family, and Cornet Kerr who was both adjutant and relation to Colonel Gardiner. This is the same Kerr who had fetched Gardiner from Bankton amidst those chaotic scenes west of Preston, and who would give testimony in support of Fowke at the inquiry. Now he put on 'an air of gaiety' according to Carlisle and talked confidently of the army's prospects in the coming trial.[32] The strange atmosphere can perhaps be imagined, but surely both Gardiner and Carlyle found some comfort in the familiarity of a minister's table. Once the meal was done there was little need for small talk. Gardiner and Kerr attended to their military duties and Carlyle, once again at a loose end on the periphery of Cope's camp, headed back along the road between Dunbar and East Linton for the fourth time in twenty-four hours. There he found the demand for beds had swollen further still as more civilian volunteers had been gathering. It was well known now that the army would be moving out soon, and that the road west must bring it to Linton Bridge.

Thursday, 19 September 1745

In spite of all its preparations it still took time for the British army to strike camp at Dunbar. The first hours of daylight were spent moving companies into their arranged positions and loading the last essentials onto the baggage carts for departure. It was a bustling scene of beating drums and passing aides, but in due course the column had begun moving westwards along the road through Belhaven

29   Carlyle, *Autobiography*, p.132.
30   Dodderidge, *Gardiner*, p.124.
31   Dodderidge, *Gardiner*, p.201.
32   Carlyle, *Autobiography*, p.132.

View over Linton Bridge towards the village, where Carlyle re-joined the redcoats. (Author's collection)

and West Barns. If Cope's camp was indeed located at Winterfield, then the first soldiers would have been passing the inn at Beltonford, where Carlyle had found even the kitchen filled with soldiers two nights previous, before the rear-guard had quitted the campsite. The inn no longer stands, as the little settlement here was demolished in the 1960s to make way for a new roundabout. It stood just west of the fork in the road which is still mirrored in the roadways off the roundabout, where the post road offered traffic heading to England the option of bypassing Dunbar itself. On the northern side of the roundabout today the original line of the road is preserved as a tarmac path beside the sewage works: the strip of trees between the path and the new road mark the site of the smithy, cottages, and inn which the British army passed in 1745. The path soon re-joins the line of the A199, the main road to Haddington which was now blocked with marching redcoats. This route is known locally as 'the old A1', to distinguish it from the parallel dual carriageway which carries most of the traffic towards Edinburgh today.

The road continued in a pretty straight westward line towards Linton village (now East Linton), where it crossed the historic stone bridge. Linton Bridge was the most important crossing of the River Tyne, and since it carried the principal road between Edinburgh and Berwick it was strong structure with a colourful history. Two centuries before Cope arrived, the Duke of Somerset had brought an army of 17,000 men across the river here on his way to a stunning if futile victory at Pinkie Cleugh near Musselburgh. An eye-witness at the time described the scene at Linton on 7 September 1547: 'our horses and carriages passed through the water, for it was not very deep: our footmen over the bridge. The passage was very straight for an army'.[33] The bridge Somerset's army had crossed was broken down by the French army during the protracted campaigning in the area which followed, but a replacement was erected by 1560. It was this bridge that Cope's army crossed, and which still stands today.

The bridge was repaired several times in the seventeenth century but its appearance probably altered little: two great arches striding from bank to bank over a massive cutwater pier. The width of the road between the parapets was probably 10-12ft in 1745, with another two or four feet being added eighteen years later in a major widening project. This means that Linton Bridge would have been approximately the same width as the Roman Bridge over the Esk in Musselburgh remains today, which is a helpful comparison. Whether the entire army crossed over the bridge, or whether Cope sent his waggons and guns splashing through the Tyne, is open to speculation. There was less risk of a bottleneck for Cope's small army than for Somerset's large one two centuries before, and he was advancing towards an unpredictable enemy and will have wanted to complete the crossing quickly. Either way the passage of the river probably meant delays further along the column, where soldiers will have taken the opportunity to relax their postures and resettle their loads before the queue lurched forwards again. On a quiet day when there are few cars, a walk across Linton Bridge still allows one to imagine the thousands of gaitered feet tramping across its span, the clack of the horseshoes and the creak of the gun carriages. The column veered left at bridge-end and turned away from the village and off to the west.

It can only be hoped that Alexander Carlyle found more rest on Wednesday night than he had managed on Tuesday, and in the morning there was little for him to hurry for. Linton's spiritual needs were served at this time by the charming and ancient Prestonkirk, which stood north of the village on a bend in the river close to an important watermill. The main body of the church would be rebuilt twenty-five years later but the early seventeenth century bell tower still remains. Across the lane from the church was the manse in which Matthew Reid was hosting his adventurous young guest. No doubt Reverend Pyott had sent his regards along with

---

33 Patten's 'Expedition into Scotland in 1547', published in Pollard, A.F., *Tudor Tracts* (Westminster: Archibald Constable and Co., 1903), p.90.

Carlyle from Dunbar, since we know the latter had related the tale of his search for a bed to the amused Cornet Kerr over dinner. After breakfast, Carlyle and his friends made arrangements with the other civilian volunteers that they would rendezvous together at a Haddington inn. Presumably they were confident that Cope would take the Haddington road rather passing marching through Linton village onto the lesser road through Markle. That route passed close beneath the Garleton Hills towards Bangley Brae, whereas the post road offered the security of running through open farmland with the Tyne on the flank all the way to the county town. Carlyle himself waited on the army's arrival, although it was after 11am, and possibly as late as noon, before the column appeared at the bridge.[34] Since they had travelled only five miles, it seems they had left their camp at 9am.

The road west from Linton climbed up Pencraig Brae and continued more or less straight, parallel with the river. From the top of the brae, as they passed an ancient standing stone, the soldiers will have enjoyed splendid views over Haddingtonshire and across to the mighty hump of Traprain Law. Looking back they could see as far as the tower of Dunbar church, whilst the Firth of Forth glistened off to their right. The march from here was uneventful and unopposed, and perhaps the stability of the infantry gave some much needed reassurance to the jittery dragoons. The guns, probably divided in pairs along the column, in turn provided comfort to the foot and to the country-folk who observed them. Even a small professional army on the march made for a fine sight. John Home remembered how 'the people of the country, long unaccustomed to war and arms, flocked from all quarters' to witness the spectacle of Sir John's army marching to battle.[35] General Cope did not stand aloof but rode back and forth along the column encouraging the men with assurances of victory. Thus, Lieutenant Colonel Whitefoord later testified, did Cope instil in his army all eagerness to get to grips with their enemy: 'even the dragoons breathed nothing but revenge'.[36]

But the crowd of spectators, Carlyle felt, brought risks. They were permitted to mingle freely with the marching troops, sharing their own views on the coming engagement and what might be expected from the Highlanders. Carlyle, who was presumably fairly well informed on the matter, was anxious about this since 'many people in East Lothian at that time were Jacobites, and they were most forward to mix with the soldiers'.[37] As he passed Beanston, Carlyle found himself engaged in conversation with Major Richard Bowles of Hamilton's Dragoons, with whom he already had some former connection, and 'found him perfectly ignorant and credulous'.[38] What little Carlyle knew of the Highlanders and their strength was

---

34 Carlyle, *Autobiography*, p.133.
35 Home, *History of the Rebellion*, p.76.
36 Whitefoord's evidence, Robins (ed.), *Inquiry*, p.50.
37 Carlyle, *Autobiography*, p.133.
38 Carlyle, *Autobiography*, p.133.

View of Traprain Law from the Dunbar-Haddington road as it crosses Pencraig Brae.
(Author's collection)

probably drawn mainly from Home, who had at least stayed around long enough to see them first-hand, so his criticism of Bowles is perhaps a little unfair. Apparently forgetting for a moment that he was himself an uninvited civilian, Carlyle felt the country folk had undermined morale with their talk, deliberately or otherwise. But such reservations did not stop him from accepting the opportunity to talk with Bowles, who sweetened the invitation by telling his servant to dismount in Carlyle's favour.

Five miles on from Linton Bridge, the column turned to its right and marched into the county town of Haddington. The layout of the town centre was much as it is today, although the fine steeple of the town hall would not rise for a few decades yet. The army entered down Hardgate before turning onto the main east-west thoroughfare. The soldiers did not therefore pass the battered but marvellous church of St Mary, which shows the scars of the Rough Wooing even today. Cope took his army straight through the town and out the other side, where he ordered a halt. It was still only early afternoon, but Cope was advised that there was little ready water available along the next stage of his march and so he decided to make camp.

Only vague clues are left as to where the army encamped; the location is simply described by those present as west or north-west of the town. A century later, local tradition informed the Ordnance Survey that the site of the camp was an area known as The Banks, a gently sloping area of open fields between St Lawrence House and Peghdeloan. St Lawrence House still stands, and Peghdeloan appears to have been a lane on the western edge of Haddington, later the site of a gasworks and now of the houses of Station Avenue. If Cope camped on the south side of the post road, then at least part of the area of his encampment is still open field.

If, however, he camped on the north side of the road, which appears more likely given his own recollection that it was north-west of the town,[39] then the site is now covered by Somnerfield Crescent and Roodlands Business Park, bisected by the line of the old railway. The first edition Ordnance Survey map marks wells to the north and immediate west of this location, satisfying Cope's anxieties over water, and a burn running along its western side to provide not only water but a measure of defence.[40] The soldiers could look forward to an afternoon of rest, readying themselves for the next stage of the march to recover Edinburgh.

Alexander Carlyle was by now ensconced at the inn where he had arranged to meet the other civilian volunteers who had gathered the previous night at Linton. There were about twenty-five of them jostling for space with 'sundry officers of dragoons and those on the staff' who were also seeking refreshment.[41] Presumably most infantry officers were still busy in camp, since their men had tents to erect! Fortunately the inn, presumably The George, was a large establishment with a courtyard and spacious stabling at the rear. Whenever Carlyle talks of dinner it seems to be about 2pm, and it is likely that Thursday was no different since the army had doubtless arrived by then. Now known as the George Hotel, the building was altered in subsequent generations, not least by the imaginative addition of a crenelated tower, but still retains the core of a grand old coaching inn. The stables were demolished in the twentieth century but a rear yard remains, and after the hotel closed it has been standing empty in recent years. In 2016 work began to convert the building into flats, a café, and an art gallery. Here it was that the British staff officers in their fine laced coats were crowded and hassled by Carlyle and the earnest volunteers, begging for the arms and responsibilities General Cope had shown such reluctance to give them. But such considerations, and dinner for that matter, would have to wait.

News swept through the British camp and through into Haddington that the enemy had been sighted. In a scene reminiscent of the debacle at Lucky Vint's in Prestonpans on Monday night, the officers rushed into the courtyard calling for their horses. Or at least most of them did, for Carlyle noted several who showed markedly little enthusiasm for rushing to arms when dinner was so tantalisingly close. Whilst the rear courtyard filled with the whinnying of horses and the barking of orders, Carlyle headed out the front onto the High Street and spotted Gardiner showing no signs of hurry. The old colonel had no doubt seen it all before: this would turn out to be a false alarm, he said, so why bother rushing about like these youngsters. In the main camp the alarm was being taken seriously however. The entire army drew up in battle order, perhaps with the burn to their front and St Lawrence House to their left, the camp immediately to the rear between themselves and the town. But false

---

39 Cope's evidence, Robins (ed.), *Inquiry*, p.35.
40 The burn can still be found, running with steep wooded banks between a row of back gardens in the St Lawrence area.
41 Carlyle, *Autobiography*, p.133.

Haddington Cross. The blue and white castellated building is the George Inn, where Carlyle dined with the dragoon officers before the false alarm on 19 September. (Author's collection)

alarm it was. Lieutenant Colonel Whitefoord tells us that Cope, putting a gloss on the episode commended the men for their alertness and was greeted with a cheer.[42] Reassuringly, the line had been formed with admirable speed, and in that regard at least the exercise would prove to have been a valuable one.

The false alarm at Haddington is attributed to a curious cause: the arrival of a wedding party. A little over eight miles to the south-west of Cope's camp stood the fine house of Prestonhall, home to the dowager Duchess of Gordon. Her daughter had lately married, in grand style, Francis Wemyss-Charteris who had already inherited the considerable wealth of his controversial grandfather Colonel Charteris. Some of that wealth had been won from poor Morison of Prestongrange, who had fallen in with the notorious rake before losing his estates. Amongst the guests at the wedding had been David Wemyss, Lord Elcho, the groom's older brother. On 15 September, with the ceremony complete, Elcho informed Francis that he was riding from Prestonhall to throw in his lot with the Jacobites. The younger brother, with new responsibilities on his shoulders, declined to get involved. He had nevertheless given Elcho the key to his writing table and permission to use whatever money was kept there.[43]

---

42   Whitefoord's evidence, Robins (ed.), *Inquiry*, p.48.
43   Elcho, *Affairs*, p.65.

This table stood in Francis' house at Amisfield on the eastern edge of Haddington, over the Nungate Bridge and beyond the ruined church of St Martin. Elcho had ridden there that afternoon and stayed the night. On the morning of the 16th he had ridden to Edinburgh, carrying his brother's £1,500 into the Prince's grateful hands at Gray's Mill. Amisfield had once been a significant commercial site called New Mills, but Colonel Charteris had bought the area at auction when the business failed and gentrified the estate. In ten years' time Elcho's brother would commission a grand new house to be built over the one he had inherited, which would stand until 1924. A golf club now stands on the site. It was to Amisfield then that Francis Wemyss-Charteris and his bride Lady Catherine (Kitty) Gordon now made their progress. Presumably their carriage was escorted by baggage and retainers, and this happy little procession had been mistaken for the vanguard of the Jacobite army.

As Sir John Cope led his army back into its encampment, Carlyle and the Volunteers returned to the George Inn. Their ardour not diminished, they continued to seek useful employment and found a champion with the arrival of George Drummond, the former and future Lord Provost of Edinburgh who had so nearly led them out to Corstorphine with the City Guard. This veteran of the '15 agreed to make their case to the general, who would find it harder to ignore Drummond's presence than Carlyle's persistence. Nevertheless it took some time before the Volunteers' captain returned and the answer was nothing better than a compromise. Cope had no intention of arming a small band of untrained civilians however eager they might be, as much because they were likely to get themselves killed as for their lack of military value. Instead a party of sixteen was chosen who could serve as outriders to maintain a watch on the roads between Edinburgh and Haddington. They would go out in pairs in two waves, one starting out at 8pm and the other following at midnight. With almost six hundred horsemen under his command, reconnaissance should not have been a major problem for Cope, but the more eyes on the road the better. The plan also removed the most enthusiastic volunteers from under his feet.

Carlyle naturally volunteered to scout the road he knew best, the one which led along the coast to Prestonpans. He left Haddington at 8pm with his companion William McGhie, a medical student who went on to be captured after the Battle of Falkirk, and, in happier times, to befriend Samuel Johnson. Heading out into the gathering darkness must have been quite a thrill, the comparative safety of the army disappearing behind them as they rode west. At least they had been provided with horses, and they made good use of them and covered the ground along the low road down to Longniddry. They called in on Carlyle's parents at the manse in Prestonpans, who agreed to delay supper whilst the bold scouts pressed a little further ahead. When they found the roads still quiet as far as West Pans the decision was taken to return to the comfort of the manse and a good meal by the home fire. There was some excitement in Prestonpans however as Hepburn, the baron bailie, had just arrested a young medical student called Myrie who had arrived in the village bearing arms. The accused insisted that he intended to join the British army, but the locals were clearly suspicious. As the climax of the campaign loomed, it was becoming hard to know who to trust. Being a student of medicine himself, McGhie was able to vouch for Myrie and the latter was released from his improvised incarceration in a tavern and brought round to supper at the manse. For Myrie the company of volunteers was not enough: he wanted to join up as a regular. No amount of persuasion it seems could forestall him. By 1am Carlyle and McGhie had returned to Haddington and found, as had so often been their experience in recent days, that there was not a bed to be had. To their chagrin, some volunteers were taking up beds to themselves, which left the returning scouts to sleep on benches and chairs in the kitchens.

Carlyle had been closer to risk than he probably realised at the time. The Jacobite army had riders out that evening too. In a story often repeated since, and joyfully recounted by Sir Walter Scott a generation later along with a heavy dose of literary license, Francis Garden and Robert Cunningham endured a regrettable encounter during their mission out of Haddington. They pushed a little further towards Edinburgh than Carlyle had, but the quiet roads lulled them into security. Just west of Fisherrow harbour Garden and Cunningham succumbed to the appeal of a pleasant supper at Crystal's Inn, which stood between the road and the shore. Enjoying their local oysters along with a bottle of sherry, these young gentlemen were silhouetted against the window by the back-light; they caught the attention of another nocturnal rider. The tide had risen so the only way back across the river was to cross the Roman Bridge, where a pistol-wielding Highlander now lay in wait. By accusing them of being Jacobite spies, the silver tongued agent successfully induced the volunteers into earnest expressions of loyalty to King George, thereby talking themselves into their own net.[44]

These two gloomy scouts, all their bravado long since evaporated, at least had the satisfaction of falling into the hands of the heroic John Roy Stuart rather than some eager ruffian as Scott has it in his version. Even so, it was proposed they should be hanged as spies, probably in order to rattle some information out of them. Cunningham and Garden were therefore given somewhat cool treatment, fearing for their lives until a Jacobite acquaintance of theirs interceded on their behalf.[45] After questioning they were kept under the guard of the Atholl Brigade. Cunningham later claimed to have been badly treated by his captors, an accusation which Murray of Broughton rebuts in strong terms which sound the ring of truth.[46]

---

44 Carlyle, *Autobiography*, p.136.
45 Chambers, R., *History of the Rebellion of 1745*, Fifth Edition (Edinburgh: W & R Chambers, 1869), p111.
46 Murray of Broughton, *Memorials*, p.199.

The Causeway, Duddingston, where Charles Edward Stuart held his Council of War on 19 September. (Author's collection)

The future General Cunningham and the future Lord Gardenstone were interrogated not in the Jacobites' original camp at Holyrood, but in their new one at beside Duddingston village. The army had been moved during the day to the south-eastern side of Arthur's Seat, where it could concentrate on the road east without being sighted by the castle garrison. Most of the clansmen simply settled in their marching positions along the side of the road, whilst the officers occupied what shelter could be found around the village. Viscount Strathallan's little cavalry force from Perthshire is said to have camped in ground east of the village, the current site of the Holy Rood RC High School and its adjacent golf course. The splendid Duddingston House would not be built on this site for another two decades, or else the Prince would no doubt have taken up residence. The area is still known today as Cavalry Park, supposedly in memory of Strathallan's Perthshire Horse.[47]

---

47 See Historic Environment Scotland, 'Duddingston House', at http://portal.historicenvironment.scot/designation/GDL00147.

Shifting the camp to Duddingston had been triggered by reports that Cope's army was on the march west. Charles sent scouts forward to bring in confirmation, suspicious that Cope might yet try to deny him a battle by falling back on reinforcements at Berwick-upon-Tweed. The Prince prepared the army: the guard posts in the city were placed on alert, with orders to withdraw discretely the following morning. In the evening Charles Edward moved to Duddingston in person, expressing 'a great deal of satisfaction' that the enemy was approaching.[48] A council of war was called in a house at the Causeway, an event proudly recorded on a large stone plaque above its door today.

The only plan the Prince's really intended to consider was to march out and engage the enemy. It appears to have been agreed without dissent that it was better to march forward and seek to engage Cope on reasonable terms than to risk getting caught between the army and a vengeful castle garrison. James Johnstone, although probably not sufficiently senior to attend the council himself, felt that battle was necessary politically as well as militarily if they were to convert sympathisers into supports and cow the potentially hostile.[49] At the council meeting Charles also informed the chiefs of his intention to lead the attack in person, but this proved more controversial. He was forced to back down by a flurry of protestations that if Charles fell then the war was lost in a stroke. The Jacobite cause could not survive the loss of its new Dundee. Compromising, Charles agreed to lead the second line as opposed to the first.

By this stage neither Charles nor Cope could afford anything other than a decisive engagement, and it seemed likely that the battle would be fought close to Musselburgh and its strategic bridge across the Esk controlling the road to Edinburgh. Certainly that was Cope's objective: he could either fight it out there, with the river protecting his front, or, if unopposed, he could halt there before a short final march to link up with the castle garrison. General Guest had already been briefed and knew to sally out and breach the town walls to admit the British army. The Prince had to stop that from happening, and when John Roy and George Hamilton came into camp with their captives and reported that Musselburgh was clear of the enemy, he knew what to do. The Jacobite army would march out to secure the bridge before Cope could come up, and if possible press on beyond it to seek advantageous ground. In the meantime, the Highlanders snatched what sleep they could: 'the army lay out in rank and file in one line, and the Prince and the principal officers lay in houses and barns'.[50] It was one month since the Standard had been raised at Glenfinnan; one month since Cope had marched north. The climax of the campaign was upon them at last.

48 Murray of Broughton, *Memorials*, p.199.
49 Johnstone, *Memoir*, p.34.
50 Elcho, *Affairs*, p.265.

6

The Battle: Day One

Friday, 20 September 1745

Before the sun shown its rays over the shoulders of Arthur's Seat, the sounds of rousing Highlanders spread along the roadside. It must have looked as if the earth itself was breathing life into these shadowy forms; human shapes materialising from beneath the dark tartan plaids spread in lines along the roadside. The anticipation of battle was starting to course in their veins and the mood was already high. Charles Edward Stuart was amongst his men where he was at his happiest, mingling with the Highlanders with encouraging words and little care for rank or status. His grasp of Gaelic was sufficient now for him to exchange simple phrases with the men, and the Prince's efforts were well received. On the brink of the greatest test of their courage, these Highland warriors could not fail to be moved by 'the joy yt he had painted in his face'.[1] Charles was busy 'setting every Regimt in order', for he was not the sort of commander to leave the management of his army to others, whatever his detractors might later avow.

As darkness faded into light, the last pickets withdrew from Edinburgh and joined with the army at Duddingston in accordance with the previous day's orders. There were too few troops to spare a garrison for the capital. With them came a number of surgeons and coaches which had been 'ordered for the Conveniency of the wounded, so certain was the prospect of a battle'.[2] They must have been a rather sombre sight, if the Highlanders even noticed them amongst their preparations. Even victory would bring losses. But if Cope could be beaten, Charles' cause would be immeasurably strengthened. If Cope could be beaten decisively, then Charles would control all of Scotland beyond the walls of a few isolated garrisons.

But if victory went to the enemy the Jacobite army's position was weak. Much that had been achieved so far had been down to boldness, bravado, and the momentum

---

1   O'Sullivan, quoted in Taylor, *1745 and After*, p.75.
2   Murray of Broughton, *Memorials*, p.199.

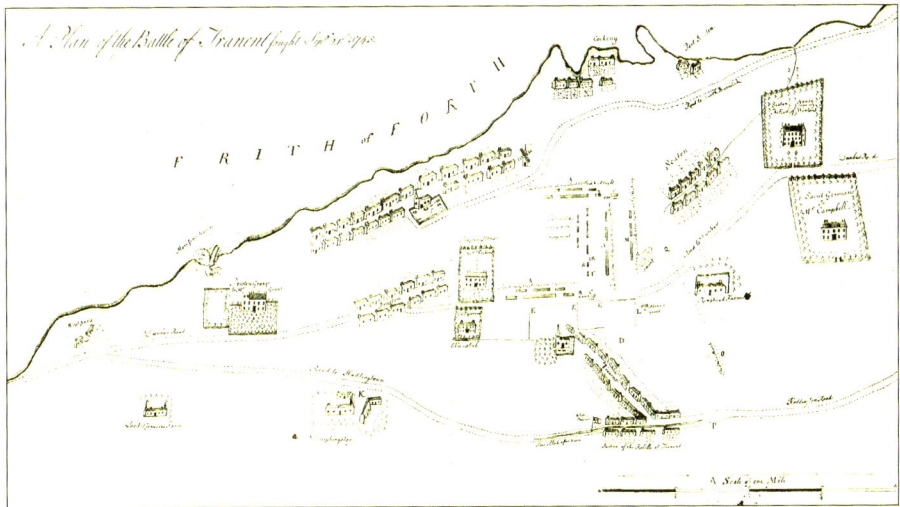

'A Plan of the Battle of Tranent', a contemporary illustration showing the various redeployments of the British line. (Reproduced with permission of the National Library of Scotland, Edinburgh)

of forward motion which created the sense of a cause in the ascendant. If that momentum was now checked, the façade would quickly begin to crack. A defeated army falling back on Edinburgh would not only be vulnerable to its pursuers but also to the garrison of the castle in its rear. Even a victory won at too high a cost might expose the army to such a risk. The Jacobites had learned in 1689 how easily triumph could turn to disaster, suffering heavy losses and a fallen commander in their victory at Killiecrankie. So it is hard to imagine how Charles Edward could have kept his army south of the Forth in the wake of a defeat in East Lothian. Even if he was able to hold the Highlanders together, he would probably have to withdraw northwards or end up like Montrose at Philiphaugh a century earlier. Blakeney could make life difficult from his base at Stirling, and until the Jacobite army reached the Highlands it would be desperately short of supplies and prey to hostile civilians. Those who had kept their heads down as they had passed would now raise their hands, and in the north news of a victory by Cope would see a sudden rush of loyal clans to arms in the King's service, previous doubts vanishing in the scramble to settle scores and expand influence. In short, even if a defeat on the field was not decisive in itself, the Jacobite cause would be unlikely to survive it for long.

This morning, however, was no time to allow the mind to wallow in the what-ifs of defeat. Instead it was time for Charles to place his fortunes into the hands of God and the Highlanders. And in appraising the enemy's performance so far, there was comfort to be found. Although the British Army's advantage in cannon and horse was a concern to them, Lord Elcho observed that 'the foot they did not mind upon account of their having Shun'd fighting in the Highlands'.[3] If they had known the relative state of the dragoons and the improvised nature of Cope's artillery crews, the Jacobites might have been more confident still. Their priority was therefore to find ground where they could meet the enemy on their own terms, neutralising the discrepancy in firepower and denying the dragoons the opportunity to get around their flanks. To maximise the benefit of the Highlanders' aggressive tactics and prowess in close quarters, they needed open ground with a gradient to give their charge momentum. What they certainly could not afford to do was allow the enemy to select his own ground, nor permit him to get close enough to Edinburgh to concert his actions with the garrison. So the Highlanders must march west and intercept the enemy on the best ground they could find.

As the sun rose the clan regiments formed in their appointed places along the column. Gentle Lochiel saw to his 600 Camerons, the largest regiment in the army, whilst Charles Stewart of Ardsheal ordered the ranks of the 200-strong Stewarts of Appin. Recently arrived, Lord Nairne was present with 250 Athollmen who were brigaded with their neighbours, 100 Robertsons of Clan Donnachaidh. Lachlan MacLachlan had also brought out 100 men, as had Patrick Grant of Glenmoriston, whilst the Duke of Perth's regiment contained over 200 men. Amongst the latter were a good number of MacGregors, many poorly armed but supported by two sons of the famous Rob Roy. The MacDonald clans were out in strength too of course: Ranald MacDonald the Younger led 200 men of Clanranald; Angus Og MacDonald had 400 Glengarry men; and Alexander MacDonnell of Keppoch had brigaded his 250 with 100 from Glencoe under the chief of MacLain, along with a further complement of MacKinnons of Skye. In total, this gave the Prince a total of around 2,300 infantry for the coming engagement. The vast majority were Highlanders drawn from the corridor of operations in which the campaign had so far played out. In addition there was the Perthshire Horse, the army's first cavalry force, which comprised of 36 men and their servants led by William Drummond, Viscount Strathallan. The ever-modest artillery complement had petered out almost entirely for the time being, down to just 'one small iron gun' which an eye-witness saw lying on the bed of a cart.[4]

As to the appearance of these men, it is possible to gain a pretty clear picture of their dress and equipment. Visual sources range from David Morier's famous depiction of a scene at Culloden in 1746, which shows front-rank Highlanders with their full terrifying panoply, to the anonymous observational drawings of the Penicuik Sketches, which show a rather more rough-around-the-edges look. The reality is that the officer class, the chief and his tacksmen, and the gentlemen who made up the front ranks of the clan regiments, were well-dressed and finely equipped. Behind them the quality and colourfulness of the dress depended as

---

3   Elcho, *Short Account*, p.266.
4   Home, *History of the Rebellion*, p.75

much on wealth and status as did the amount of weaponry available. Many wore the belted plaid, some wore breeches and hose, and amongst the gentlemen fitted tartan trews could also be seen.

There is little reason for us to doubt the detailed depiction of the Highlanders given to General Cope by John Home:

> about 1400 or 1500 of them were armed with firelocks and broad-swords; that their firelocks were not similar or uniform, but of all sorts and sizes, muskets fusees and fowling-pieces; that some of the rest had firelocks without swords, and some of them swords without firelocks.[5]

Once the Edinburgh stores had been distributed it is clear that there were more firearms amongst the Jacobite forces than is commonly assumed, something further supported by both the eye-witness reports and recent archaeology from the battlefield. Several clansmen are shown in the Penicuik Sketches with their heavy woollen plaids drawn up over their shoulders, armed only with muskets and bayonets. One of them is busy having his head deloused.[6] Not all of the muskets were of the latest style, and Patrick Crichton saw 'things licke guns of the 16 centurie', presumably heavy old matchlocks.[7] These would have been the first weapons discarded once more modern ones became available. The lack of uniformity amongst the firearms could cause logistical problems as different calibres required different sized balls, and whilst the majority needed ready access to shaped flints for firing their pieces, any old-fashioned matchlock musketeers needed a supply of match-cord instead.

As for swords, Home's description shows that not all of those carried were the famous – and expensive – basket-hilted broadsword, but the rather cruder French weapons brought over by the *Du Teillay*. There were also several companies which were armed with nothing more than 'the shaft of a pitch-fork, with the blade of a scythe fastened to it, somewhat like the weapon called the Lochaber axe which the town-guard soldiers carry'.[8] These improvised Lochabers are mentioned also by Captain James Johnstone, who has them belonging particularly to the MacGregors.[9] Actual Lochaber axes are shown in the Penicuik Sketches, in the hands of some of the scruffiest and most forlorn looking characters, but these formidable weapons gave the bearer a long reach.[10] The hooked ends were excellent for catching into the belts and clothing of enemy horsemen and pulling them to the ground, where they would be vulnerable to the axe-blade. It was no doubt their good reach and ability

---

5   Home, *History of the Rebellion*, p.75.
6   Brown, I. & Cheape, H., *Witness to Rebellion*, (Edinburgh: John Donald, 2010) pp.68-9.
7   Crichton, *Woodhouselee MS*, p.83.
8   Home, *History of the Rebellion*, p.75.
9   Johnstone, *Memoir*, p.37
10   Brown & Cheape, *Witness to Rebellion*, p.73.

to trip and snag opponents that appealed to the Edinburgh City Guard, who used Lochabers on urban patrol throughout the eighteenth century.

This then was the army which formed along the road leading from the King's Park through Duddingston village at dawn on Friday 20 September. For all it may have lacked in drill discipline it would have been a formidable sight, well-rested and eager for battle. The column was just three men wide according to Home – who had already left the city by this time – meaning that it would have stretched back about a mile if it assumed the men did not march in particularly close order. Once the day was fully dawned, Charles Edward Stuart called the staff and senior officers together. As well as the numerous clan chiefs and regimental commanders, there were also: the two lieutenant generals, Perth and Murray; John William O'Sullivan as adjutant-general; Sir John MacDonald as inspector of cavalry, a largely honorary and certainly not yet onerous task; and John Murray of Broughton, although as secretary of state he had no formal military duties. There were doubtless others too who strained their ears from beyond this historic assemblage in order to catch the words of their royal commander-in-chief. John William O'Sullivan records them for us:

> You are all agreed upon yr ranks, & the order & conduct yu are to observe this day; you cant be ignorant yt our good succes depends very much upon it, & [I] can assure yu, as I often told yu all before, yt I wish it to be as much upon your own acts to deliver you from the Slavery yu lie under as I do upon the King's, who thinks as I do, or upon my own; remember past actions, & yt yu fight for a good cause, while our enemis consciences will reproach them to fight against their King & Contry, & will be half overcome. So God will protect us.

At which point the Prince put on his blue bonnet with its white cockade, and drew his broadsword with a flourish:

> "Now Gents" says he, "the Sword is drawn; it wont be my fault if I set it in the Scabert before yu be a free & happy people. I desire yu may retire to yr postes, inform yr men of what I said, & march."[11]

Their blood fired, the officers did as they were instructed and repeated the words to their clansmen. By the time it reached the printers in Edinburgh it had been reduced to the famous lines: 'Gentlemen, Follow me; by the Assistance of God, I will, this day, make you a Free and Happy People!'[12] The Highlanders heard the words, cast their bonnets in the air as they had done at Glenfinnan, and let out a

---

11   Taylor, *1745 and After*, p.75
12   National Library of Scotland, NLS: PDP.10/23(4)

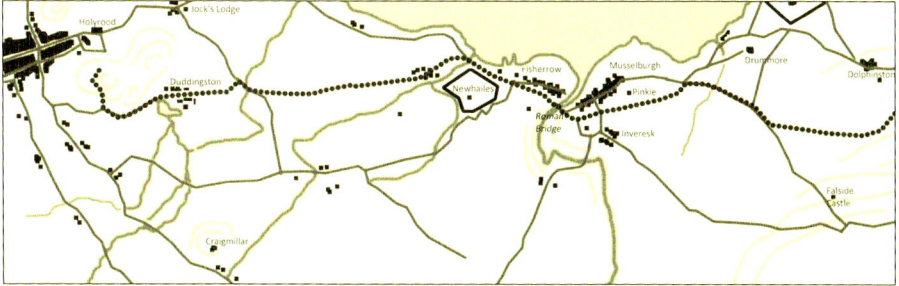

Map 7 The Jacobite army's march from Edinburgh to Tranent.

great cry which O'Sullivan felt would have shaken the hearts of their enemies with fear. Charles had spoken to them in a language they understood even if the words themselves required translation: these men were not rebels; they were the true soldiers of their king and country. Their opponents, many of whom were Scots, were already half-beaten by their awareness of the injustice of their cause. God was on the side of the Jacobites, and a Stuart Prince was at their head. At 9am Charles 'made a Signal with his hat' and set his army in motion.[13] The Perthshire Horse trotted off in the van, scouting the road ahead and searching for the enemy. The march to Prestonpans had begun.

Fifteen miles to the east the sun had risen on a rather different scene. The British army awoke in its camp, and, before the beating of drums could call the companies of Sir John Cope's army into their ranks and files, there was the ordered bustle of striking tents and creaking waggon-wheels. Hundreds of horses stamped and tossed their heads, whilst soldiers inured to the ritual shuffled and muttered into position. All those present, veterans and green troops alike, knew that whether it happened today or tomorrow this march could only end in contact with the enemy. After a month of tramping the length and breadth of Scotland, that might well have held some appeal. Canteens filled from the wells and burns around St Lawrence, the men braced themselves for whatever the day might bring.

If Cope addressed his officers or troops that morning then his words are not preserved. It seems unlikely that he did, not least since he had received no confirmation that the enemy intended to intercept him immediately. The battle might yet be a day away. There does survive, however, a speech which is attributed to the general prior to the engagement, and since it is almost certain that he never gave it there seems no great harm in mentioning it out of place, where it might be contrasted with that of his opponent. Indeed, the two speeches were printed together at the time so that that the contrast would be evident to all readers.

---

13 Murray of Broughton, *Memorials*, p.200. Elcho, *Affairs*, p.266, recalls it as 6am, but this earlier departure is difficult to reconcile with the later timings, which are otherwise in alignment.

According to a broadsheet, Sir John Cope addressed his men in the following terms:

> Gentlemen, you are just now to engage with a parcel of Rable; a parcel of Brutes, being a small number of Scots Highlanders; you can expect no Booty from such a poor despicable pack. I have Authority to Declare, That you shall have Eight full hours Liberty to Plunder and Pillage the city of Edinburgh, Leith and suburbs, (the places which harbour'd and succour'd Them), at your Discretion, with Impunity.[14]

Not only did Cope have no such authority, the speech is so ludicrous that not even the meanest redcoat could have believed it. Edinburgh was the financial and civic heart of Scotland, and had done nothing to deserve a punitive plundering which could only have succeeded in setting all of Scotland ablaze. Amongst Cope's forces were many Scots from both the Highlands and Lowlands, serving as officers, privates, and volunteers, and such words as these would have outraged them to the point of desertion or mutiny. Edinburgh was the army's objective, but it was not their target. Little more need to be said, except to notice that in the broadsheet Charles Edward's speech is labelled as that of 'the Prince Regent', whilst Cope is billed as 'General of the Usurper's Army', which is telling of the printer's sympathies. This speech is as bogus as the more famous 'no quarter' order reputedly given by the Jacobites before Culloden, although far less deadly in its result. This one at least was intended to rouse supporters rather than to justify slaughter. Either way, the words never passed Sir John Cope's lips.

As the British army readied for its departure from Haddington, the Earl of Loudoun circulated the order of battle. The flanks were to be formed by the dragoons, two squadrons of Gardiner's on the right under Gardiner himself and Lieutenant Colonel Shugborough Whitney, and two squadrons of Hamilton's on the left under Lieutenant Colonel William Wright. In the centre was the infantry, with the artillery distributed along the line in close support, arranged from right to left: two cannon and mortars; Lee's Regiment (5 companies) commanded by Lieutenant Colonel Peter Halkett; Guise's Regiment (2 companies) brigaded with Lascelles' Regiment (8 companies), commanded by Major John Severn; two cannons; then the only complete regiment, Murray's, under Lieutenant Colonel Jaspar Clayton; and then the final two cannon. Behind the main line was a *Corps de Reserve*: the remaining squadron of each dragoon regiment on the flanks; 1 company of the Black Watch and 4 weak companies of Loudoun's Highlanders in the centre, supported by the Volunteers from Edinburgh under George

---

14   National Library of Scotland, NLS: PDP.10/23(4).

THE BATTLE: DAY ONE 131

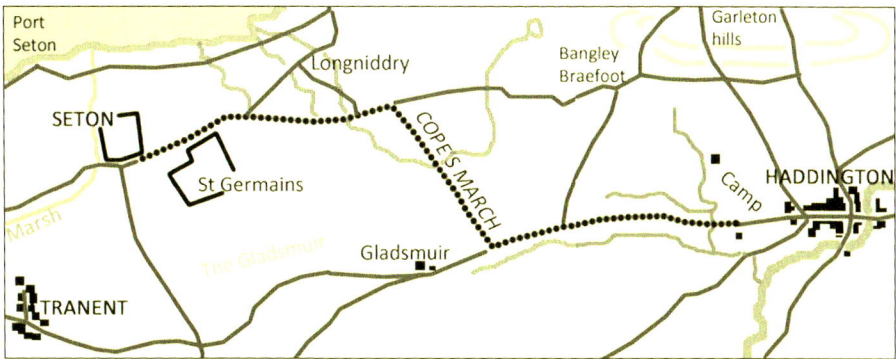

Map 8 The British army's march from Haddington to Preston.

Drummond.[15] At last it seems Cope had allowed these enthusiastic civilians to have an official posting. If battle were joined, everyone in the army now knew their place. Although Cope's actual returns were lost in the wake of the battle, he had at his disposal about 1,500 infantry and 567 dragoons, not including officers, sergeants, and drummers.[16] The total was close to 2,400 men.[17]

By 9am on Friday 20 September, just as the Perthshire Horse was riding out from Duddingston, Cope's column recommenced its advance along the post-road to Edinburgh. No doubt still weary from his night's adventures and stiff from an uncomfortable kip on the kitchen bench at the George, Alexander Carlyle and his friends in the Volunteers marched with them. William Robertson expected that he would soon be passing his own manse and the church at which he was minister, as this road led up the rising ground towards Gladsmuir village. That was also the birthplace of Colonel Gardiner's mother, Mary Hodge. Beyond the village lay the open heath of the Gladsmuir itself, over which the road would pass until entering the more enclosed land around Tranent. Gladsmuir lay barely three miles from the camp and would soon be reached. But then, just shy of the village the army suddenly turned off to the north.

This apparent diversion had presumably been agreed between Cope and his officers at council, although naturally enough nobody had informed young Carlyle who was left to express his 'great surprise'.[18] It seems most likely that outriders

---

15 Drummond was a veteran of Sheriffmuir, but is best known for his role in the foundation of Edinburgh's Royal Infirmary and, later in his career, in driving plans for expanding the capital by creating the New Town.
16 Sensible estimates vary within relatively narrow margins. See Reid, S. *1745: A Military History of the Last Jacobite Rising* (Staplehurst: Spellmount, 2001), p.32.
17 See Margulies, M., *The Battle of Prestonpans 1745* (Stroud: Tempus, 2007) p.126, for an excellent evaluation of the many estimates offered by both contemporary and secondary writers.
18 Carlyle, *Autobiography*, p.136.

from one of the mounted regiments did indeed press along to Tranent to make use of the ridge in watching for the enemy, but the main army instead took a lesser road which struck off from the post-road at a right angle and headed north past Trabroun and Elvingston. This route took the army off the ridge and towards the coast, where the ground was flatter and more open. In Cope's assessment this was a more suitable route for his army in case of attack, and although Carlyle could not understand the case for yielding that the high ground, the professional military men knew their business. Cope explained his reasoning at the inquiry:

> If we had marched forward by the Road leading to Edinburgh, we had Defiles and Inclosures immediately before, where our Horse could not act, and which we could not get passed before the Rebels might come up to us.[19]

In contrast, the flatter coastal plain was 'very proper for us'. The enclosures around Tranent and the layout of the village itself, at a right angle to the main road with the steep-sided heugh along one side, held more risks than advantages. It would be hard to deploy a regular line and difficult to find a clear field of fire, whilst the army's advantages in cannon and horse would be neutralised. This was the main road in and out of Scotland, one which Cope himself would have travelled between London and Edinburgh, and there were also local men like Gardiner on hand to identify the potential hazards and alternatives. There was Alexander Carlyle too, of course, although he was clearly not asked!

Carlyle describes how the army then turned west again, passing the village of Longniddry to the north and the estate of St Germains to the south. William Roy's military survey, commissioned in the wake of the Rising, shows the Elvingstone road following the same route as it does today, heading westwards and by-passing Longniddry on the coast to the north. From here the road was enclosed on both sides as it passed between St Germains and the larger estate of Seton Palace, with its faded magnificence and neglected turrets. The two estates were not directly aligned however, in the way that those of Preston and Bankton were to the west, and so the potential bottleneck was more easily passable. But just as the column was passing between the two estates, the order was given to halt. The army had marched just under six and a half miles and it was approaching midday. No doubt the soldiers shuffled anxiously at the delay, taking slugs of water from their canteens. Whether they were permitted to rest in the fields beside the road or whether they were kept in their places is unknown, but they were here for nearly an hour. For at last there was news of the enemy.

The Jacobite army left Duddingston behind at 9am and followed the road east past a mill and on through the little village of Easter Duddingston. Sticking

---

19 Cope's evidence, Robins (ed.), *Inquiry*, p.37.

View from the Gladsmuir, looking north-west towards the actual site of the battle.

to the main road, the Highlanders kept to the north side of the Niddrie Burn, across which were the estates of Brunstane House and Newhailes House (formerly Whitehill). The latter belonged to Sir James Dalrymple, a cousin of the Earl of Stair who had commanded for King George at Dettingen in 1743 and therefore knew Sir John Cope. In a year's time, Sir James would erect an obelisk commemorating his cousin's role at Dettingen, which can still be seen in the grounds of Newhailes today. But on 20 September 1745, beyond the trees at the edge of his park, Dalrymple would have seen the march of the Highland army.

The clansmen crossed a little burn near the north-west corner of Newhailes estate and continued past Crystal's Inn, the waterside hostelry at which the unfortunate Garden and Cunningham had been arrested after their oysters the previous night. Perhaps there were now a few jocular jabs in the ribs from their captors as they passed. At this point, three miles into their march, the Highlanders were following the road through open ground as they approached the village of Fisherrow. Here they were seen by a certain Mrs Handasyde, who passed on her memory of the event to Robert Chambers in 1827. Charles Edward, she said, rode with a party of officers to the side of the column, preferring the grass and stubble to the roadway, his tartan coat catching the breeze and allowing the sunlight to glitter on the badge of St Andrew hanging around his neck: 'even those who were ignorant of his claims, or who rejected them, could not help wishing him good fortune, and at least no calamity'.[20] Some other poor woman lost her broom, snatched up by

20   Chambers, *History of the Rebellion*, Fifth Edition, p.114.

a Highlander who waved it aloft to great cheers, promising to sweep the enemy from the land! The army turned down Market Street, angling away from the coast towards the old stone bridge across the Esk.

The Roman Bridge today looks much as it did in 1745, although its ends were originally ramped rather than stepped. Tradition held that the Romans first built the crossing here, and indeed the rise overlooking the west bank had once been occupied by an important Roman fort. The bridge had been rebuilt many times across the centuries, not least in the wake of the Battle of Pinkie in 1547 when it had been fired upon by an English galley lurking in the river mouth. Over its wide arches now came the Camerons, leading the rest of the army to the safety of the far side. By reaching Musselburgh the Jacobites had achieved their first objective, denying this natural line of defence to their enemy and clearing a potentially dangerous bottleneck. From here they had three choices of road: the broad High Street of Musselburgh to the north; the road through Inveresk village, past the church of which Alexander Carlyle would one day become minister, heading south-east towards Carberry Hill; or the middle route, the back road, which ran along the south side of Musselburgh before heading east past Pinkie estate.

Either the High Street or the Pinkie road would have served their purpose, as they joined up further to the east before approaching West Pans. They chose the Pinkie road and so the army passed behind the back gardens of the Musselburgh residents as the road hooked behind the town before straightening out eastwards. The Jacobites now passed along the southern boundary of the Pinkie House estate. Pinkie was a fine tower, which boasted a splendid gallery with a stunning painted ceiling. It belonged to none other than John Hay, Marquess of Tweeddale and Secretary of State for Scotland. And it was here that the army received the news the Prince so desperately wanted to hear. Some of Strathallan's doughty horsemen were now riding up with excited and urgent reports: the enemy had been sighted.

Four and a half miles to the east, the situation in Cope's army was very similar. The halt at St Germains had been ordered when the Earl of Loudoun came galloping along the road from Preston. Earlier in the morning he had ridden forwards with the Earl of Home and Lieutenant Colonel Whitefoord. Their mission was to reconnoitre the ground on which Cope intended to establish what Loudoun called 'a strong camp near Musselburgh'.[21] Their way took them past Lord Drummore's estate near West Pans and the owner rode out to accompany them. This was an uncommonly prestigious scouting party! Drummore later recalled that the new camp was intended for 'a Field near Pinkie', which suggests the ground immediately south-east of Musselburgh, between Pinkie estate and Inveresk.[22] This is confirmed by Alexander Carlyle, who wrote: 'I understood afterwards that the

---

21 Loudoun's written submission to the board, Robins (ed.), *Inquiry*, Appendix, p.27.
22 Letter from Drummore to Cope, Alnwick, 24 October 1745, Robins (ed.), *Inquiry*, Appendix, p.36

The Roman Bridge, Musselburgh. The Jacobites crossed from right to left on the way to Prestonpans. (Author's collection)

General's intention was (if he had any will of his own) to occupy the field lying between Walliford, Smeaton and Inveresk'.[23]

Again mistaking Cope's failure to confide in him as failure to know his business, Carlyle nevertheless accepted the strength of such a location both in terms of access to supplies and defensibility. If the Jacobites attempted to engage him here, Cope would have had the benefit of the river to his front, obliging the enemy to attack over the narrow bridge or down the steep banks. The high ground around Inveresk church and the site of the old Roman fort would have played to Cope's advantage in firepower. But of course Cope's intention was not solely defensive, and if not attacked then the Musselburgh camp would be the final staging post before his push towards Edinburgh and the castle garrison. But this camp would never be, as Loudoun's party soon detected movement along the road. In their accounts, Loudoun and Drummore do not give their precise location where they spotted the Jacobites, but it is likely that they rode forward to the excellent vantage point of Inveresk church, as their view would ahead have been severely restricted if they had remained near Pinkie.

The scouting party watched the advancing Jacobites through their spy-glasses, probably as they were crossing the open ground between Crystal's Inn

---

23 Carlyle, *Autobiography*, p.137.

and Fisherrow. Once the scouts were satisfied that this was the main body of the enemy and not just a feint, Loudoun rode back to Cope. Home stayed on to watch a little longer before riding back himself. Lord Drummore, perhaps after falling back a little with Home, then waited until the Jacobite vanguard was 'distant not above four hundred Yards', at which point he too rode off.[24] The whole party was lucky to get away, as riders from the Perthshire Horse must have been dangerously close, bringing back their own report. It seems they had followed the post road onto the ridge, spotting some cavalry outriders at Tranent before turning about. The capture of a clutch of senior officers, including two earls, would have been an auspicious prelude to battle. Instead, both commanders were now informed that their opponents were marching towards them and that battle was surely imminent. How that battle would play out would be determined by the choices they each were now about to make.

Sir John Cope advanced his army past Seton village and over the simple wooden bridge which carried the road across the eastern extremity of the drainage channel from the Tranent Meadows. The road itself hugged the edge of the ditch eastwards along its whole length until it passed through a narrow passage between the estates of Lord Grange (Preston House) and Colonel Gardiner (Bankton). The ditch and road formed the southern boundary of a large open plain which sloped gently downwards as it approached the coast. The coast road from Prestonpans to North Berwick, passing through Cockenzie and Port Seton, was a little less than a mile to the north of the ditch and roughly in parallel, marking the northern edge of the plain. The long walls of Preston House estate formed the western boundary and Seton Palace the eastern. Between them was around one and a half square miles of fine unenclosed farmland, crossed north-south only by an old cart track and the waggonway from Tranent. The only enclosed area which projected into the plain was the Cockenzie warren park to the west of the waggonway. The harvest had just been completed, so the fields were clear of the crop down to a short stubble.

Onto this plain marched the British army at 1 pm, crossing the wooden waggon rails half way across the field before forming in line facing westwards towards Preston House walls. If the Jacobites continued their march due east they could only come at the redcoats through the bottle-neck between Preston and Bankton, or else over the small piece of open ground between the back gardens of Prestonpans and the northern wall of Preston estate, a gap barely 300 yards wide. Neither approach would give them room to deploy, and even if they came through both they would be at the mercy of concentrated musket-fire and grape-shot. In the judgement of James Johnstone, aide to Lord George Murray and on occasion also to the Prince, Cope's battle-line was 'fortified by nature, and in the happiest position for so small an army'.[25] The British general was satisfied: 'we took up this

---

24 Letter from Drummore to Cope, Alnwick, 24 October 1745, Robins (ed.), *Inquiry*, Appendix, p.35.
25 Johnstone, *Memoir*, p.35

Ground, to give us the Command of the Outlets from the two Defiles, through which only we could be attacked; and to guard our being attacked in Flank'.[26]

Cope could have chosen to press the army forwards rather than deploying for battle. He had two possible options. Alexander Carlyle, benefitting from hindsight by the time he wrote his account but having gained little in military knowledge, still maintained there was time to regain the high ground at Tranent. To do so the army would have had to cross the drainage ditch over the raised bed of the waggonway and the cart track, which Loudoun considered too narrow for such a march, and then cross the Tranent Meadows uphill into Tranent, surrounded as it was by coal-pits and enclosures. Had the Jacobites caught up with them at any stage of this operation then the army would have been in serious peril. It therefore probably occurred to nobody except Carlyle to even consider it. The slightly more plausible alternative was to continue the advance and, since the enemy was too close for them to reach Musselburgh, offer battle on the western side of Preston. But here the Jacobites might well have gained the advantage of the higher ground around Dolphinston and Rigley Hill, and as Lord Drummore pointed out there were enclosures all around, including his own, which would prevent an easy deployment and facilitate and ambush. With the enemy already past Pinkie, Cope decided the best option was to let them come to him.

And so the British army was ordered to form line and prepare for battle according to the orders passed out by Loudoun earlier that morning. The soldiers stood in the area now known as Thorntree Fields, in a line facing west. The warren park enclosure protected their right flank and the drainage ditch their left. The sloping ground immediate south of the warren was known for generations after as Johnnie Cope's Hole.[27] All Cope's scouts had now drawn in, including Lord Drummore, who understandably preferred remaining with the army to returning to a house directly in the path of the enemy. The outriders up at Tranent, after being spotted by Strathallan's men, had fallen back to the main body too. As the breeze stirred the King's Colours above the dressed ranks, as the horses tossed their mains and pawed the ground, the soldiers of the British army waited for their enemy to show themselves. All eyes watched those two roads from Preston. Then, around 2pm, the Jacobite army came into sight at last. But they were not at Preston.

The Jacobite response to the reports of Strathallan's scouts was very different to Cope's. Rather than halting the army for almost an hour and evaluating the options, the news had spurred the Highlanders into a rapid and immediate advance. Lord George Murray, commanding the head of the column, tore off at once: 'there was no time to deliberate, or wait for orders', he recalled; 'I was very well acquainted with the grounds, and as I was confident that nothing could be done to purpose except the Highlanders got above the enemy, I struck off to the

---

26 Cope's evidence, Robins (ed.), *Inquiry*, p.38.
27 Ordnance Survey Name Book: OS1/15/37/43.

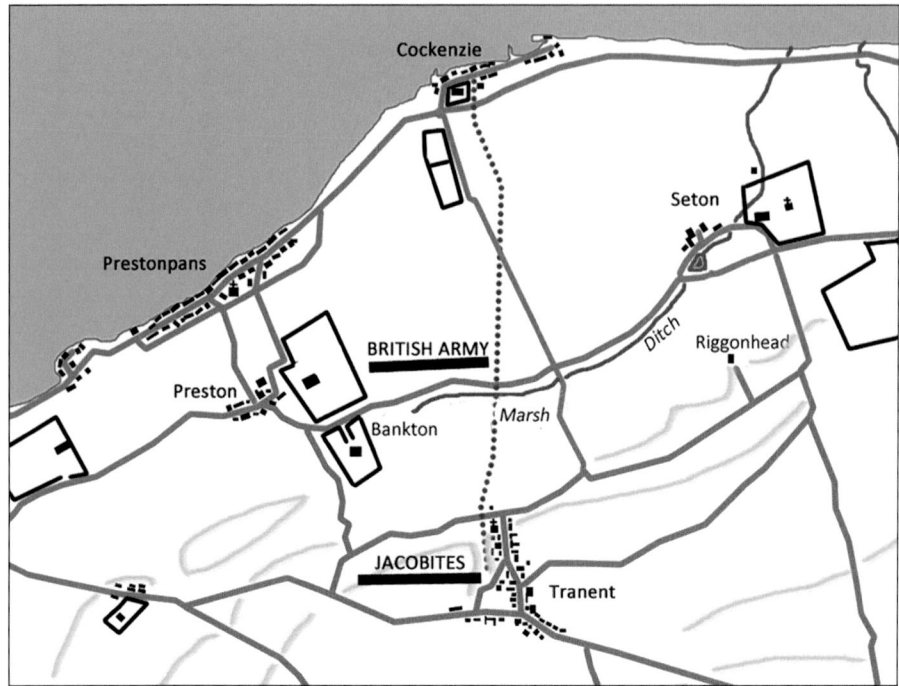

Map 9 Positions on the afternoon of 20th September.

right'.[28] In the words of Sir John Macdonald, Murray had 'taken upon himself more authority than was his due', and this sudden rush was in fact potentially reckless.[29] In his eagerness to gain the high ground Murray split the army. As he admitted himself he did not wait for orders, and in his rush forwards the rest of the army was simply left behind. Most Jacobite sources put a gloss over the incident, Elcho simply stating that the army went up the hillside 'in two Colums', but Murray's own tone is defensive: 'after I had got possession of the ground, I intended waiting till the rear was fully joined'.[30] In the event no harm was done, but had the Jacobite intelligence been faulty or out of date, there were potentially two regiments of dragoons nearby which could have cut the army in half.

And the intelligence was faulty: when Murray arrived on the high ground he saw that Cope's army was not at Tranent but down on the plain below in full battle order. Strathallan's first riders had seen only the scouts at Tranent, not the main body down near Seton. The Prince was being brought up to date as he drove

28 Murray, 'Marches', p.36.
29 Taylor, *1745 and After*, p.76.
30 Elcho, *Affairs*, p.266.

View from the Jacobite's first position, on Birslie Brae, across to Cope's position in the north-east. (Author's collection)

the main body up the hill, presumably with more detailed reports now from the Perthshire Horse. No more were needed however, as the red-coated troops of the British army now stood out clearly amongst the yellow stubble fields to the north-east. In their rush the Jacobites had struck off from the main road, and instead of following it round the northern side of Drummore's estates towards Morrison's Haven they had taken a track heading south-east towards Wallyford House (now demolished) before going cross-country onto the shoulder of Falside Hill. The army marched onwards onto Birslie Brae to the west of Tranent, where they regained the post-road which had come up the hillside through Dolphinston. Had Cope not taken the low road at Elvingstone, it would have been here on Birslie Brae that the armies now clashed. That of course is what he had feared, and now Cope's decision not to follow the post-road left the Jacobites on top of the hill and he at the bottom. Garden and Cunningham were now simply released without ceremony from their unhappy but benign captivity, for the clansmen now had more important things to think about than them. It was 2pm.

At first sight of the Highlanders upon the hill, notwithstanding the fact that the enemy were not at all where they had been expected, the redcoats cheered. Carlyle recalled their shouts, which released not only the tension of this last anxious wait but also the pent-up frustration of the past month. At last, for better or worse, the moment of truth had arrived. But soon the cheers were cut short as aides and officers rode along the British line with orders for it to redeploy. The enemy were not coming by Preston after all but from the ridge to the south, and this placed them off left Cope's flank. The army was ordered into a new position, so that Drummore could later remember to the general, 'you alter'd your Disposition, or rather Situation, and made your front extend along the Ditch, which was at first upon your Left, but a pretty good distance from it'.[31]

Cope and Loudoun both describe the manoeuvre in the same terms, although only Drummore gives the impression that the new line was some distance back (north) from the ditch. This is plausible: with his left flank remaining effectively where it was, Cope could have wheeled the line so that the whole swung like a door towards the ditch. After a month on campaign the soldiers had by now gained enough experience in large formations for such manoeuvres to be performed with efficiency. From his new position Cope then had the liberty to advance forwards as near to the ditch as he pleased, with a free field of fire before him.

Most contemporary plans of the battle show the army in fact drew up close to the ditch, although there is a very fine map – available in 1745 for two shillings and sixpence – which does shows the line held back as Drummore recalled it. The map proclaims that it was informed by 'an officer in the army who was present', although some of the local detailing (the ornamental gardens of Preston House, the medieval tower overlooking them, and Mr Nisbit's parks to the west) could suggest somebody like Drummore had input too. That might explain why the plan pulls the line back away from the ditch in concurrence with his testimony.

Either way, Cope brought his army into a new position shortly after 2pm so that it faced due south and was anchored on the right by Lord Grange's long wall. Parties were detached from the battle-line to set breaches into this wall so that the enemy might not be permitted to shelter behind it should they still chose to come through Preston. As Drummore noted, the walls were too high for anyone to fire from the parapet, but the breaches would at least allow the redcoats to move into Preston rapidly should they need, perhaps to enfilade an attacking column passing between there and Prestonpans. Cope and his staff were clearly contemplating how they might respond to several different situations. None of them probably realised how critical these walls would soon prove to be for their chances of survival. At the same time as the walls were being breached, the waggons of the baggage train were being drawn into the relative security of the Warren Parks and the artillery was concentrated in one group on the left flank. Still lacking decent crews, it was not plausible to spread the pieces along the line as intended.

There was now an anxious period of waiting, both sides eyeing the other across the marshes of the Tranent Meadows. A certain Lieutenant Craig of Wynyard's 4th Regiment of Marines, who had somehow become attached to the army as a volunteer, perhaps whilst on leave like the Earl of Home, rode forward during the redeployment to observe the Jacobites on Birslie Brae; he reported that 'to the best

---

31 Letter from Drummore to Cope, Alnwick, 24 October 1745, Robins (ed.), *Inquiry*, Appendix, p.36.

of his Judgment [sic] they seemed to be more than 5000'.[32] This would suggest the enemy's strength had doubled since the report of John Home at Dunbar, and from here on the British staff was working under the mistaken assumption that they were heavily outnumbered – an error they persisted in repeating in the subsequent inquiry, fuelled by false figures which some of them would later receive directly from the Jacobites.

Cope soon found further employment for Lieutenant Craig, despatching him to Edinburgh with a final urgent appeal for General Guest to release trained artillerymen to man his cannon. It was a potentially risky mission, but of serious importance. At Haddington the previous night, at about 7pm, a certain Richard Jack had been interviewed by the general after arriving in camp professing to be an engineer who had aided in preparing the walls of Edinburgh for a defence. Jack appears to have been a maths teacher with a high opinion of his usefulness, but now on Friday afternoon he suddenly appeared amongst the artillery train and informed master-gunner Griffith that he had been instructed to aid the artillery crews. Notwithstanding his claim to understand the theory of gunnery, he had to be shown how to load a cannon. Accepting Jack's offer of aid, assuming he ever actually did (Cope could barely remember their meeting), would come back to bite the general a year later when Jack caused trouble at the inquiry.

With little sign of activity amongst the Jacobites, Cope was itching to know what they were about. Ever helpful, Colonel Gardiner now reminded the general that Alexander Carlyle was both local and eager to be useful. One of Cope's aides – we know two of them to have been Lieutenant Cooney and Major James Mossman of Lee's – therefore sought out the young volunteer and offered him a chance at last to perform a valuable service for his King and Country. The aide bore 'a message to inquire if I could provide a proper person to venture up to the Highland army, to make his observations, and particularly to notice if they had any cannon, or if they were breaking ground anywhere'.[33] Here was an invitation to glory. There were obvious risks, but Carlyle was not one to shy from his moment: he wasted no time in locating his father's church-officer, 'a fine stout man', and sending him off towards the enemy! When asked a little later, Carlyle did agree to climb the church tower in Prestonpans and observe what he could from there. The ruin of Preston Tower would have offered a better vantage point, but it was on the wrong side of the walls and therefore potentially exposed to the enemy. Walter Grosset, the customs collector at Alloa, also volunteered to head over the marshes to get a clearer sense of what the enemy might be up to.

General Cope was not the only commander sending scouts over the marshes that afternoon. The Jacobites had the advantage of the heights and so none of Cope's activities were hidden from them, but they needed to know for sure whether the

---

32   Craig's evidence, Robins (ed.), *Inquiry*, p.59.
33   Carlyle, *Autobiography*, pp.138-9.

The ridge west of Tranent, Birslie Brae being to the right, as viewed from the Tranent Meadows. Walter Grosset observed the Jacobites' initial position from near here. (Author's collection)

ground before them could be crossed or not. It did not look promising from the summit; Murray recalled there were 'meadows, and deep broad ditches, betwixt us and them'.[34] His namesake, the secretary, says that the Prince only had to look across the ground to realise the problem: 'so soon as the Chevalier had taken a view of the Enemy he judged it impossible to attack them in the post they was then in, having a deep ditch in their front... where he must have sustained great loss before he could pass it'.[35] Nevertheless, Lord George sent Colonel Henry Kerr of Graden – not to be mistaken for Cornet Kerr of Gardiner's Dragoons – into the Tranent Meadows. 'He rode in at a gate, and went to the meadow next the enemy;' Murray recalled, 'several of their men got alongst the ditches and shot at him. He did his business very coolly, and then returned'.[36] Cope must have had a screen of pickets out in front of the line, especially if he was drawn a little way back from the ditch as Drummore suggests. Kerr's report, gained at such risk, was hardly necessary. As was to be expected he found that the ground was too enclosed with ditches and walls to allow an easy approach, and that the lower portions were too boggy to facilitate an attack. So much for Murray's confidence that he knew this ground.

---

34   Murray, 'Marches', p.37.
35   Murray of Broughton, *Memorials*, p.200.
36   Murray, 'Marches', p.37.

It seems Charles Edward had already determined there could be no attack that way, for even as Murray was sending Kerr into the firing line the Prince was ordering a party of Camerons into Tranent churchyard. Both Elcho and Murray of Broughton attribute the order to Charles, whilst Lord George implies it was done on a whim by O'Sullivan, 'for what reason I could not understand'.[37] This was an important moment as it led directly to the opening shots of the battle. The order to occupy the churchyard was, regardless of Murray's derision, a perfectly natural one. As it does today, the churchyard stood on a high platform fronted to the north by a tall and buttressed retaining wall. In front, across a cut path, was a large lectern doocot on a raised platform. On its western side the churchyard was protected by the steep-sided heugh, at the bottom of which ran the waggonway, and which was lined with trees. This was therefore a defensible position forward of the main battle-line, from which the enemy's motions could be closely observed and from which any attempt to pass up the waggonway or cart road could be blocked. Its occupation as a forward strongpoint should therefore have been comprehensible to anyone with formal military training. Nobody other than Murray criticised the reasoning behind it.

The Jacobite accounts are not clear as to how many men were actually detailed to the churchyard. Broughton refers to 'a detachment', Murray identifies 'fifty of Lochiel's people', and Elcho raises that to '300 men'.[38] Murray's recollection is the more likely, and as he appears to have witnessed O'Sullivan ordering them out he was well-placed to know. What is clear is that they did not simply occupy the graveyard itself, but also the wooded area around the heugh and there was probably also a forward picket at the doocot. From here a Jacobite soldier would not only have a clear view across open ground to his opponents, but could also prevent the doocot becoming a blind spot for those watching from the churchyard wall. Although they were now within easy range of Cope's artillery the clansmen had clearly been ordered to keep their heads down, something which probably required little formal instruction now that they were less than half a mile from the enemy line. There are roughly 745 yards (680 metres) between the doocot and the ditch.

It was now almost two hours since the armies had come within full sight of one another. Walter Grosset offered once more to scout forwards towards the enemy, proving himself to be one of Cope's more useful civilian volunteers. As he had done earlier, Grosset headed up the waggonway. The wooden rails were barely discernible as the sleepers had been covered with earth and permitted to grass in order to provide a fair footing for the waggon horses. More obvious was that the path was slightly raised from the ground as it approached the ditch and marsh, not only to prevent the rails becoming waterlogged but also to ease the gradient down from the heugh. The waggonway passed close to Cope's left flank so the path was

---

37 Murray, 'Marches', p.37.
38 Murray of Broughton, *Memorials*, p.200; Murray, 'Marches', p.37; Elcho, *Affairs*, p.267.

an obvious one for Grosset, who appears to have been positioned with the guns on the left. There was a path running westwards from the bottom of the heugh along the foot of the ridge and it is possible that this was where Grosset was hoping to get his close view of the Jacobites on the hill above. The path is still there today, known as Brickworks Road.

But this time Grosset, perhaps complacent after his earlier successful scout, was in for a shock. The trees lining the Heugh ahead burst forth with deadly sounds. Muskets cracked close at hand, flashes of orange light in the darker undergrowth followed by blasts of smoke and fire. Grosset, in his own words, had been 'surprised by a Party of them, who lay concealed in the Church-yard on one side of the said hollow Way, and a thicket of Wood on the other'.[39] They had waited until he was 'fairly betwixt them', and so the location was the crossroads where the east-west pathway intersected the waggonway heading into the darkness of the heugh. How many shots were fired and by how many of those fifty Camerons is not recorded; it was probably just the outermost pickets who engaged. But to Grosset it must have felt as if he had stumbled into the entire Jacobite army, and the sudden panic at being attacked from close range can readily be imagined. As the balls whipped about him, the customs collector managed to keep his head and flee the way he had come.

Still no doubt driven by adrenalin, Grosset gained the redcoat line and on finding Eaglesfield Griffith proposed they should return fire with the mortars. Griffiths protested that these were not able to fire at present, so Lieutenant Colonel Whiteford of the Marines responded with his cannon instead. Loudoun reports that 'Sir John advanced two Gallopers' to the edge of the ditch, which were then loaded by the sailors of HMS *Fox*. Whiteford and Griffiths themselves took up the linstocks, and the two 1.5 pounders blasted forth their iron shot. These came crashing through the branches towards the Camerons who had now revealed their position to the enemy. Elcho recalled the cannon firing 'briskly', the improvised crews evidently doing good service.[40] The redcoats 'huzzaed at every discharge', according to Murray, who admits that 'they soon wounded a man or two'.[41] Lochiel himself came up into the churchyard to judge the risks his men were exposed to, and in consultation with Murray he quickly withdrew the picket deeper into Tranent.

The first shots of the Battle of Prestonpans had now been fired, late in the afternoon of 20 September. The first had come from Cope's pickets sniping at Henry Kerr, followed shortly after by the first actual exchange of fire up the line of the waggonway around the heugh. It is telling that the musket fire from both sides had been utterly ineffective, especially that from the Camerons which was clearly much

---

39 Grosset's evidence, Robins (ed.), *Inquiry*, p.87.
40 Elcho, *Affairs*, p.267.
41 Murray, 'Marches', p.37.

The Heugh, from which Walter Grosset was attacked on his scouting mission. Tranent church is on the left, with its defensible walled churchyard. (Author's collection)

hotter than the pot shots taken at Kerr. Walter Grosset had been caught in a trap at relatively close range but had got away without injury and with a fine story to tell that would shame Alexander Carlyle, who watched the firing from the safety of his father's steeple. Cope's gunners had performed well at their first test, presumably because the teams had been able to concentrate on just two pieces whilst not themselves under fire. Richard Jack had proved himself inept at the arts, however, so Whitefoord had set him aside. The redcoats had drawn first blood, and no doubt the sight of their cannons firing had given them a boost. Loudoun thought they had 'killed about a Dozen of them', which presumably was the common belief amongst the army.[42] Cope had reason to feel satisfied.

But then there was immediate movement on the ridge, so soon in succession to the events at the churchyard that some of those who witnessed it could not recall which occurred first. A large body of Highlanders was now in motion, heading back along Birslie Brae towards the west. Carlyle spotted it from the church, rushing down the steps and leaping onto his horse. Meeting an aide, he passed on

42 Loudoun's written submission, Robins (ed.), *Inquiry*, p.87.

his report that the 300-400 Highlanders were heading towards Dolphinston and then returned to his post. He had at last made a contribution to the campaign, although the activity must have been clearly visible through the officers' glasses in the field. Perhaps they had already begun to move before Grosset had unexpectedly triggered the action at the churchyard, which distracted everyone's attention for its duration. At the same time, the rest of the Jacobite army appeared to be moving eastwards off Birslie Brae, in the opposite direction. To Cope and his staff there could only be one explanation: the enemy intended to attack from both east and west, taking the army on each flank.

The British army now shifted its line again, some time before 5pm: 'I ordered the Baggage to move towards the East of Cockenny [Cockenzie], and made the Line face obliquely cross the Field with a South-west Aspect', recalled Cope.[43] This meant that his main fire was facing towards the road passage between Bankton and Preston, whilst the dragoons on his flanks could cover both the track from Prestonpans in the north-west and the waggonway/cart road paths to the south-east. But whilst the redeployment made defensive sense, it was becoming increasingly clear that Cope now had no plan of his own other than to wait and see what the enemy did. This realisation was dawning on the Highlanders, and it 'added so much courage to the Princes [sic] Army'.[44] But then, with the light already beginning to fade into evening, the detachment of Highlanders suddenly began to withdraw again. Cope assumed it was as a result of his own movements, which had deterred them from their attack. In dutifully rushing down the steeple steps to report the latest news, Alexander Carlyle was accosted by the church-officer he had sent up towards the enemy. He had returned full of stories of the enemy's strength and vigour, although one wonders if he ever actually went very far. Carlyle sent him on to Cope to bear both of their reports and then, apparently considering his duty done, sought out Colonel Gardiner. The British army was by then redeploying once again, returning to its south-facing position along the north side of the ditch.

This flurry of activity had been set in motion by Charles Edward's assessment that there was no possibility of attacking the enemy across the Meadows. He was therefore consolidating his position whilst weighing up his options. The Prince's main concern was that Cope might attempt to slip away without engaging, either eastwards towards the border or, more dangerously, westwards to the security of Edinburgh. In the latter case the Jacobites would be in a very exposed position, locked out of a walled city which would this time be stoutly defended by both castle and army. With some justification, Charles accepted that although he could not attack the enemy, neither could Cope attack him: the most important immediate objective was therefore to prevent the redcoats marching westwards. The road to Edinburgh had to be closed.

43 Cope's evidence, Robins (ed.), *Inquiry*, p.39.
44 Elcho, *Affairs*, p.267.

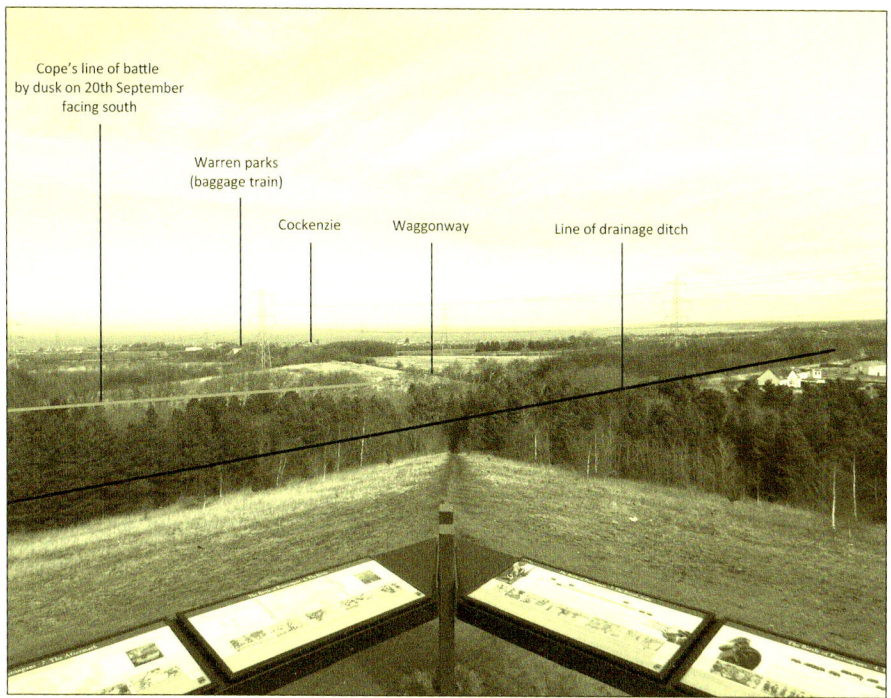

Looking north-east across Cope's position at the end of day one. The Jacobites would appear off to the right the following morning. (Author's collection)

Lord Nairne was ordered to march the Atholl Brigade towards Dolphinston to watch that road. At the same time Murray withdrew the Camerons from the churchyard, sending the army's vanguard eastward through Tranent in the hope that the other side of the Meadows was more amenable for an attack. The rest of the army was drawn back from the lip of the ridge at Birslie Brae so that their position was not so visible to the enemy, allowing the Prince a chance to pass close enough to Windygoul to be brought a glass of wine by the lady of the house. Its owner, John Anderson, had been out in the '15 and his son Robert had already joined the Jacobite staff. In making these dispositions the Prince impressed the more experienced soldier O'Sullivan, who judged that he 'behaved on this juncture as the most experienced General in [the] posting of his Guardes to cover his army'.[45] Lord George Murray disagreed.

What followed was a confusing set of orders and counter-orders which must have bamboozled the Highlanders as much as they do the historian. The timings are difficult to follow, no doubt because there were several things happening at

---

45   Taylor, *1745 and After*, p.77.

the same time but not in concert. Murray rode onto the Brae to order the main body to march east through Tranent, without feeling any compulsion to inform either his commander-in-chief or the adjutant-general. The latter now came up in a frenzy of anxiety, as the Murray was sending men through the town in full view of the enemy without either reconnaissance or consultation. He had also abandoned the forward position at the church without discussion too, even though this new eastward march was exactly the kind of manoeuvre for which such forward outposts were required. After all, even though there had been a few casualties the churchyard picket had in fact done its job, preventing any further scouting up the waggonway.

But whilst Murray was dismissing O'Sullivan's concerns about both the churchyard and the eastward motions, he noticed the absence of his own brigade of Athollmen. Spotting the Prince, he asked him 'in a very high tone' where the brigade had gone, and when he was told it was moving towards Dolphinston it was Murray's turn to fume.[46] As O'Sullivan, and admittedly only he, gleefully recalls, 'he threw his gun on the Ground in a great passion, & Swore God, he'd never draw his sword for the cause, if the Bregade was not brought back'.[47] The strains of the day were showing. Only Charles Edward kept his cool, ignoring the presumption of his subordinate and for the sake of the peace ordering the Atholl Brigade to return to Birslie Brae. O'Sullivan went off with the order, no doubt chafing at the injustice of it, and poor Nairne duly turned his brigade about. It was this withdrawal which Carlyle had seen from the steeple.

But by the time O'Sullivan was back at Tranent, he found that whilst the main body was continuing around to the east of the town that Lochiel had calmed Murray's temper and induced him to contrition. Accepting the Prince's former reasoning, Murray suggested the Atholl Brigade should indeed be left to observe the Edinburgh road. His anger at not being consulted had initially blinded him to military reasoning, and so the Athollmen were halted on Birslie Brae. It was now around 8pm, and the Jacobite army was strung out across the ridge in perhaps three bodies, with its senior officers at loggerheads and confusion. Nairne's brigade lingered on the shoulder of the ridge west of Tranent for several more hours, keeping the enemy guessing and keeping a wary eye on the road to the capital.

Unaware of the confusion in his enemy's camp, and most likely giving them too much credit for their ability to keep him on the back foot, General Cope had also accepted that a full engagement was now unlikely today. The presence of Highlanders west of Tranent made him anxious for his right flank, but it soon became clear that the main body was preparing to camp in the east. The eastern Tranent Meadows were no more open for an assault than the west: although there were fewer enclosures, the ground was still too marshy and the ditch from here

---

46   Taylor, *1745 and After*, p.78.
47   Taylor, *1745 and After*, p.78.

Colonel Gardiner's home, Bankton House, viewed from north through the avenue of trees along which it was once approached. (Author's collection)

was waterlogged all the way to Seton and the little wooden bridge. The British army therefore took up its night-post. A subaltern's guard was placed in Colonel Gardiner's gardens at Bankton, the most vulnerable position if the enemy came from the west. A grand-guard of 100 dragoons, presumably from Gardiner's, was posted to watch the breaches in the park walls of Preston House, along with the reserve squadron which patrolled nearer the coastal route through Prestonpans. A matching guard was set to the east: the reserve squadron of Hamilton's Dragoons was posted to watch the open ground between Seton and the sea, where the coast road came in, whilst another grand-guard of 100 dragoons watched the more inland routes. They were to patrol in three groups, the northernmost, closest to the other squadron, being 30 troopers and a cornet, the second being 30 men and a lieutenant, and the one closest to the crossing at the wooden bridge being 40 dragoons led by their captain. Colonel Lascelles reported that the main frontage along the ditch was watched by infantry pickets, with a main guard in the centre.[48]

No sooner had the orders been given for these postings, than shots split the air. They came from the south-west: the picket at Bankton was under attack. Cope immediately ordered an officer forward to reinforce the position and hold that crucial road onto the plain. Little was made of this at the inquiry, although it is surely the same incident which is described by Loudoun as having taken place

48   Cope's evidence, Robins (ed.), *Inquiry*, p.39.

a little earlier in the day, in which only his timings appear to be mistaken: 'the Rebels detached a Party down by a Quarry and a hollow Road, that led to behind Colonel Gardener's House, which we took Possession of'.[49] Lascelles called what happened 'a pretty brisk Firing about Colonel Gardener's House', which suggests it was a little hotter than is implied by the fact that it got so little attention at the inquiry.[50] Like the exchange at the churchyard nearly four hours earlier, these preliminary skirmishes are often overlooked, but they were significant enough for those who took part in them. In the twilight a party of Athollmen had come down the road which would later be named after the British commander, and opened fire on the sentries there from the western side of the grounds. Not only is this where the road led them, but also where musket balls have recently been found by locals. Presumably, once it became clear that the picket had been reinforced – one good volley down the road would give sufficient notice of that – the Jacobites pulled back, satisfied at having perturbed their opponents before they took to rest.

Nairne's men were probably just frustrated, baffled as they were by orders to march back and forth along the road to Dolphinston. The firefight at Bankton might well have been their way of letting off steam, and it might therefore have occurred without much in the way of authorisation. None of the senior Jacobite commanders mention it in their accounts, which might imply that they all had nothing to do with it. Lord Elcho did however remember another incident: 'about ten o'clock at night Lord Nairns Colum fired a good deal at some dragoons who were patrolling and kiled [sic] some of them'.[51] Perhaps he was recalling the same incident at Bankton, mistaking the infantry picket for dragoons. Or perhaps the Atholl Brigade was deliberately patrolling aggressively to keep the enemy's attention out to the west.

By the time the firing petered out, Peregrine Lascelles was at Bankton in person, ensuring this important post was being properly watched:

> I, considering the Importance of that Post, and the Danger the Guards were in of being surprised, as there were thick Hedges and several small Inclosures upon the Left of it, offered my Service, saw the Centries posted, and gave them and the Officers such Orders as I thought proper.[52]

Clearly he considered the situation here to be serious, the original guard posted here being inadequate for so important a location. There is no mention of casualties except by Elcho, but, even assuming the redcoats got off without a scratch, Bankton could have been easily overrun if it had been pressed, and at the very

---

49 Loudoun's written submission, Robins (ed.), *Inquiry*, Appendix, p.28.
50 Lascelles' evidence, Robins (ed.), *Inquiry*, p.65.
51 Elcho, *Affairs*, p.268.
52 Lascelles' evidence, Robins (ed.), *Inquiry*, p.65.

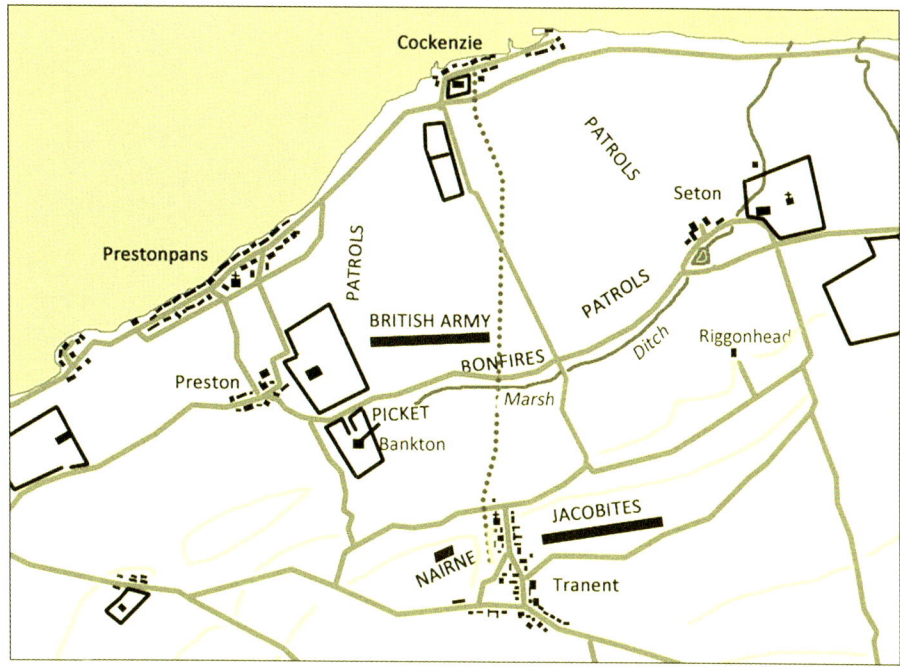

Map 10 Positions on the night of 20 September.

moment Cope's army was settling into its night-posts. It is not therefore difficult to see why most British officers keep quiet about the incident at the Inquiry, whereas Lascelles was under direct investigation so needed to prove his attention to duty.

Certainly the sounds of the firing, however brief it may have been, would have jolted Cope's men into fresh anxieties. Despite the efforts of the officers to claim that the men lay down to rest in good spirits, it is hard not to believe they were on tenterhooks. As if in response to their fears, 'about Nine of the clock that night, all the Dogs in the Village of Tranent began to bark with the utmost Fury, which, it was believed, was occasioned by the Motions of the Rebels'.[53] The noise prompted Lascelles to a new round of visits around the sentry posts, meeting Major Talbot who was responsible for them along the way. The outer guards had been posted out in the Meadows, where three large fires were built so that any attempt to cross in the darkness would be foiled.[54] These will presumably have illuminated the British sentries as easily as any lurking Jacobites, and they probably did not help the sentries' night vision either. But they would have helped to at least create a sense of safety in the British camp.

53 Lascelles' evidence, Robins (ed.), *Inquiry*, p.65.
54 Whitefoord's evidence, Robins (ed.), *Inquiry*, p.49.

Of course there was no camp as such: the tents remained with the baggage off in the rear. The train had been shifted several times as the army redeployed, but it is likely that much of it was now back in the Warren Parks enclosures. The most valuable goods, including the military treasury and the senior officers' baggage, were removed to the even greater security of the stone walled enclosure of Cockenzie House. Perhaps part of the treasury was also now removed onto HMS *Fox*, which was probably anchored nearby, although this may have already been done as a precaution back at Dunbar. The Highland companies of Loudoun's and the Black Watch were sent to guard what was left of it, along with the rest of the baggage. Lord Drummore went that way too, leaving the officers to their business. He slept in Cockenzie because he was a civilian and could enjoy that privilege: Cope and his staff did not, despite the traditions that the general slept either at Cockenzie House or the Inkbottle House. Instead the officers remained alert for most of the night, catching only a light sleep if any at all. As for the private soldiers, those who were not on duty lay in their positions on the open field and caught what rest they could after a tense but ultimately anti-climactic day. In today's landscape their position would be parallel with the road and railway line, directly north of the battlefield viewpoint, with their right flank under the housing somewhere close to Schaw Road and their left running through Thorntree Fields over the disused railway spur towards the waggonway path. One wonders whether James Gardiner, lying in the field beneath his cloak, noticed that single solitary hawthorn tree growing amongst the stubble nearby.

Alexander Carlyle had left Gardiner earlier looking 'grave, but serene and resigned'. Meeting his church officer once again, he now asked whether Cope had paid him for his troubles in reconnoitring the enemy. He said not, and so Carlyle gave him half a crown of his own, perhaps buying off a little of his guilt for not daring the risk himself. Who knows how far the reluctant volunteer ever went, but certainly Cope would have learned more from men like Grosset and Lieutenant Craig. The latter had still not returned from Edinburgh with those artillerymen. They had at least set out from the castle, but unbeknownst to Cope had somehow managed to get lost on route. He had been asking for them to be sent out to him since 3 August, but they would never show up.

Carlyle found his father's manse so filled with Volunteers that there was no room for him even at his own home. This had been his most common military experience so far. Amongst those at the manse was Patrick Simson, who was a cousin of Captain Adam Drummond the paymaster of Lee's Regiment. The captain had entrusted Simson with 400 guineas, presumably regimental funds, in two saddle bags. These were now left in the secure care of the minister at Prestonpans. Carlyle dined with his father but fell asleep at his beef: he retired to a neighbour's house where he 'fell into a profound sleep'.[55] The battle he had been waiting for was just a few short hours away.

---

55   Carlyle, *Autobiography*, p.141.

7

The Battle: Day Two

Saturday, 21 September 1745

The Jacobites had even less rest than their opponents on the plain below. The evening's confusion over the churchyard and the Atholl Brigade had finally come to an end around 10.30pm, by which time the whole of the rest of the army was in its new position in an open field to the east of the town, later known as Prince's Park.[1] The best road through into these fields had been shown to O'Sullivan by an obliging farmer, Alexander Henderson, who received a guinea for his trouble. In return he joined the Jacobite army and spent the coming days being somewhat loud about his politics. In due course his name would be passed to the government by irritated neighbours. A little to the north-east of the army's new position was the farm at Riggonhead. To the north of the camp the marshes were more open but no more accommodating. The Jacobites therefore posted their own out-guards and then sought what comfort they could from the freshly gathered sheaves which had been neatly stacked after the harvest. Sir John Macdonald was close enough at his post to hear the voices of the redcoat sentries down in the marshes below.

Cope did not wish his enemy to rest any easier than he did. Perhaps in retaliation for the probe at Bankton, he authorised mortar shells to be fired during the night towards Tranent. His four Coehorn and two Royal mortars, squat cauldron-like barrels mounted on simple wooden blocks, ought to have been capable of firing explosive shot in a high arc onto the ridge. At the very least it would keep the enemy on edge throughout the night. One letter, written later that very day and forwarded to the Chancellor of Carlisle Cathedral, says that 'Sir John threw a good many small shells into the town… which did some Execution but did not much disturb them'.[2] But Lieutenant Colonel Whitefoord told the subsequent Inquiry

---

1   Between Tranent Mains and Blindwells, neither of which appear on Roy's map. The A1 dual carriageway cuts through the Prince's Park today.
2   National Archives: SP36/68/284. The Canceller, John Waugh, states that the letter was sent from a gentleman of Edinburgh to a friend in the neighbouring area.

The Waggonway heading north across the plain. The British army slept in the field to the left, marching over the tracks the following morning to deploy. (Author's collection)

that only one shell was fired. On its failing to burst, since the fuses had been 'damnified', according to Griffith, by overlong storage in Edinburgh Castle, the attempt was abandoned. On the receiving end of this meagre shelling, Lord Elcho concurred with the British officers: '[the enemy] threw off one Coehorn'.[3] A fault with the aiming quadrant had been discovered earlier that day, which had been the reason the mortars could not been used against the churchyard. But this had now been fixed with the aid of Richard Jack the maths teacher, who was otherwise considered a liability by the gunnery officers. Understandably for a first firing, the shot 'fell short' according to Elcho. That was fortunate, for had the elevation been better or the fuse good, this random shot in the dark could have ended the war in an instant: the shot landed 'in a direct line where the Prince was'.[4]

But Charles Edward Stuart was not destined to be killed that night, and the shelling was stopped in case the Jacobites now lost their perceived fear of Cope's

---

3   Elcho, *Short Account*, p.269.
4   Elcho, *Short Account*, p.269. A mortar survives at Kedleston Hall in Derbyshire, reputedly abandoned nearby by the Jacobites in December 1745. It is possible that it is one of those which they captured at Prestonpans.

artillery. Amongst the clansmen the 'Common Conversation was how to Catch Cope' once the battle began, whilst the senior officers were focussing on 'what was to be done next morning and how to Gett at Mr Cope'.[5] Proposals to use fascines – bundles of sticks bound together and used by soldiers to cross ditches in siege operations – had been put forward earlier in the day, but whilst they might have helped at the ditch they did not solve the problems of the bog. The Prince's eye was probably still flitting west, where the Atholl Brigade were still watching the Edinburgh road, but to the east lay another alternative.

There was a track heading east from the Jacobite camp which turned northwards past St Germains and joined the old road at Seton Palace. They could cross the wet ditch at Seton Bridge, or go around the pond through Seton village and into the ground between the settlement and the sea. But Cope was watching these entry-points with almost two-thirds of Hamilton's Dragoons, and the Highlanders would be unable to deploy until they pushed through into the open ground over which Cope had marched at noon the previous day. Furthermore, a wide loop around to the east left the road to Edinburgh clear. Cope could either rush to the city as soon as he perceived the Highlanders had gone east, or, in the event of anything other than a swift and decisive Jacobite victory, he could mount a fighting withdrawal towards the castle garrison. This route was not therefore much more appealing a prospect than attacking through Preston, which at least kept the Jacobite army between Cope and the capital. After continued discussions a council of war was scheduled for midnight, leaving time for a brief rest and a lot more thought.

Perhaps around this time a certain Mr Lucas approached Lord George Murray. He was a tenant farmer from Tullibody, he explained, and the Jacobite army had taken some of his horses on the way down to Stirling. For the loss of these Lucas would be charged by his landlord, who had sent him on with a letter demanding their recovery. Murray expressed his regrets, and advised Lucas that the horses were all corralled in Tranent churchyard. If he were to recover his property when opportunity presented, Murray promised to turn a blind eye. He was no doubt motivated as much by the chance to irritate the Irish Inspector of Cavalry, Sir John Macdonald, as by a sense of justice. Murray had a particular dislike of the Prince's Irish advisors, who had the Prince's ear on account largely of having been with him the longest. Then, inspired by Lucas' bold acceptance of this proposal, Lord George offered him a commission in the army, but Lucas replied that he thought they would both be better off out of it. The story goes that Murray shrugged his shoulders with the old adage, 'in for a penny, in for a pound'.[6]

Before the midnight council, the lieutenant general had a more important visitor. Trying to doze, he was stirred by young Robert Anderson, whose own farm

---

5   Elcho, *Short Account*, p.269.
6   Chambers, R. *History of the Rebellion of 1745*, First American Edition (Philadelphia: E C Mielke, 1833), p.174.

was a few miles off at Whitburgh but whose father was master at Windygoul just a short way off. Anderson was on the quartermaster's staff and had been present in the background whilst his superiors debated their course of action. He had not felt it was his place to speak then, but immediately afterwards he had sought out James Hepburn of Keith with some pertinent information. The Andersons were well connected in the area and knew the ground well. Johnstone calls him 'proprietor of the marsh', but that is probably a simplified recollection.[7] A family of Andersons had until recently rented the farm at Riggonhead, and another branch later took up residence at St Germains. It was whilst visiting his relations that Anderson had used the marshes for hunting snipe, as the family would later inform that great collector of anecdotes Robert Chambers.[8] There was, Anderson now told Keith, a little-used track which led from Riggonhead Farm through what Murray later called 'a small defile near the east end of the ditches'.[9] The defile led to a little wooden crossing of the drainage channel, beyond which lay the open plain. It was a far shorter route than that by St Germains, and had the advantage of cutting out the choke points at Seton. But it was narrow and if the exit to the defile was guarded then, as O'Sullivan neatly put it, 'all was over'.[10]

Sensible of Lord George Murray's resistance to advice from those he saw as competitors, Keith advised Anderson to propose the idea himself. Murray liked it very much, and later claimed the lion's share of the credit for it too: 'I knew the ground myself, and had a gentleman or two with me who knew every part thereabouts'.[11] The Prince was close enough at hand to be awakened quickly. He was, famously, lying on a bed of pease-straw out in the open. Informed of Anderson's suggestion, Charles gave orders for the defile to be scouted discretely ahead of the midnight council. On 'finding it neglected' by the enemy, the Jacobite officers 'had little left to deliberate upon'.[12] Nairne's detachment was at last ordered to come in from its western position by 2am, presumably going around the rear of the town so as not to alert the dogs again. The army would be formed and ready to march two hours later. Charles Edward was now too keyed up to get much further rest and 'happyly was all night in motion', offering reassuring words to his men as they stirred along the hillside. Perhaps sensing the Prince's mood, the chiefs once more reminded Charles that he must not take any unnecessary risks when the battle came. Only his royal person held the army together, they said.

---

7 Johnstone, *Memoir*, p.56.
8 Chambers, *History of the Rebellion*, Fifth Edition, p.120.
9 Murray, 'Marches', p.38.
10 Taylor, *1745 and After*, p.79.
11 Murray, 'Marches', p.38.
12 'Neglected': Murray of Broughton, *Memorials*, p.201. 'Little left': Maxwell, J. *Narrative of Charles, Prince of Wales' Expedition to Scotland in the Year 1745* (Edinburgh: Maitland Club, 1841), p.39.

"Tis for yt reason," says the Prince, "yt they must see me; you all expose your selfs for the King and contry's cause, & I am as much obliged to it, as any of you". All they cou'd gain upon was yt he wou'd not fight a horse-back, & yt he'd laid [lead] up the Atholl Brigade; he laid it up indeed like a young Prince, for as soon as the fire began he was in the midst of 'em'.[13]

On the plain below the British officers and sentries were watching and listening. With the faint praise that the dragoons deserved, Cope reports that 'to do the Dragoons Justice, they were very alert, and their Patrols brought good Intelligence the whole Night, of every Motion the Enemy made'.[14] Lascelles concured. At 2.30am he was walking with Lieutenant Colonel Peter Halkett when by the light of the bonfires he recognised the Earl of Loudoun. Together this party of senior officers visited their general and reported that all appeared quiet. Barely half an hour later, after the officers had returned to their posts, Cope received the first indication that something was afoot: 'the Patrols reported, that the Rebels were moving towards the East'.[15] The news was the same for the next hour as the out-guards presumably detected first the movement of the Atholl Brigade around Tranent and then the main body stirring into life shortly afterwards. Despite their precautions for silence, the Jacobites were only about half a mile from the drainage ditch and are unlikely not to have been heard as they formed for the march.

The Jacobite column was a simple affair, drawn up three abreast. It was the turn of the MacDonald Regiments to have the honour of holding the right flank this day – they were alternating with the Camerons – and so they formed at the van with Robert Anderson up front to guide. The right of the line was to be commanded by the Duke of Perth, who seems to have had little to say during the previous day's events but was now marching boldly towards his first battle at the head of a division. Under his command where, from the front, the Clanranald, Glengarry and Keppoch regiments, followed by Perth's own regiment combined with the MacGregors. Behind them came the reserve, which was obliged to join the main column by the narrowness of the track. This was led by the Prince himself, on foot as agreed, and it comprised of the Atholl Brigade along with the Robertsons and MacLachlans. Bringing up the rear was the front line's second division under Lord George Murray: the Stewarts of Appin first, then Lochiel and his Camerons. The only troops left behind in Tranent were the Perthshire Horse, partly because their horses would be noisy but mainly because their numbers were so inadequate when compared to Cope's mounted arm.

Anderson guided the head of the Jacobite column through the Riggonhead defile without incident but not without detection. Cope knew they were coming

13 Taylor, *1745 and After*, p.79.
14 Cope's evidence, Robins (ed.), *Inquiry*, p.39.
15 Cope's evidence, Robins (ed.), *Inquiry*, p.40.

The Riggonhead March, by Andrew Hillhouse. (Reproduced with permission of the Battle of Prestonpans 1745 Heritage Trust)

from the increasingly alarming reports of the Hamilton's picket. The dragoons pulled back as the Highlanders entered the plain, too late to stop them at their most vulnerable point but perhaps not too late to have harassed their deployment if their own spirits had been bolder. Loudoun suggests that one squadron did face the enemy as it withdrew, deterring the latter from pressing too far forward whilst the rest of the battle line was formed. This done, the troopers fell back to the main body.[16] The enemy's intention now clear, and with his soldiers already stirring from the increasing activity around them, Cope ordered one of his cannons to be fired in alarm. The stillness of the pre-dawn was shattered by powerful thump of the signal gun.

The British army sprang into action as Cope swung his battle line around to face east. In all probability the foot arose in their positions and were faced north before wheeling forwards on the march, advancing across the wooden waggonway and the cart-track before halting a little further east than where they had first formed the previous afternoon. The artillery had rumbled along beside them on the right flank. The army now stood about halfway between the walls of the Preston House parks and Seton Palace. By now accomplished at its manoeuvres, the soldiers of this inexperienced army managed the redeployment in just a quarter of an hour, and as was repeatedly affirmed at the Inquiry the entire line was properly formed before the Jacobite attack commenced. This is important: Cope's army was not

---

16   Loudoun's account, Robins (ed.), *Inquiry*, Appendix, p.130.

caught out and unprepared as is sometimes assumed. That is not to say that the battle line was perfect, however. As on the previous day, the artillery was concentrated in one block rather than being dispersed along the line in close support of the infantry. But since the gunners had still not turned up there was little that could be done about that. They were also now on Cope's right flank instead of his left, as there was no time to haul them around to the opposite end of the line with action imminent. The artillery was vulnerable to close action, and so a guard unit of 100 men had be detached from the line and posted on the extreme right. In addition, there was no time for the 300 foot-soldiers on sentry duty to find their companies during the rapid motion eastwards, and so these men were banded together in a separate unit and placed between the artillery and Lee's Regiment.

The effect of these compromises was to over-crowd the right flank, as Sir John attested: 'there was not full enough Ground left for Colonel Gardener's Squadron; they therefore formed in the Rear of the Artillery-Guard, a few Paces behind, ready to sustain it'.[17] Only one squadron of Gardiner's Dragoons made it into the battle-line, with the second staggered in the rear and the third back in reserve. The day before, Cope had ordered the dragoons to extend into a broad line to maximise their frontage; now they had to do the opposite. Gardiner himself was posted in the second line,[18] whilst the forward squadrons of his regiment were led by Lieutenant Colonel Shugborough Whitney. Four years older than Gardiner, Whitney was an Irishman who had served in the army for over forty years. He had married his second wife, Margaret Dunbar, in Edinburgh in 1743. He was therefore an experienced hand and had probably been with his regiment longer than Gardiner. It was not unusual of course for a colonel not to have immediate responsibility for his own regiment on the field: Peregrine Lascelles was also acting as brigadier and so not with the unit which bore his name, and the same was true on the other side of the field for both Perth and Murray. Nevertheless, it is possible that Gardiner was being kept out of the front line on account of either his health or his relentless negativity. His performance in independent command at Stirling had been weak, and one wonders why Brigadier Fowke had to be brought in over his head. Gardiner seems now to have little influence over the coming events, until his own life reached its dramatic climax.

The other important issue with Cope's new deployment was that it no longer had the support of a full *Corps de Reserve*. The two rear squadrons of dragoons remained, that from Hamilton's out to the left and that from Gardiner's to the right, but between them there was no infantry line at all. The Highland companies were all still at Cockenzie House and the Warren Parks guarding the baggage. Reid suggests that some of Cope's Highlanders were so new as to not even have received their uniforms, meaning they would anyway have been virtually

---

17 Cope's evidence, Robins (ed.), *Inquiry*, p.40.
18 Ker's evidence, Robins (ed.), *Inquiry*, p.90.

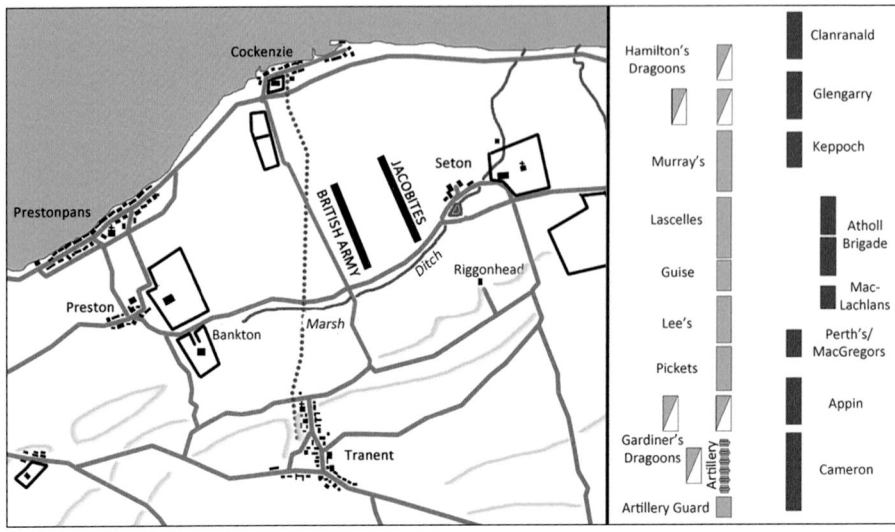

Map 11 Positions at dawn on 21 September.

undistinguishable from their opponents.[19] Certainly they were amongst Cope's greenest troops, and so the decision to keep them out of the main line was understandable. Now there was no time to bring them up from their enclosures anyway, and since George Drummond and his civilian Volunteers were scattered amongst the beds of Prestonpans and Cockenzie there was no infantry reserve at all should the front line be pierced. Nevertheless, with his line deployed and ready, Cope had good reason to hope that would not happen.

Opposite Cope's muzzles the Jacobite army was rushing into position with somewhat less order. There was a light mist upon the plain, and although usually referred to as being flat the ground in fact slopes down towards the north. As the Duke of Perth led the MacDonald regiments into position, these factors combined with the army's inexperience to draw the Jacobite right further up the field than was necessary. Following behind was the Prince, who chose to leap across the three or four foot ditch rather than waiting his turn on the bridge. James Johnstone was beside him at the moment Charles 'fell upon his knees on the other side. I laid hold of his arm and immediately raised him up'.[20] Was this an omen of bad luck? The Prince dusted himself off and pressed forward, taking his column into its place as the second line. Unburdened by the complexity of formal drills, the Jacobites simply faced to their left when in position and thus the column became the line. Behind Charles came Murray, who discovered 'that the front had advanced too

---

19 Reid, *1745*, p.33.
20 Johnstone, *Memoir*, p.37.

far, which proceeded from them not being able to distinguish the line, as the day was but just beginning to dawn'.²¹ There was now a considerable gap in the centre of the Jacobite line which, if it had been perceived, was an invitation for a counter-attack which could have torn the army apart. Fortunately for the Highlanders, the murk of the morning meant that this gap could not be made out when the engagement began, especially as any view of it from the west would have looked straight through to the Atholl Brigade behind to give the illusion of a continuous line.

It was now around 5.15am, the time recorded by Lord Drummore as he rode up from Cockenzie towards Hamilton's Dragoons, along with George Drummond. As a civilian with no military pretensions, Drummore recognised the folly of getting tangled up in the battle lines: 'as I had nothing but a Whip in my Hand, I stop'd about 150 Yards from the Left, and resolved to see the Fate of a Battle in which I was most sensibly interested'.²² He was not a little amazed to see how well-dressed the MacDonald lines were ahead of him, recalling that 'though their Motion was very quick, it was uniform and orderly, and I confess I was surprised at it'. At the opposite end of Cope's line the Earl of Loudoun was less impressed as he watched Murray's wing deploy. 'There seemed to be a great Confusion among them', he recalled, 'but [they] still kept on, and in a few Seconds were formed into five square Bodies or Columns, that on the Left the largest, and about twenty deep'.²³ This larger body was presumably the Camerons, so Loudoun meant the Jacobite army's left rather than the left hand side as he saw it.

Immediately as the Jacobites were fully in sight the first cannon on Cope's right opened fire. The army let out a loud huzzah, but the Jacobites returned it with equal gusto. The Prince, after visiting Perth and Clanranald at their stations on the right, was returning through the MacDonald lines towards the Reserve when he spotted Alasdair MacMhaighstir Alasdair of Dalilea, his tutor in the Gaelic. With a smile and no doubt a wink, he called out to the bard, '*Gres-ort! Gres-ort!*' – 'Make haste! Make haste!' The Highlanders needed no urging. Guided by little more than the instinct to drive forward, they began to advance without further pause. More cannons fired, belching ball, grape, and canister across the stubble field, each gunner loading whatever was to hand. Fragments of these deadly blasts have since been found upon the field. The Camerons, directly opposite the guns, 'seemed to shake, but the men kept going on at a great pace'.²⁴ The rest of the Highland front had slowed briefly, waiting in Loudoun's judgement to see whether the cannon had stopped the Camerons. On seeing that it had not, the whole line surged forwards once more in 'Columns, Clews or Clumps'.²⁵ After initially forming in silence, the

21 Murray, 'Marches', p.39.
22 Letter from Dummore to Cope, Alnwick, 24 October 1745, Robins (ed.), *Inquiry*, Appendix, p.37.
23 Loudoun's written submission, Robins (ed.), *Inquiry*, Appendix, p.30.
24 Home, *History of the Rebellion*, p.85
25 Drummore to Cope, Alnwick, 24 October 1745, Robins (ed.), *Inquiry*, Appendix, p.37.

View from just forward of the British left towards the Jacobite right. The MacDonald regiments would have charged over this stubble field straight towards the camera. (Author's collection)

Highlanders now 'sett up a hideous noise', as they advanced; the sounds of pipes, drums, and battle cries filling the air as the last of the mist dispersed under the first rays of the sun.[26]

General Cope was meanwhile over on the left wing, where he observed that the Highlanders had considerably out-flanked him. This was on account of Perth deploying too far north, but it now gave them an opportunity to overwhelm Cope's left. The Jacobites saw the chance: 'we have outwing'd them!' cried O'Sullivan.[27] Cope sent Major Mossman to Whitefoord and Griffith to call two of the gallopers over to the left. This is precisely what such guns were for: a single pony or a small team could clatter them at great speed to wherever the need for fire support was most pressing. But Mossman reached the guns only to discover that the 'Artillery Horses… were all gone away'.[28] At that very moment, the Camerons and Stewarts began their advance and so the cannon were anyway required here. Whilst riding back along the line Mossman met Lieutenant Cooney, who told him Cope was already riding along the front towards his

---

26 MacDonald, *The Clanranald of Gormoran*, p.364.
27 Taylor, *1745 and After*, p.81.
28 Mossman's evidence, Robins (ed.), *Inquiry*, p.59.

The view of the charging Camerons and Stewarts as they headed towards the artillery and Gardiner's Dragoons. (Author's collection)

right. Cope remembered this moment too, galloping across the face of his army 'encouraging the Men, as I went along the Line, to do their Duty'.[29] For all his possible flaws, Cope was no coward. He was a veteran officer and would behave as coolly under fire as any man.

The general was riding south because he had seen the Camerons outstripping the advance of their comrades, and the commencement of the artillery fire had not stopped them. But before he arrived, things were already unravelling at that end of the line. The sailors were the first to flee. Below-decks gunnery against French and Spanish privateers on the high seas was a very different experience to standing in the open plain and facing down a Highland Charge. If one is inclined to be understanding, these men were in a totally alien environment and totally unprepared for what was coming at them. Knowing how to fire a cannon was not the same as being an artilleryman. When they fled, the sailors and invalids took the priming flasks with them. Nevertheless, Whitefoord and Griffith manned the pieces themselves, the former firing five cannon and the latter the six mortars. At least one shell burst amongst the enemy according to an officer of the artillery guard, and this firing had put the first men cold to the

---

29 Cope's evidence, Robins (ed.), *Inquiry*, p.40.

ground. Richard Jack, still claiming to be a key part of the artillery team, says he mounted a horse and saw several Highlanders fall. Cope, who angrily dismissed just about everything Jack told the Inquiry, says he could not have seen that since the light was still poor.

Unable to reload their pieces, the remaining artillery crews ran after the sailors. The Jacobites were now firing themselves, too high and at too long a range to do much damage. Maxwell of Kirkconnell admits the men 'could not be prevented from giving the first fire',[30] and Lieutenant Colonel Whitney dismissed its effectiveness:

> I find their Fire is only a Bugbear, for not being acquainted with kneeling, & stooping, the fire of their Center, & Rear Ranks, went over our Heads. Had all the Shot that they pour'd in upon my Squadron, been given according to Art, I think not one of us cou'd have escap'd.[31]

Clearly there was no shortage of guns amongst the Jacobites. But even this inaccurate musket fire was enough to cover the Cameron advance, which was close now to overrunning the gun line. This was the moment for the dragoons to show their worth. Whitney's squadron advanced, wheeling to the right so that they could charge into the flanks of the mixed mass of Camerons and Stewarts charging toward the smoking cannon. According to Loudoun, who was near at hand, Whitney got 'within Pistol-shot of their Flank; when, on four or five Shots coming from the Flank of the Highlanders, the Men stopt, and could not be got along any further'.[32] At this crucial moment, when only he could stiffen his men's resolve, Shug Whitney received a musket ball in the left arm: 'it was broke half way betwixt my Wrest & my Elbow. The small bone much shattered'.[33] Painful for Whitney, it was disastrous for his squadron. At the very moment they needed encouragement and leadership they instead saw their officer seriously wounded. They turned about and broke.

The artillery-guard meanwhile, according to Adjutant Kerr of Gardiner's, 'by falling into Confusion, had come into the Rear of the Artillery'.[34] They were probably shying back to receive some protection from the guns, as the failure of the cannon to halt the attack would have left this small band totally exposed on the extreme flank. From here they fired a volley at the Camerons as they came

---

30 Maxwell, *Narrative*, p.41.
31 From a letter from Whitney to Lieutenant Archibald Campbell, aide to Major General Humphrey Bland, dated Edinburgh, 26 November 1745. The letter is in a private collection, but is reproduced in the appendix.
32 Loudoun's written submission, Robins (ed.), *Inquiry*, p.130.
33 Letter from Whitney to Campbell, Edinburgh, 26 November 1745. This is the dramatic moment depicted by Peter Dennis on the cover of this book.
34 Kerr's evidence, Robins (ed.), *Inquiry*, p.96.

THE BATTLE: DAY TWO   165

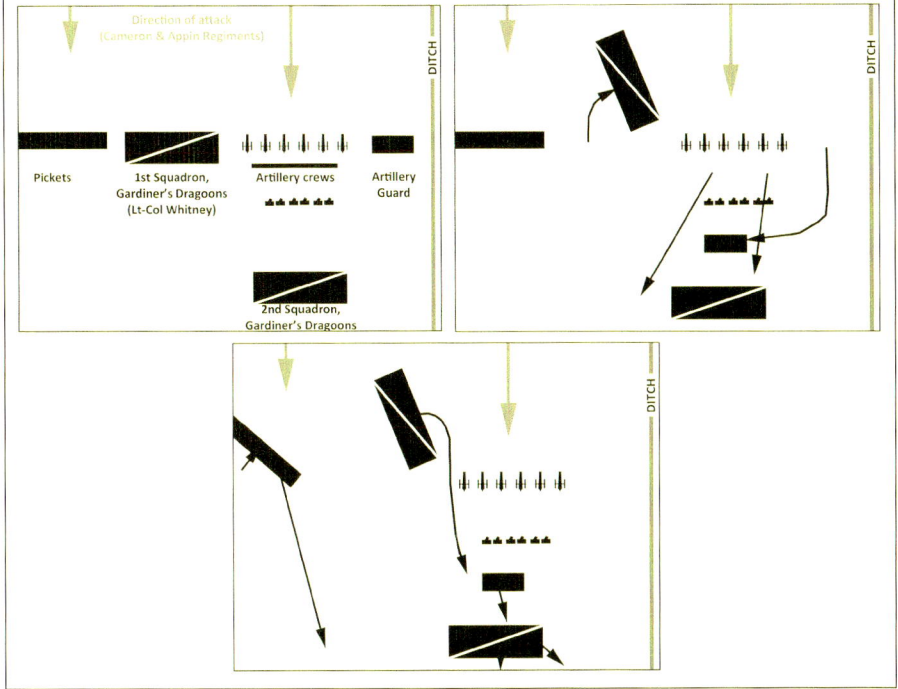

Map 12 The collapse of the British right wing.

on towards the empty cannon, but this was soon blocked from their view by the sudden appearance of Whitney's squadron. The dragoons, themselves now exposed since they had wheeled forwards, abandoned all thought of charging and instead turned their horses' heads and rode straight through the gun line and into the artillery guard that they unexpectedly discovered behind it. The horses carried these forlorn foot soldiers with them as they ran, but worse was to follow. To their immediate rear were the other two squadrons of the 13th. Whitney had lost four men, and at least twice that many were wounded; now the sight of these empty saddles leading the squadron's flight was enough to persuade their comrades to run as well. The whole of Gardiner's was then in flight, despite only a third of the regiment having been engaged.

Meanwhile the Camerons and Stewarts had taken the artillery with only the officers left to resist them. Whitefoord was determined to hold his ground, thrusting with his small sword, but he was soon wounded. Alexander Stewart of Invernahyle was at last able to save him from beneath the Lochaber axe of one of his own men, a miller, by prevailing upon Whitefoord to surrender. Master-gunner Griffith was also captured. Before Cope ever reached his right flank, it was gone.

Now the infantry were in serious trouble. They had given 'one good fire from right to left', according to James Maxwell; Elcho calls it 'a very regular fire'.[35] As had been shown at Killiecrankie in 1689, the Highland charge was not only vulnerable to well-ordered volleys from the front, but also, because of the tight clusters of men they formed, to flanking fire. Colonel Lascelles ordered the foot on the right to wheel back and fire into the momentarily disordered Stewarts and Camerons, but was thwarted by their creeping timidity:

> Some Files of the Platoons upon the Right; were crouching and creeping gently backwards, with their Arms recovered, which was occasioned by a continued irregular Fire over their Heads; which I soon set to Rights by my Example and Reproaches.[36]

For all his cursing Lascelles could not get them to execute the manoeuvre. These men were the pickets: they had slept the least and were not fighting with their familiar officers and friends, so their collective morale was weak. And in that instant of hesitation their chance was lost. The clansmen now fell on their exposed flank with broadswords and targes. Lascelles stumbled and fell.

Things were faring no better for the redcoats at the far end of the line, where their flank hung in the air. The MacDonalds were coming on in good order, their line extending so that the Clanranald men were threatening to turn their opponents. Lord Drummore, his palm no doubt sweating as it held his horse-whip, looked on in amazement at what happened next:

> The Fire of small Arms appeared to me to begin up on the Right, nor did I observe any Fire upon the Left before Hamilton's Dragoons gave Way and went off, not in a Body, but quite broke in two's or so; and when they were gone above 400 Yards, I saw the Left of our Foot standing naked; which I apprehend I could not have seen had there been any Fire upon the Left ; for the Morning was still, and the Fire from our Right (of the Foot I mean) and the Highlanders Right, took that Part of the Line quite out of my Sight.[37]

This is damning. The Duke of Perth was within 'three score yards' of Hamilton's regiment, according to Secretary Murray, when they turned about before even receiving a shot. O'Sullivan recalled there being 'a very irregular discharge' of shots, but clearly the firing here was less intense than on the south side.[38]

---

35   Maxwell, *Narrative*, p.41. Elcho, *Short Account*, p.272.
36   Robins (ed.), *Inquiry*, p.66.
37   Drummore to Cope, Alnwick, 24 October 1745, Robins (ed.), *Inquiry*, Appendix, p.37.
38   Taylor, *1745 and After*, p.81.

Pulling back to avoid being outflanked, Hamilton's would have inevitably inclined towards the centre-rear, coming up toward their own reserve squadron. But there was no safety to be found as they had left now Murray's Regiment totally unsupported and for them to stand alone would have been suicide. Those MacDonalds not falling on Murray's were able to keep the pressure on Hamilton's, and as the latter now fled south-westerly they gained enough of the slope to see the right flank. Out of the banks of smoke there came streaming all three squadrons of Gardiner's, and it was a matter of a moment's instinct for both horse and rider to spur themselves off in their wake. They paused briefly by the park walls, but Drummore was following them and saw that they came under 'a good deal of Fire there, and many an empty Horse came down' towards him. The two regiments of dragoons had lost only a handful of men each, and if they had turned about they might have saved the infantry yet. Cope laments that 'they stood with their Croops to the Enemy; and here they received a good many Shot; but they could not be prevailed upon, by all that their Officers could do, to rally'.[39] They broke once more, flying to the passageway between Bankton and Preston. Their general observed that they went so fast that it was hard to know which Regiment had routed first.

> Seeing the Dragoons go off in this Manner, I went to the Foot, to try by their Means to retrieve the Affair. The other Bodies of the Rebels kept advancing, obliquely, towards us, in the same Manner that the Body upon the Left did. Our Foot gave them their Fire; but the right Flank being exposed, by the going off of the Dragoons, and attack'd by a large Body of the Rebels, broke from the Right. The Motion of the Rebels was so very rapid that the whole Line was broken in a very few Minutes.[40]

The collapse of the infantry line was now inevitable. Without a reserve to relieve them and abandoned by their cavalry, they were stranded in an open field without cover or support. The gap in the Jacobite centre had been plugged both by the MacGregors, who inclined towards the Stewarts as they charged, and by the Prince and his second line which he was leading up close behind the first. The British infantry line was now a scene of the most terrible carnage: broadswords, Lochabers, and scythes falling on unprotected shoulders; pistols cracking at point-blank range; targes batting aside bayonets as clansmen screamed their war-cries. Captain John Stuart of Lascelles' Regiment was determined to hold his post, with what Broughton called a 'mistaken notion of honour'. Though repeatedly called upon by Ensign Donald Stewart to yield, this officer insisted upon fighting until the latter finally struck him down. Captain Stuart, from Physgill in the south-west

---

39 Cope's evidence, Robins (ed.), *Inquiry*, p.41.
40 Cope's evidence, Robins (ed.), *Inquiry*, p.41.

of Scotland, had only joined the army after a lawsuit had stripped him of his inheritance, obliging him and his brother to seek employment.

This dreadful clash of arms was mercifully short. The British line reeled back, fractured, and then shattered virtually by platoon from right to left. Even if they could have repelled the frontal charge, the foot would soon have been surrounded and trapped without a hope of mercy. Before that could happen, they fled. What followed was, according to O'Sullivan, 'a general deroute, & never such a one I believe in any other action'.[41] Cope did his best to rally his fleeing men, riding amongst them. Captain Pointz remembers him crying out, 'For shame, Gentlemen, behave like Britons; give them another Fire, and you'll make them run'.[42] But it was to no avail, and, seeing that the foot were not to be rallied, Cope turned to the dragoons lingering by the park walls. But they soon made their way off again, and all the general's endeavours were in vain.

Cope was not alone in these efforts, as the officers were later at pains to prove. Brigadier Fowke tried to stiffen his jittery cavalry throughout the action, but they were no cooler under fire than they had been in their humiliating retreats from Coltbridge or Musselburgh. Colonel Gardiner was having no better luck. His own horse had become 'troublesome' merely at its rider drawing his sword, prompting the Earl of Home to recommend he change mounts. Whether Gardiner had leisure to do so is unlikely. Lord Drummore had meanwhile realised that 'it was full time for a Pen-and-ink Gentleman to provide for his Safety, which I did by riding off, but I hope with more Discretion and Deliberation than the Dragoons did from the Line'.[43]

As the British line disintegrated into chaos, the soldiers fled west across the plain. They ran back over the waggonway towards Thorntree Fields, many casting aside their arms and accoutrements as they went. But the Highlanders were amongst them and their blood was up. A month of anticipation had led to this moment and now the enemy was utterly at their mercy. Swords and axes cut men down as they fled. James Gardiner rode amongst the fugitives, attempting to rally them. But he knew the army was beyond saving: 'O my God, all is gone!' he cried. A musket ball struck him the right thigh. Close to that solitary hawthorn tree, the colonel managed to rally seventeen desperate men to face the enemy and make a stand. Another ball struck him, this time in the shoulder, with enough power to throw him from the saddle. Others say it was a scythe such as those carried by the MacGregors which brought him down from his horse.[44] Then Gardiner was overwhelmed, swords and Lochabers striking him six blows across the head according to Adjutant Kerr, who had the details from the surgeon who later tried to save him.

---

41 Taylor, *1745 and After*, p.81.
42 Pointz's evidence, Robins (ed.), *Inquiry*, p.92.
43 Drummore to Cope, Alnwick, 24 October 1745, Robins (ed.), *Inquiry*, Appendix, p.37.
44 Dodderidge, *Gardiner*, p.208.

It was a brutal, gruesome end. 'I have but one life to give for my country', Gardiner once had said.

Elsewhere, Cope's aide Major Mossman had become trapped beneath his horse, whilst Peregrine Lascelles had been overrun on the right flank. His own account of what happened so bizarre that it might just be true. In attempting to wheel the infantry and prevent the right from breaking, he moved too fast and 'had the Misfortune to fall'.[45] Perhaps he was momentarily stunned, but on rising he was surrounded by sixteen Highlanders and ordered to give up his sword. On obeying the officer, Lascelles expected to be taken prisoner, but instead the clansmen rushed off and left him. He was then able to walk quite without interference to Seton, where he managed to find a horse and escape via Haddington. It is hard to believe that a full colonel would present so implausible a story, without any corroborating witnesses, unless he really believed it was true. It also seems incredible, however, that a Jacobite officer and his men would not understand the value of securing a high ranking prisoner resplendent in gold lace. Brigadier Thomas Fowke, meanwhile, was disorientated in the confusion of the rout and became cut off from support. He rode northwards towards the coast, where he linked up with a Captain Christie from Murray's Regiment and together they were able to loop around the rear of the Jacobite army and head east to Berwick.[46]

The rest of the senior officers now felt that the only possible means of stemming the rout was to get ahead of the fugitives, and so Cope drove his horse through the chaotic crowd trying to squeeze down the narrow road at Bankton. The sight of him doing so probably gave rise to mutters, but we must accept him at his word as to his purpose. On the other side of the enclosures he found that Loudoun and Home were already ahead of him, the two earls threatening the dragoons and shaming them into obedience. Home was brandishing his pistol, and the language being used can readily be imagined. Loudoun led the horsemen into a field 'adjoining to the Road leading to the Village, and lying South of it'.[47] This appears to place the rallying point in the fields west of Bankton House and south of the railway station today. The staff succeeded in assembling about 450 dragoons, along with Major Mossman, Major Singleton, Captains Wemyss and Forbes, several other officers, and the commander of the absentee Volunteers, George Drummond.

Whilst this was happening, Lieutenant Colonel Peter Halkett had managed to rally fourteen men and five officers. He led them into the ditch beside the road close to the edge of Bankton estate, and began firing on the Jacobites, who by now were in a state of considerable disorder. In this way Halkett endeavoured not only to preserve his men's lives but also to cover the flight of their comrades. Seeing this, Lord George Murray gathered about a hundred men and faced them off; Halkett

---

45 Lascelles' evidence, Robins (ed.), *Inquiry*, p.68.
46 Fowke's evidence, Robins (ed.), *Inquiry*, p.72.
47 Cope's evidence, Robins (ed.), *Inquiry*, p.68.

and his men surrendered on good terms. Murray claimed 'nothing gave me more pleasure that day, than having it so immediately in my power to save those men'.[48] Lochiel had also rallied a large body of Camerons by summoning them together with his piper, and so much of the Jacobite left was by now back under control and ready for further orders. It was therefore either a group of Camerons or of Stewarts who advanced along the Preston road only to see the unwelcome sight of 450 formed dragoons waiting in the field beyond.

Halkett's short stand in the ditch now assumes more significance, as it had clearly bought the dragoons enough time to rally unmolested. Cope and his brother officers now induced them to take their revenge by charging down those Highlanders who had ventured too far into Preston. The clansmen 'stood in awe', temporarily immobilised by the sudden realisation that they were in grave danger. But the dragoons would have none of it, caring little for their own honour and far less for their officers'. Cope did all that remained possible of his duty: he led the only formed troops left under his command off the field to safety. As was appropriate in a retreat, the officers posted themselves at the rear as the squadrons began to withdraw up the pathway up the hillside to Birslie Brae. But the men were too eager to be restrained and they set off at a gallop. Only by posting themselves at their head could the British officers keep the dragoons in order, or so at least they would later claim. Three times, Loudoun says, they halted to face the enemy, in a vain attempt to add a veneer of dignity to the flight. The road from Bankton to Birslie Brae is still known today as Johnnie Cope's Road. At the top, on the same spot from which Charles Edward Stuart had first looked down upon the British army the previous afternoon, Cope and his officers agreed there was nothing to be gained by heading to Edinburgh and so they turned instead towards Berwick-upon-Tweed. They headed for the Lammermuir Hills, meeting Lord Drummore at Fala as they moved with impressive speed towards Coldstream.

With the dragoons and most of the senior officers now gone, the remnants of Cope's army back at Preston were totally alone. Trapped by the park walls, most of them were unable to make their escape: 'they would have been cut to pieces in a moment, but for the interposition of the Prince and the Gentlemen of his army'.[49] The Jacobite accounts show that the senior officers mounted as soon as they were able, by which means they became both more visible and more mobile, and therefore better able to restore sufficient order to start saving the lives of as many of Cope's men as possible, especially the officers. Once it was clear the battle was won it would have been the work of just a few minutes to bring horses down the waggonway from the corral in Tranent churchyard, straight to where they were needed. Charles Edward now rode about the field demanding that his men give

---

48 Murray, 'Marches', p.40.
49 Maxwell, *Narrative*, p.42.

quarter, whilst other officers endeavoured to regain control of their men. There was still the potential for grave danger. The battle had happened so quickly that there were pockets of redcoats all around who had to be disarmed quickly before they realised the vulnerability of the disorganised Highlanders. Most were too stunned of course to resist, and groups of redcoats were surrendering to individual Highlanders.[50] There was a false alarm when a body appeared to be forming on the hillside near Tranent, but on rushing the Camerons halfway up the waggonway Murray discovered them to be a party of Jacobite officers' servants mingling with curious locals. It was not quite 6am.

The actual engagement had been dramatically, mercifully, short, but there was still much to do. Nothing was more urgent than the removal of the final military threat: at Cockenzie House there remained almost 200 enemy soldiers from Loudoun's and the Black Watch. It seems unlikely that all of these men had originally been posted in the walled enclosure of the house, as the space was inadequate to accommodate both them and the baggage train. More plausible is that the cartloads of canvas tents and camp equipment were still in the Warren Parks, whilst the more valuable baggage had been moved to the place of greatest safety. It also seems likely that any of Cope's Highlanders posted in the parks had by now fallen back on the more defensible perimeter of Cockenzie House. The indefatigable Camerons were sent to oppose them. The Prince had other formed regiments that could have been used, for his second line had barely been engaged and should therefore have been in good order, but it seems that Murray wanted to be everywhere. The Camerons were also a large, well-equipped and disciplined unit, and if the baggage guard resisted then that might be critical.

Lochiel's men had an easy march to the enemy, as they were already on the waggonway line which led straight to Cockenzie. Here was a potentially difficult task, and in the hour of victory few Jacobite officers would have been keen to throw away lives. The garrison fired a volley from the walls, but, aware of the battle's loss, they had little stomach for futile gestures. Most of these troops were green, and some of them at least lacked enthusiasm for their service. Lord George Murray now brought up his prisoner, Peter Halkett, who agreed to give the baggage guard a way out. He gave them positive information about the army's defeat and confirmed that the Jacobites were now in possession of the British artillery. Halkett probably had an easy job in persuading Sir Patrick Murray that it was not worth fighting on. Murray of Broughton says it was Captain Basil Cochrane of Lee's Regiment that acted as the emissary, presumably on Lieutenant Colonel Halkett's authority.[51] The baggage guard surrendered and the Camerons rushed in to secure the haul. A vain attempt had been made to hide the war-chest and the general's papers under the stairwell of the house. Thus did the Jacobite army acquire, at no cost to itself, all

---

50   Johnstone, *Memoir*, p.40.
51   Murray of Broughton, *Memorials*, p203.

The Surrender of Cockenzie House, by Andrew Hillhouse. (Reproduced with permission of the Battle of Prestonpans 1745 Heritage Trust)

the carts, tentage, and supplies which it was lacking, along with at least £2,500.[52] Alexander Henderson, another volunteer who came to the field too late for the battle, thought there was a higher figure of £4,000 in the treasury, and that there had been a great deal more until Cope had wisely put some aboard HMS *Fox*.[53]

The Volunteers, once so eager to be a part of the battle, had been left behind as stranded observers to its final moments and immediate aftermath. Carlyle had been woken by the signal cannon, and after dressing at speed he went to his father's manse. The Reverend William was already up the steeple observing events as best he could, but he soon came back into the house with news of the defeat. Carlyle rushed into the garden and found its highest point: 'the whole prospect was filled with runaways, and Highlanders pursuing them. Many had their coats turned as prisoners, but were still trying to reach the town in hopes of escaping'.[54] The Highlanders were still firing at the fugitives as they ran. Lord Elcho suddenly appeared before Carlyle with 'an air of savage ferocity which disgusted and alarmed', demanding directions to a public-house where comfort might be found for the wounded. Shortly afterwards came the Duke of Perth, who spoke 'in a very different tone' whilst ordering some wounded British officers to be taken to the customs collector's house in Prestonpans.

The minister was now growing anxious lest his son be recognised by anyone as having been in arms with Sir John, so they decided to slip away from the uncertain

---

52 Elcho, *Short Account*, p.27. According to the Bank of England's inflation calculator, this figure could equate to around £544,188 today.
53 Henderson, A., *The History of the Rebellion, 1745 and 1746*, (London: A. Millar, 1753), p.87.
54 Carlyle, *Autobiography*, p.142.

situation. They mounted and rode towards the coast, riding eastwards across the beach to avoid attention. They had not got far when they saw two or three of the army's waggons attempting a desperate escape from the Jacobites approaching Cockenzie. A group of Highlanders got ahead of them and demanded that the foremost driver halt. When he refused he was shot dead. No doubt the other waggons now reigned in, but the sight so shocked Carlyle and his father that they wheeled about and rode home. There Carlyle replaced his riding boots with shoes in the hope that nobody would suspect him of having been out of the house. He then went to the collector's house a few doors down to offer his aid to the surgeons. There were two, Cunningham and Trotter, who as army surgeons had known their duty and surrendered to aid their comrades. One of their patients, Captain Blake of Murray's Regiment, lay with a slice of his skull resting on the table beside him. Despite Carlyle's assumption that nothing could be done for such a man, the surgeons were confident they could save him as long as they had proper instruments. Their medical chests were amongst the baggage, and so they invited Carlyle to recover them. Another officer, Captain James Clarke of Hamilton's Dragoons, suffered a very similar injury to that described by Carlyle and had a silver plate fitted over the hole. He was fit enough to give evidence to the inquiry a year later, and his damaged skull is now in the collection of the Royal College of Surgeons in London. It returned to Prestonpans in 2012 for a special exhibition on the role of the dragoons.

Granted a guard from the Duke of Perth's staff, Carlyle now headed once more towards Cockenzie. On their way they met a pair of grooms leading four good horses, and when the Highlander challenger them they admitted being Sir John Cope's coach team. A few paces on they found a British officer's servant with another two horses and a bag of clothes. Along with the coachmen they were ordered by the Highlander to the collector's house as prisoners, where they all duly reported without demur. At Cockenzie House, Alexander Carlyle saw two different sides of the Jacobite army, much as he had with Elcho and Perth. The clansmen he saw were 'of low stature and dirty', but he found Lochiel 'polished and gentle'.[55] Carlyle's request triggered a search amongst the baggage but no medical equipment was found and he was obliged to leave empty handed.

On his return, walking on the fore-shore beside Prestonpans, on the southern edge of what is now Greenhills Park,[56] Carlyle saw the British officers who had been taken prisoner that morning:

> I then saw human nature in its most abject form, for almost every aspect bore in it shame, and dejection, and despair. They were deeply mortified

---

55 Carlyle, *Autobiography*, p.147.
56 The northern half of Greenhills is reclaimed land relating to the former power station which stood adjacent from the 1960s until 2015.

with what had happened, and timidly anxious about the future, for they were doubtful whether they were to be treated as prisoners of war or as rebels.[57]

The officers had little need for anxiety, as the Prince had given strict orders about the treatment of both prisoners and the wounded. The main focal point for the latter was Bankton House, which was quickly secured as a field hospital. Surgeons from Edinburgh were brought in, including John Rattray who was famed in the capital as a sporting archer and excellent golfer. He had in fact signed the first ever formal regulations for the game. George Lauder, 'Lang Sandy' Wood, and Alexander Monro also answered the call, meaning that some of the finest surgeons of the day were on hand at Prestonpans. The coaches that Secretary Murray reported as assembling at Duddingston were now put to work, carrying the badly wounded off the field. Most went to Bankton House or into other houses in Prestonpans closer to where they had fallen. Wounded private soldiers were treated in the gardens at Bankton. All of the sources concur that the greatest care was taken of the wounded, and that this was done by the personal order of the Prince as well as by the general humanity of the Jacobite officers. Only Andrew Henderson disagrees, but his account is relentlessly partisan. Murray of Broughton goes so far as to say that in their attendance of the British wounded the Jacobites in fact neglected their own, whose 'wounds festered, being all gun Shott and mostly in the legs and thighs'.[58]

Ironically, Colonel Gardiner was one officer who did not make it to the field hospital at his home, although amazingly he was still alive. He was found by a servant of his, who had fled to a mill and disguised himself, which seems an elaborate precaution. On returning to the battlefield he found Gardiner beneath the thorn tree beside which he had attempted his last stand. The servant told the story to the colonel's friend Phillip Dodderidge, who soon published it in his hagiographic but immensely popular book on Gardiner's life:

> The hurry of the action was then pretty well over, and he found his much-honoured master, not only plundered of his watch, and other things of value, but also stripped of his upper garments and boots, yet still breathing... In this condition, and in this manner, he conveyed him to the church of Tranent, from whence he was immediately taken into the minister's house and laid in bed; where he continued breathing and frequently groaning, 'till about eleven in the forenoon, when he took his final leave of pain and sorrow.[59]

---

57 Carlyle, *Autobiography*, p.148.
58 Murray of Broughton, *Memorials*, p.205.
59 Dodderidge, *Gardiner*, p.210.

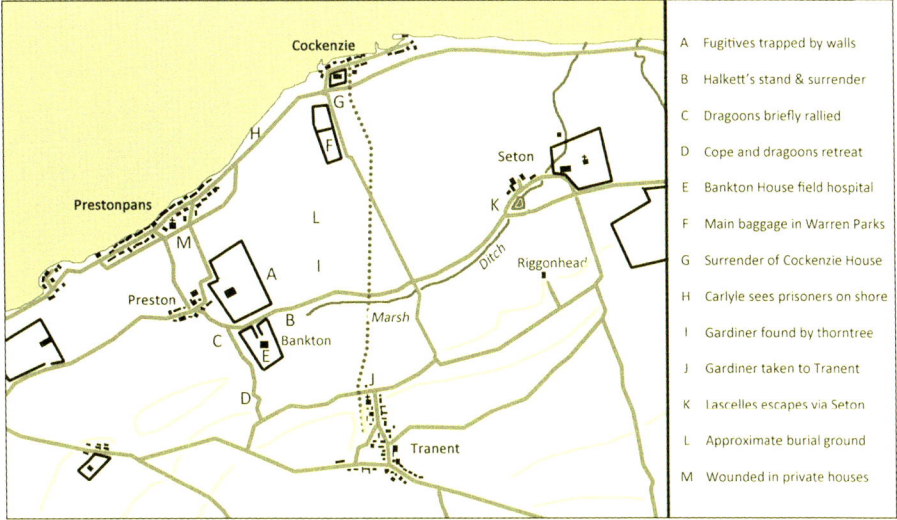

Map 13 Events following the main engagement.

Gardiner was taken upon a cart up the waggonway path, this being the most direct route from the thorn tree to the church. He was tended there by the Reverend Cunningham, who of course knew the colonel well, and somehow a surgeon was brought up too. He later gave Cornet Kerr evidence as to Gardiner's wounds, as reported at the Inquiry. Also in attendance were Beatrix and Mary Jenkinson, daughters of the late minister at Athelstaneford and nieces of the present minister Cunningham of Tranent. They had previously encountered the Prince at Duddingston, where he had flattered them with gifts. Now, according to the tradition, one sister comforted the dying officer whilst another distracted the prowling Highlanders who came in search of food. Charles Edward had called these sisters the bonniest lassies he had yet seen in Scotland.

Whilst the surgeons were doing their best for the wounded across the battlefield area, arrangements were being made to secure and identify the prisoners. This was no small task. There were more than 80 captured officers, including the commanders of all the principal units at the battle: Lieutenant Colonel Jaspar Clayton of Murray's; Lieutenant Colonel Peter Halkett of Lee's; Major John Severn of Lascelles'; Lieutenant Colonel Wright of Hamilton's; Lieutenant Colonel Whitney of Gardiner's; and from the artillery train, Lieutenant Colonel Whitefoord and Major Griffith. Many of the officers were wounded. Elcho provides a detailed list.[60] This was a major haul of senior officers, most of whom were given honourable

---

60   Elcho, *Short Account*, p.275. This list has been corrected with additional information in Reid, S., *1745: A Military History of the Last Jacobite Rising* (Staplehurst: Spellmount, 2001), p.38-40.

paroles on condition not to serve in arms against the Prince again. In total there appear to have been around 1,200 British soldiers who were taken prisoner, half of Cope's total strength. Only about 114 of these were dragoons, which correlates with the relatively low numbers of casualties amongst Gardiner's recalled by Whitney: 'we had only about 16, or 18 Men killed, & about thirty wounded'.[61] Assuming Hamilton's Dragoons also left only a small number of dead behind, Cope's figure of around 450 survivors amongst the dragoons is not unreasonable if perhaps a little high. A small number of fugitives succeeded in reaching Edinburgh Castle, where General Guest refused to open the gates until he was sure there was no immediate danger.

The prisoners were of course the lucky ones. The exact number of the fallen has proved impossible to calculate with any certainty without Cope's detailed muster rolls from before the battle.[62] Jacobite estimates vary wildly, but Secretary Murray's report is the most credible: 'according to the best Computation that could then be made, there were seven or eight officers with about three hundred private men killed, and betwixt four and five hundred wounded'.[63] The *London Post* agreed with this figure, although the *Newcastle Journal* halved it. It is hard to make the mathematics of Cope's army work, however, as there is a sliding balance which must reconcile the number of prisoners, the number of escapees, the number of dead, and the total number on the field. None of these figures can be given with absolute certainty or consensus. But if the army numbered around 2,400 officers and men, an estimate of 300 dead and 1,280 prisoners (including officers) leaves more than enough room for the 450 dragoons heading to Berwick with Cope and the 170-plus infantry said to have escaped by Home. It also leaves around 200 unaccounted for, who could be added with plausible deliberation to the fugitives, the fallen, or the escapees, or else subtracted from the initial starting figure. But attempts to be too precise are built on shifting sand, and the debate is also largely academic. The headline remains the same: the British field army in Scotland no longer existed.

Jacobite losses are a little easier to evaluate; they were considerably lighter and primarily occurred as the army passed through the enemy volleys before crashing into their line. The margin of difference between the estimates is lower than that of the redcoat fallen. O'Sullivan remembered 'we had above sixty wounded & very few killed'.[64] Elcho places the figure slightly higher, as he did with Cope's casualties: 'about 50 private men [killed], and 80 wounded'.[65] James Maxwell says 40 dead and 60-70 wounded; Murray of Broughton 30 killed and 70-80 wounded. The

---

61   Whitney to Lieutenant Archibald Campbell, 26 November 1745: see Appendix II.
62   See Margulies, *Prestonpans*, p.150 for a discussion of the estimates.
63   Murray of Broughton, *Memorials*, p.205.
64   Taylor, *1745 and After*, p.84.
65   Elcho, *Short Account*, p.274.

London Post reported the following week that the rebels had lost 50. Lord George Murray, who was very well placed to have accurate information, does not number the dead in his narrative of the campaign but does in his letter to his brother on 24 September: 'our loss may be about 36 kill'd; and 50 wounded; theirs 600 killed, as many wounded, and 12 hundred prisoners besides'.[66] The Jacobite casualties are therefore known to within a far smaller margin of uncertainty than those of the British army, and some of the discrepancies may lie in the sad reality that not all wounded men stay on that side of the list for long. If ten of Secretary Murray's wounded men were to die of their injuries, then his figure would be an exact match for Maxwell of Kirkconnell's figure.

Amongst the Jacobite dead was Captain Malcolm MacGregor, who had lain in the stubble with five balls in him crying out, 'My lads, I am not dead! And by God I shall see if any of you does not do your duty!'[67] He died of his wounds shortly after. Captain Robert Stewart of the Appin Regiment was killed, as were Lieutenant Allan Cameron of Ludavra and Ensign James Cameron, both Lochiel's men. It is to be wondered whether the ensign was carrying the famous yellow and red striped standard of his regiment. All these officers were in the centre and left of the line, but Captain Archibald MacDonnell was on the right with the Keppochs. He was the brother of the chief. These officers would all have been leading the charge in the front ranks when the volleys crashed in. It is all too easy given the scale and speed of the Jacobite victory to forget the courage it took to run forwards into the volleys of regular soldiers. Elcho also reports another casualty, the unfortunate David Threipland of Fingask in Perthshire. He was one of Strathallan's horsemen, who had been too few to block Cope's departure but were at least able to round up strays. In chasing a party of dragoons beyond Preston, Threipland's horse stumbled and a dragoon officer wheeled about and shot him dead. He was the brother of the Prince's own physician. Tradition says that he was buried where he fell, in the fields between Preston and Wallyford, and that a factor from the family estate later identified his horse at a sale and brought it home.

One point on which there is consensus is that the Prestonpans battlefield was a dreadful sight to behold on that fine clear morning. Captain Johnstone, who had charged at the Prince's side, described it as 'a spectacle of horror, being covered with heads, legs, arms and mutilated bodies'.[68] These were the results of the hand-to-hand fighting, deadly swords and Lochabers inflicting horrific injuries. But if the scene was shocking for the victors, imagine how much worse it was for one who supported the vanquished. Andrew Henderson, arriving on the battlefield too late to participate, was staggered by the scale of the disaster:

---

66 Burton, J. H., *Jacobite Correspondence of the Atholl Family* (Edinburgh: Abbotsford Club, 1860), p.24.
67 Johnstone, *Memoir*, p.37.
68 Johnstone, *Memoir*, p.41.

> Stepping forward, [I] survey'd the Field, which was one Scene of Horror capable of softening the hardest Heart, being strew'd not so much with the Dead as the Wounded; the broken Guns, Halberts, Pikes, and Cantines, shewing the Work of the Day; in my Progress I asked the [captured British] Soldiers what had become of Cope, which none of them knew, tho' all, but especially the English, spoke most disrespectfully and bitterly of him: Then turning to the Road-side, I saw the young Chevalier.

Although Alexander Carlyle had encountered Elcho, Perth, and Lochiel, of the Volunteers it was Henderson who got closest to Charles Edward Stuart at Prestonpans:

> I went to the Road-Side where the Chevalier, who by Advice of Perth &c had sent to Edinburgh for Surgeons, was standing. He was clad as an ordinary Captain, in a coarse Plaid and blue Bonnet, his Boots and Knees were much dirtied; he seemed to have fallen into a Ditch, which I was told by one of his Lifeguards he had. He was exceeding merry: Speaking of his Army, he said twice, "My Highlandmen have lost their Plaids". At which he laughed very heartily.

It was not uncommon, as had been observed in previous risings, for clansmen to un-belt their great plaids during the charge. This allowed them to discard the cumbersome weight of wool about their waists and shoulders. Their long shirts preserved their decency. Clearly some of the Highlanders had done so, to the amusement of their commander. But Henderson, distraught at the scenes around him, was unable to look beyond appearances and now saw only the negatives in the Stuart prince.

> When talking of the Wounded, he seemed no Way affected. There were seven Standards taken, which when he saw, he said in French, a Language he frequently spoke in, "We have missed some of them". Then he refreshed himself upon the Field and with the utmost Composure ate a Piece of cold Beef, and drank a Glass of Wine, amidst the deep and piercing Groans of the wounded and dying, who had fallen a Sacrifice to his Ambition.[69]

All the other sources demonstrate how keenly interested Charles was in seeing to the wounded. As to his dining amongst the dying, a more rational account is revealed by the Jacobite sources. O'Sullivan explains that after ordering up the surgeons and ensuring all his instructions were being attended to, the Prince was prevailed upon to eat since he had not do so for so long. He initially refused 'in

---

69 Henderson, *History of the Rebellion*, pp.88-89.

a most feeling way', until after he had spoken with the surgeons. When he finally agreed to take refreshment, having barely slept or eaten since arriving on Birslie Brae, he did so beside the captured cannon. Since virtually everybody at this end of Cope's battle-line fled before contact, this was probably one of the areas which had the least likelihood of being covering with dying men. Charles had already done all he could for any that were still on the field. Sir John Macdonald, disappointed that Strathallan had not used his cavalry to more effect in capturing prisoners, saw Charles by the guns listening to a long blessing over the claret and cold beef that had been brought up. Murray of Broughton was outraged when he read Henderson's more critical account: 'He [Charles Edward] breakfasted on the field, but not amongst the dead and within hearing of the groans of the wounded, as has been falsely asserted by a little ignorant Scholl master who has pretended to write a history of an affair of which he could be no judge'.[70] Henderson taught at the High School in Edinburgh.

Charles mingled amongst his men a while longer, commending their valour and meeting those singled out for excellence. These included a fourteen year-old who had apparently struck down a redcoat for each of his years. Rumours later circulated that Charles also visited Colonel Gardiner, either on the field or at Tranent, but even Dodderidge accepted that these stories were baseless. O'Sullivan remembers how Charles Stewart of Ardsheal now suddenly realised in the calm after the storm that no form of bodyguard had been identified to protect the Prince's person whilst he had been charging across the field under fire. The Prince replied that 'he was oblidged to 'um all, for the care & tendernesse they had of him; yt he only did what he ought to do, & yt he'd never forget their behaviour yt day'.[71] Since this seems to have been the opportune moment, it was probable now that Charles Edward commissioned Lord Elcho to form a new regiment of mounted Lifeguards. Now taking to the saddle – he had been given Gardiner's horse to add to his own – the Prince quit the field at midday, at the end of a long and bloody morning's work. As he left he repeated his orders for the 'the dead to be buried and all arms secured'.[72]

Sir John Macdonald was surprised when he noticed 'the dead all fully dressed', at least until the time the Prince departed, which suggests that after the initial wave of looting some decorum had been imposed during Charles' near presence. Now O'Sullivan passed on the Prince's parting instructions and parties were sent amongst the houscs to ensure 'the inhabitants shou'd come wth speads [spades] & other instruments, to bury the Dead'.[73] For the villagers this would not have been a pleasant exercise, but it might at least have been profitable if they found something

70 Murray of Broughton, *Memorials*, p.205.
71 Taylor, *1745 and After*, p.83.
72 Murray of Broughton, *Memorials*, p.209.
73 Taylor, *1745 and After*, p.83.

the Highlanders had missed. Alexander Carlyle avoided this duty as his father was still eager to get him out of Prestonpans. They passed over the battlefield between 11am and noon, and he noticed the bodies were 'mostly stript' although still guarded.[74] The Inspector of Cavalry later heard some had been 'stripped by the women who followed the English Army', who were certainly present as they are reported by both Carlyle and Henderson as being in considerable and noisy distress. That anything of value would be removed from the bodies is to be expected, although there is a nineteenth century reference to the discovery of a few bodies in Thorntree Fields which were apparently still clothed. Robert Chambers also records an anecdote which tells of a Highlander spotting that a dragoon was being buried in a pit with his boots still on. He ordered the villager to give him the boots but was instead told to take them off himself if he wanted them so badly. It was a bold retort, but apparently this was a bold fellow: when the clansman entered the grave he was struck over the head and buried along with both the dragoon and the boots. It is a good story, even if it never happened.

Most of the bodies were buried in shallow pits in the western sector of the battlefield close to where they had fallen in the greatest quantity. A sketch drawn by William Blakeney at Stirling shows a cluster of pits in the open field roughly level with the north-eastern corner of Preston House park. The map is not precise, but the location drawn correlates with the area of Thorntree Fields. Bones were located there at the end of the 18th century during draining works near Thorntree Mains farm (which post-dates the battle), and again in the 1950s and '60s when the railway spur and pylons were constructed for Cockenzie Power Station. In the south-west corner of this field once stood the now famous thorn tree, where tradition says others were also buried. Visible rises in the ground are mentioned by Chambers, writing about eighty years after the battle. Another local 19th century tradition was that soldiers had been buried in the sheep park near Cockenzie House, but these would have to have been transported a fair distance. Bones were indeed found here prior to house-building in the late 20th century, but they proved to be rather more ancient than the battle. Locals had probably found bones here previously and then made an erroneous connection to the battle, which in time made its way into the Ordnance Survey Name Book.

The main army began moving out towards Edinburgh in the early afternoon, taking with it the prisoners. John William O'Sullivan, after accompanying the Prince off the field, was sent back to Cockenzie around 3pm to formally inventory the captured guns and baggage. On arriving there he found that Lord George Murray, despite having apparently been there for four hours, had done nothing beyond listing the prisoners from the Highland companies. To his further chagrin, he was then told by Lochiel that sixteen carts had already been sent off by Murray before any accounting could be done. The mystery of where they went is

---

74 Carlyle, *Autobiography*, p.149.

Thorntree Fields, later the site of Thorntree Mains farm. The fallen are believed to be buried in this area. (Author's collection)

solved by Murray's own account: 'I had got some of their own biscuit carried from Cockenny to Colonel Gardiner's courts and gardens'.[75] The redcoat wounded were being fed with their own provisions, an eminently reasonable arrangement even if it confused O'Sullivan's attempts to coordinate the army's logistics.

Lord George Murray then moved out to Musselburgh after handing care of the baggage to the adjutant-general. Here a newly-decorated house had been secured as his billet, but instead he filled it with wounded British officers, sharing with them his 'cold provisions and liquor'. They initially made their beds on the straw as the house was unfurnished, but beds were later brought in. The prisoners were afraid they might be attacked in the night and so Lord George calmed them by sleeping on the floor amongst them. This must have been a curious scene indeed. Could a lieutenant general really not have found a guard that he could have trusted?

Charles Edward was also in Musselburgh, occupying the Marquess of Tweeddale's residence at Pinkie House. He arrived less than twenty-four hours after he had stopped at the walls of the very gardens he now occupied to hear confirmation that the enemy had been sighted. The Prince must have felt satisfied the day's work. There survives a letter which he reputedly wrote from Pinkie to

75 Murray, 'Marches', p.43.

his father in Rome. It is probably not a genuine work of his hand, as it contradicts the letter he later sent and which is quoted in the prologue to this book. Instead this was probably a propaganda device circulated for a public audience, officially or otherwise. Nevertheless it comes close to revealing how Charles may have felt as he sat at Pinkie:

> If I had obtained this victory over foreigners my joy would have been complete; but as it is over Englishmen, it has thrown a damp upon it that I little imagined. The men I have defeated were your Majestie's enemies it is true, but they might have become your friends and dutiful subjects when they had got their eyes open to see the true interest of their country, which you mean to save, not to destroy.[76]

Charles Edward Stuart was not a man to gloat over his enemies, and these sentiments are fully in keeping with his behaviour and sensibilities. But even if he never wrote the letter, the Prince had at last bought himself some time to reflect. He was master of Scotland.

Twenty-five miles to the south, meanwhile, Sir John Cope and his horsemen had reached Lauder. From here they would ride to Coldstream where they would rest before heading to the safety of Berwick in the morning. At Lauder the general took the time to gather his wits and compose a letter to the Secretary of State for Scotland:

> At the Dawn of Day, the Enemy attacked us. Our Troops expected the Enemy, so that it was no Sort of Surprise. Notwithstanding this, our Troops gave Way; and all that the Officers could do, to carry them on, or to rally them, was to no Purpose, and we lost the Day… The Battle was fought in a Field near Preston Pans. I have dispatched Expres to the Coast, that if possible the Dutch may be sent to land Southward. I have been unfortunate, which will certainly give a Handle to my Enemies to cast Blame upon me. I cannot reproach myself.[77]

Every word written must have hurt. After a month-long campaign, the work of a quarter of an hour had ruined him. He was already theorising over the cause of the panic, blaming the speed and manner of the enemy attack and the men's inability to endure it. What more could he really have done? He sent ahead his letter, notifying his rival Lord Mark Kerr at Berwick that the army was lost. Thus he gives

---

76 The National Archives, Treasury Papers, T 1/321/32: [Lord George Murray] to Charles Edward, the Young Pretender, concerning the battle of Prestonpans.
77 Cope to Tweeddale, Lauder, 21 September 1745, Robins (ed.), *Inquiry*, Appendix, pp.77–8.

the lie to those who call him the first general to bear the news of his own defeat. He sent it on ahead.

Earlier on that same momentous day, four hundred miles from the battlefield, the Marquess of Tweeddale had settled down at his desk in Whitehall to compose a letter to Lieutenant General Cope in Scotland:

> This Morning I received yours of the 18th Instant from Dunbar, which I immediately laid before the King. You may believe, we were all much surprised and concerned to hear, that the City of Edinburgh had capitulated with the Rebels, especially, when there was so near a Prospect of your coming with the Army under your Command to their Assistance. His Majesty is pleased to find by yours, that you intend to proceed, without Loss of Time, to retrieve this Misfortune. I heartily wish you good Success.[78]

Before his quill had touched the paper the army was already lost, and Scotland with it.

---

78 Tweeddlate to Cope, Whitehall, 21 September 1745, Robins (ed.), *Inquiry*, p.177.

8

Beyond the Battle

Word of the Jacobite victory spread like wildfire. It needed to, because the implications for King George's government were frightening. Any deficiencies the Highland army had once had – in arms, materiel, confidence or experience – would all now vanish. So on both sides of the conflict there was an urgent need to spread news of the battle: one to capitalise on the opportunities it offered; the other to brace for whatever might follow in its wake.

On the morning of 22 September, barely twenty-four hours after the battle, a messenger reached Lady Aemilia Murray at Tullibardine with the first news of the engagement and how 'the enemy's Horse very soon gave way, but the foot fought resolutely'.[1] Generous to the enemy, even this early report is fairly reliable in its information. The only glaring error is its report that Cope fled by sea on 'a man of war which was lying near Cockeny', presumably HMS *Fox*. Most importantly to Lady Aemilia, the messenger confirmed that her husband Lord George was safe and well, as were all those of note. The report came from a clansman who had fought at the battle then remained on the field for two hours, until around 7.30am, before rushing with the news to Stirling almost fifty miles away. He arrived there before 11.00pm, at which time another messenger headed north to Lady Aemilia. Informed of the battle early the next morning, she in turn sent word on to her brother-in-law the Duke of Atholl.

The restored Duke was 'most agreeably Surprized with your Ladyship's delightfull letter, giving the only distinct Account as yet come here of the victory'.[2] It was midday when he received it, although it would be 6.00pm on 24 September before Lord George decided to notify his brother in writing personally, blaming 'the fatigue and various Duties I have been oblig'd to undergoe'. This letter goes on to exhort Atholl to raise more of his reluctant tenants and to continue raising funds. Importantly, Murray also confirms that the army was now capable of equipping its new recruits: 'we have got above 1000 stand of arms more than we

---

1 Burton (ed.), *Atholl Family*, p.22.
2 Burton (ed.), *Atholl Family*, p.23.

want at present; 2000 targets [shields] and 500 tents are furnished by the Town of Edinburgh, which, with what we have got from Cope's armie, will serve near duble our number'.[3] Thus encouraged, on 25 September Atholl was busy at his table dictating letters to chiefs and lords across the Highlands, calling them to arms and forgiving their earlier hesitations.

In the meantime Reverend George Kelly was sent to Paris – no easy commission now that the Royal Navy was on full alert – in the hope that news of Prestonpans would trigger French aid for the cause. It did, as an ambassador was formally sent to attend upon Charles and treaty terms were agreed. Franco-Irish and Franco-Scots soldiers were despatched to Scotland in due course, as were arms, cannon, and cash. But this was a trickle rather than a flood, designed to keep the war going rather than to end it. The Paris *Gazette*, which reported the Battle of Prestonpans on 23 October (New Style), summed up the French priority: 'as a result of all this, the King has determined to recall all the English troops from the Allied Army'.[4] A more detailed account of the battle was printed the following week.

King George's agents were no less efficient in passing on their reports. On Monday 23 September, Chancellor John Waugh of Carlisle was able to forward to the Duke of Newcastle three different accounts of the battle. One anonymous letter from Edinburgh had reached the Provost of Annan before heading to Carlisle and being sent on from there. Other information came via Dumfries and Dalkeith: 'we have several people out for intelligence', writes Waugh.[5] The reports he had received were obviously informed by eye-witnesses but were not wholly accurate in their details of the battle. One describes how 'Gardiner's Dragoons did great execution till their Colonel was wounded in the thigh & many of themselves cut to pieces, after which they retired'. The detail about Gardiner is close, but the performance of his regiment greatly overestimated. Here also is an early criticism of General Cope: 'the Highlanders seem to have surprised them in the morning before they knew what they were about; Sir John having lighted a great many fires gave them an Opportunity of seeing his motions in the night'. The same source mistakenly reports John Murray of Broughton as being amongst the dead.

Another of Waugh's informants reports that the 'two armies Cannonaded one another the whole night', which is a rather grandiose assessment of a few failed shells, but more interestingly the letter goes on to report that fugitives from Hamilton's Dragoons claimed that 'the Dragoon horses would not stand fire'. Considering the jitters reported of even Gardiner's own horse at the start of the battle, it is clear that the horses had not been adequately trained for the battlefield. That may not have been that uncommon in itself, but two full regiments breaking

---

3   Burton (ed.), *Atholl Family*, p.23.
4   Author's translation, from an original in his possession.
5   The National Archives, State Papers up to 1782: SP 36/68/284. The enclosed accounts are included in this same listing.

in simultaneous flight was. Neither can gunfire be blamed for the dragoons' previous performances at Coltbridge and Preston. Whatever faults there were with the horses were matched by those of the riders.

Fortunately for the government, the best accounts of the battle arrived exactly where they were most needed, Berwick-upon-Tweed. England's bastion north of the Tweed, Berwick's stunning Tudor ramparts made it a far more defensible town than any in Scotland. In addition to its vast walls there was a substantial barracks built in the wake of the earlier Jacobite risings, and within the fortifications was a quayside facilitating reinforcement and resupply from the sea. Its military governor was Lieutenant General Lord Mark Kerr, an experienced soldier who had been Cope's rival for the Scottish command. News of Prestonpans first arrived here from the mouths of Brigadier Thomas Fowke and Lieutenant Christie of Murray's Regiment, who had escaped along the coast from the battlefield. They had ridden east until they reached the hamlet at Beltonford, just outside Dunbar.[6] Christie says they stayed there for 'some time', presumably at the inn which Alexander Carlyle had found so filled with redcoats just four days before.

Perhaps it was here that they were caught up by Colonel Lascelles, who had found a horse at Seton and ridden on through Haddington. From here the post road passed through Beltonford and it may have been for the very reason of waiting for others that Fowke had paused there. He could not have known that Cope's route to Berwick would be rather more circuitous than his own. After catching their breath the party rode on through Dunbar, where the citizens discovered the fate of the army that had so recently encamped there, and down the road to the Border. They reached Berwick that same night, where Lord Mark is said to exclaimed: 'Good God! I have seen some battles, and heard of many; but never of the first news of a defeat being brought by the general officers before!' The brigadier and the colonel would have felt keenly the shame of his words.

Cope himself arrived early the next morning at the Scots Gate, still the main entry into Berwick from Scotland. Beyond its arch was the guardhouse and he presumably led his dragoons straight from there to the barracks before attending upon Kerr, perhaps at the fine governor's house which overlooks the eastern ramparts. The meeting was awkward but professional. Cope in fact held seniority and so on his arrival the companies at the barracks and the expected Dutch auxiliaries all came under his command. Kerr wisely chose to remove himself from the potentially uncomfortable situation, and after contemplating a break-through to Edinburgh he instead went south to check on the situation at Newcastle. Sir John Cope would not be relieved from command until Marshal Wade, commander-in-chief of all forces, assumed personal control of the northern army. In the meantime, boats had been sent out by the customs officer at Berwick to prevent those much-anticipated Dutch from trying to land any further north. Once the Dutch

---

6 Fowke's evidence, Robins (ed.), *Inquiry*, p.78.

had arrived, they camped beside Cope's forces at Tweedmouth on the south side of the river, protected by the town. Messengers passed between Berwick and Carlisle: the two traditional border bastions were each on high alert.

There was of course a rush to attribute blame. Cope knew this would happen, as the defensive tone of his letters attests. Major General William Blakeney, based on detailed information from survivors arriving at Stirling and from 'a very intelligent clergyman', criticised Cope's deployments:

> In my opinion, had Sr John Cope placed his right at Preston-panes and his left at Cockenzie his Foot and Cannon on the right and left, and the Dragoons in the Center, he certainly would have defeated the Rebells, for they never could have surprised him, nor make him alter his Disposition so often as he did; besides, it is a maxim in the art of War, not to place Horse on any Wing of an Army that is near woods or Inclosures, from whence they may be anoyed by Infantry without being able to offend them.[7]

If so, then all Cope's senior staff were equally culpable as there were enough experienced officers around the general to have advised him of any obvious alternatives. Blakeney had the advantage of both hindsight and distance, but his letter went off to Henry Pelham nevertheless. Colonel Lascelles, responsible for the infantry, not unnaturally blamed the dragoons, but he received a furious response from the wounded Lieutenant Colonel Whitney when he got wind of it. Lord Drummore overheard some of Cope's dragoons discussing the battle in the weeks that followed, and heard them 'first mutter somewhat in their own Defence, and afterwards they grew a good deal bolder, and in my Hearing, some of them took the Liberty to blame the Officers'. Sir John read accusations of both cowardice and treachery levelled at him, but Dalrymple assured him that 'so false and malicious they are that these Scandals soon will vanish'.[8] But as early as 11 October the *Derby Mercury* was reporting rumours that officers from Prestonpans might face a court martial.

At Athelstaneford in East Lothian, the minister Robert Blair was stunned when he heard what had happened:

> The action at Preston was as Shameful as it was Unfortunate. Never was I more Confounded in my Life, than upon the morning of the Engagement, to hear that the Kings Army was Entirely Defeated, & that their Artillery baggage &c. had faln into the Enemys hands. How far the General officers

---

7 Letter from Brigadier William Blakeney to Henry Pelham, Stirling, 18 October 1745, Nottingham University, Manuscripts and Special Collections: Ne C 1708/1.
8 Drummore to Cope, Alnwick, 24 October 1745, Robins (ed.), *Inquiry*, p.39.

did their duty, it is not my business to Enquire: If their Conduct is aprovd of by their Superiors, it do's not become private persons to find fault. However I canot Help thinking, If all of them had behavd as did my worthy Friend & Gallant Countryman Collonell Gardner, this present Rebellion had never Arivd to such a head as it has done.[9]

In contrast, when the Ormiston brewer Robert Robertson heard the news – which would have been fairly quickly since he was only four miles away – he poured himself a drink and repeatedly toasted the health of King James and Charles, Prince of Wales.

The *Newcastle Courant* meanwhile printed a Jacobite eye-witness' account, within a week of the battle. With considerable irony the same page features an advertisement for purchasing copies of Humphrey Bland's *Treatise of Military Discipline*. The Newcastle article again featured the report that Cope had escaped aboard HMS *Fox*, also mentioned by Patrick Crichton in Edinburgh. For these rumours to have gained any currency the *Fox* must therefore have been anchored close at hand during the battle. One contemporary map does in fact depict a three-master lying just off the western end of Prestonpans, although none of the eye-witnesses specifically mention seeing the *Fox*. One wonders how many of Cope's fleeing sailors made it back to their ship after abandoning the guns.

The same source quoted in Newcastle also informed the anonymous author of the pamphlet *A True and Full Account of the late Bloody and Desperate Battle fought at Gladsmuir*, which appeared in Edinburgh and featured prisoner lists and the latest news of those who had perished from their wounds. It also details how the prisoners have been 'most humanly and civily used… The Officers were lodged in Queensbery House, but are since at Liberty upon Parole, not to depart from the City, nor correspond with the Garison of the Castle'. Queensberry House stands now within the Scottish Parliament complex. Just a little way up the Royal Mile is the Canongate Kirk and Tolbooth, where most of the private soldiers were incarcerated until they could be moved.

Some preferred to accept the invitation of the Prince to enlist in his ranks, however, and it was later claimed that Captain George Hamilton of Redhouse had entered the Canongate Kirk and threatened to kill those who did not enlist. Some of those who did were unsurprisingly uncommitted to the cause and would melt away when opportunity arose or when the tide of war appeared to be turning. Others, however, were enthusiastic volunteers, like Alan Stewart of Loudoun's Highland Company and his more famous namesake Allan Breck Stewart, who would be immortalised in *Kidnapped* almost a century and a half later. If they were caught with the Jacobites there would be little mercy, as Robert Paterson

---

9   Means, J. 'Robert Blair to Henry Baker: A Report on the '45', *Studies in Scottish Literature*: Vol. 24: 1 (1989), p.160.

from Haddington found out after deserting from Guise's Regiment in favour of Perth's: he was executed a few days after the Battle of Culloden.

Most of the prisoners did not turn coats however, and these were later transferred further behind the lines so that the burden of housing, guarding, and feeding them would not interfere with the army's main duties. As early as 26 September a large group was on its way north to Logierait in Atholl's territory, guarded by a hundred men. Arrangements were made for them to be quartered in different houses and reviewed twice a day to deter escapes. Lord George Murray suggested that 'the jaile is at hand if any of them should be obstreperous'.[10] Each prisoner was allocated two pecks of oatmeal a week, or one peck of meal and the equivalent in mutton. Over the coming weeks, as the Jacobite army began to concentrate resources for the march south, conditions clearly relaxed. On 9 October Sir Thomas Sheridan instructed the Duke of Atholl to release George Muschet of Gardiner's Dragoons and William Collier of Lascelles' Regiment, 'upon condition they swear never more to bear arms against him [the Prince]'.[11] Muschet was released after so swearing, but apparently no such person as Collier could be identified. Perhaps he had slipped away already; if so he was not the only one.

On Thursday 2 October two British officers reached Preston in Lancashire and informed post-master John Nocks that they had escaped from captivity. Nocks sent a report to London which confirmed their names and appearance: both men wore light coats over red waistcoats and breeches. One, Captain Charles Tatton of Lee's Regiment, was described as 'about 5 foot 6 inches high, some pock holes in his face, about 30 years old'. The other was Ensign Hardwick of the same regiment, 'about 22 years old'.[12] Two weeks later, Major General Blakeney wrote to the Prime Minister that his garrison at Stirling had been strengthened by the addition of yet more escapees, whom he had added to his strength: 'wanting all necessarys, I take care to furnish them with linnen, shoes, stockings, and watchcoats, the weather being very Cold and Wet'.[13] Whether they lacked these essentials on account of their captors' negligence or the difficulties of their escape and subsequent flight, is open to debate.

Officers not so bold as Tatton and Hardwick, or honour-bound not to escape after receiving clemency, were granted the liberty of Perth and a loose confinement. Sir Patrick Murray, taken at Cockenzie House when he surrendered the baggage guard, wrote on 13 October of the 'kind usage meant towards us', asking 'what libertys we have reason to expect'.[14] He clearly did not feel intimidated. That same

---

10 Burton (ed.), *Atholl Family*, p.30.
11 Burton (ed.), *Atholl Family*, p.74.
12 Letter from John Nocks, Postmaster at Preston, to the Postmaster General, Preston, 25 September 1745, The National Archives, State Papers up to 1782: SP36/70/158.
13 Letter from Major General William Blakeney to Henry Pelham, Stirling, 18 October 1745, Nottingham University, Manuscripts and Special Collections: Ne C 1708/1.
14 Burton (ed.), *Atholl Family*, p.86.

day Lieutenant Colonel Wright of Hamilton's Dragoons wrote to the Jacobite Duke of Atholl citing the poor health of some officers and the pressing business needs of others as the reasons behind repeated appeals to be released on parole. He was still asking nearly a week later, and the Jacobites responsible for their upkeep were soon expressing their support. But Atholl had more immediate concerns: it no easy task to raise the numbers of men being asked of him by the Prince, whilst under the constant pressure of increasingly insistent demands that he march south in person.

Prisoners, especially officers, were at least more fortunate than the wounded. Many of their comrades were still quartered around the battlefield area for several days after the fighting had ceased, including a good number who lay on straw mattresses in the Prestonpans schoolroom. Captain John Maclean commanded the guard detail overseeing the wounded at Bankton House until Monday 23 September when they were transported to Edinburgh. They travelled with what remained of the captured baggage train, presumably making use of the carts as much as possible. The following day another wave of surgeons went out to the battlefield to attend those too sick to be transferred. Amongst the latter was James Sandilands, Master of Torphicen, an officer of Lee's Regiment who has suffered no fewer than twenty injuries. His sister came to Bankton to attend him, and although he survived he was never well again and died only three years later. Helping the wounded was not without risk however: a year after the battle Robert Randall languished in the dungeons of Carlisle Castle, relying on a Mrs Elizabeth Watson of Newbigging in Musselburgh to testify that although he had cared for wounded redcoats at her father's house he had not been 'in Highland dress, had no arms or cockade' and was therefore helping out as a civilian, not a rebel.

On 24 September, Colonel James Gardiner was laid to rest in Tranent Churchyard, which Dodderidge says was well attended despite the continued presence of the Highlanders. Gardiner was buried beside seven of his children, near the south-west corner of the church. The graveyard that had so recently served as the horse corral for the Jacobite army had now returned to its intended uses. A little to the north, Captain John Coltrane Stewart was buried in the Prestonpans churchyard. In due course his father-in-law would erect an elaborate stone monument on his behalf. William Carlyle presumably led the service.

By now Reverend Carlyle's son had had his fill of military adventure. The Prince issued a proclamation that any former Volunteers who reported to his court at Holyrood in appropriate quick time would be pardoned for their former folly. Carlyle cut his losses and travelled to Edinburgh to make sure he was on that list. Charles Edward had returned to the capital on Sunday morning, entering the city at the head of a strong column to the stirring tune of 'When the King Enjoys His Own Again'. Cope's captured standards were carried triumphantly aloft. But this was the limit of the official celebrations, for although the Prince could not miss the chance to demonstrate the scale of his success he forbade any bonfires or further public displays. A formal court was established at Holyrood with all the proper etiquette and routine, and he set about governing Scotland. It was into this strange new environment that Carlyle arrived, checking in with the clerks in the Great Gallery at Holyroodhouse before at last finding an opportunity to see the Prince himself. Carlyle watched as he rode out to review the latest reinforcements that were arriving at Duddingston camp, where the army was now properly camped. Carlyle now turned his mind back to his studies, which he would now complete at Leiden in the Netherlands. He left the uncertainties of the civil war behind him.

Back in his home town the mood remained tense and sombre. There were still Highlanders about, and Captain MacLean was back in Prestonpans in early October with a party of soldiers. According to Elcho, 'Ardsheil's battalion [the Stewarts of Appin] was order'd to East Lothian to facilitate the levying of the publick money in that county'.[15] This involved collection of the salt duty, and it seems the army enlisted the help of the local workforce. At least fourteen salt workers from West Pans, Prestonpans, and Cockenzie would later be reported as having aided the Jacobites in the collection of the duty. Some, like James Reid and William Rannie, did no more to assist the Prince than to continue in their normal duties, whilst the Prestonpans brewer Andrew Sherriff both helped to collect the tax and put up Captain MacLean during his process.

Others were even more helpful to the Jacobites. The labourer Christopher Ramsay, from Seton village, joined their army and marched with them to the bitter end. So did Alexander Henderson of Tranent, who had earned his guinea from O'Sullivan by directing the army through the village. Also from Tranent was the mason Henry Davidson who rode off to join Lord Balmerino's troop of the smart new Lifeguards regiment being created in Edinburgh, as did the farmer John Dodds of Setonhill near Longniddry. Both were later captured; Dodds was transported. From Prestonpans itself, salt officer William Brown, the butcher John Dicks, and the fifty-two year-old tailor William Cowan, all signed up with the Duke of Perth's Regiment. All were later tried, and Cowan was transported.[16] With others housing and feeding the wounded or their guards, and those who had done their part by helping to bury the dead, there were few families unaffected by the drama that had been visited upon their community. This battle did not just happen *in* Prestonpans, it happened *to* Prestonpans.

Charles Edward Stuart left Edinburgh on 1 November, dividing his army of almost 6,000 men into three columns on three different roads to baffle the preparations of his enemies. Converging on Carlisle, the army invaded England. Marshal Wade had by now replaced Sir John Cope in command of the British army, but although the Prince waited eagerly at Brampton the redcoats failed to show. The Jacobites were then able to push as far as Derby, just 120 miles from London, without anybody getting in their way. It was here, in the first weekend of

---

15   Elcho, *Short Account*, p.282.
16   Livingstone, A. & Aikman, C. (eds.), *No Quarter Given: the Muster Roll of Charles Edward Stuart's Army, 1745-6* (Aberdeen: Neil Wilson Publishing, 2001), p.70.

Memorial to Captain John Coltrane Stewart of Lascelles' Regiment, Prestonpans churchyard. (Author's collection)

December, that the tide of war turned irretrievably against the Jacobites. As the army began a long and arduous retreat through terrible winter weather, the spell of Prestonpans was finally broken. The Duke of Cumberland had returned to Britain at the head of veteran regiments and the chase was on. He attempted to slow the Prince down by attacking the Jacobite rear-guard at Clifton in Lancashire, but Cumberland got a bloody nose. Still Wade failed to intercept the enemy.

Whilst the Jacobite army was in England there occurred a tragic post-script to the Battle of Prestonpans. On the night of 14 November a terrible gale blew across the south-east of Scotland. Considerable damage was done along the coasts of the Firth of Forth, and the *Happy Janet* was driven aground at Queensferry. Captain Knight managed to get her afloat again, although the ship needed repairs. Less fortunate by far was HMS *Fox*, which was caught in the storm as she rounded the rocks north of Dunbar harbour. Ripping her bottom out as she went, *Fox* was driven into Belhaven Bay where she broke up with devastating speed. Edmund Beavor and almost all of his 145 crewmen perished. Tradition says that the *Fox* had on board the remains of Sir John Cope's war chest, and if so it still lies today at the bottom of this beautiful bay. A letter reported in the *Derby Mercury* on 22 November confirms that the locals had successfully recovered at least eight of the ship's cannon and were hoping to retrieve some of the rigging too: the bay is not deep. No doubt some looked for the gold. Considering the great events that were happening elsewhere, the loss of HMS *Fox* was largely overlooked and so information is scarce, but it is impossible for us to pass over it without wondering whether the sailors who had fled from the Camerons at Prestonpans had done so only to be overcome by nature less than eight weeks later.

On its return to Scotland after the retreat from Derby, the Prince's army was strengthened considerably by linking up with fresh recruits and the first French regulars. It was soon pushing towards 10,000 in number; a far more formidable force than it had been at Prestonpans. In a howling rainstorm on 17 January the army smashed into General Hawley's army of equal strength on Falkirk Muir. The battle was a confused affair, clarity not aided by the weather, but Hawley's army was broken and driven off. Both Gardiner's and Hamilton's Dragoons had been given the opportunity at Falkirk to redeem themselves. Colonel Francis Ligonier had taken command of Gardiner's leaderless regiment, but like his predecessor he was already a sick man when he took to the field. The Highlanders had no fear of these men, although the dragoons at least attempted to charge this time. But when the Jacobites gave them a disciplined fire at close range and followed with the sword and targe, the dragoons broke again. Gardiner's Dragoons were routed once more. They left behind a green guidon fringed with gold, which bore the motto 'Britons Strike Home', a line from a popular opera song which was trumpeted as the cavalry charged forwards at Dettingen. Presumably Gardiner's had carried this flag at Prestonpans too, but now it was adopted by the Prince's Lifeguards and borne by them at Culloden. It was later burned by the public hangman of Edinburgh, along with all the other captured Jacobite colours. Shortly after his regiment's defeat at Falkirk, Ligonier died of his illness. As his monument in Westminster Abbey proclaims, 'the disease proved more victorious than the enemy'.

Shug Whitney was also a casualty of Falkirk. His wound from Prestonpans healed, Whitney had managed to get himself back to his old regiment. Whilst recuperating, he had advised his brother officers that in order to avoid a repeat of Prestonpans the dragoons should be dispersed along the infantry line and used in close support. Instead Henry Hawley had launched them onto Falkirk Muir into the teeth of the gale, completely without any support of their own. The dragoons rushed forwards into the point-blank fire of the Jacobite right and centre, then routed before their counter-charge. Whitney fell as his regiment fled, much like Gardiner had before him. Two defeats at the hands of the Highlanders were enough to put both Ligonier's/Gardiner's and Hamilton's out of the rest of the war, both regiments being posted to patrol duties. Later: they were both sent to Ireland, where they had been stationed previously. As late as July 1747 the government issued orders for '199 Firelocks, 209 bayonets & 239 Case of Pistolls' to replace those 'lost at the Actions at Preston Pans and Falkirk against the Rebells'.[17] Both regiments remained in Ireland for a generation. The Jacobite victory at Falkirk, muddled as parts of it were, showed that an army larger and more experienced than Cope's could be beaten by the Prince's men. Prestonpans was no fluke.

It was not until 16 April 1746 that the British army finally overcame their opponents on the bloody fields of Culloden. By then the Jacobites had successfully captured Ruthven Barracks, Fort Augustus, and Fort George, and had put Fort William to siege. But at Culloden the battle was less evenly-matched than ever before, and for the first time the Prince's army was exposed to efficiently-manned artillery and the sustained firepower of a larger enemy deployed in sufficient depth to absorb its attack. The treatment given by the Jacobites to those captured or wounded at Prestonpans was so shamefully at odds with what they endured in return. There were still instances of honour however: Lieutenant Colonel Whiteford heard of the capture of Stewart of Invernahyle, who had saved his life at Prestonpans, and intervened on his behalf. In August Lieutenant Colonel Halkett sent a statement to Carlyle which had been signed by Eaglesfield Griffith on behalf of several captured British officers who wished to evidence Robert Taylor's 'remarkable care' over them at Bankton. Taylor claimed he had only joined the Jacobites because his shoemaking business was failing and he was desperate. He had been captured rather ignominiously by the Edinburgh Castle garrison, triggering Griffith's testimony in October 1745. He was later transferred to Carlisle for trial, at which point Halkett re-issued the earlier appeal for clemency. There are other similar instances: even in the dark days in the aftermath of Culloden some honour could still be maintained at least.

---

17 Request for the Supply of Arms to Hamilton's Dragoons, 16 July 1747, the National Archives, State Papers up to 1782: SP 41/18/90.

With the last Jacobite rising over and the Prince on the run, a board of senior officers gathered in the Great Room at Horse Guards on Monday 1 September 1746 to open an official inquiry into the conduct of Lieutenant General Sir John Cope, Colonel Peregrine Lascelles, and Brigadier Thomas Fowke, the three most senior surviving officers from the Battle of Prestonpans. There was considerable demand for the investigation, not least from Cope, who knew he had already been condemned in the court of public opinion. As was soon pointed out by Benjamin Robins, the anonymous author of the preface to the board's report, the defeat and the problems which stemmed from it were most commonly 'imputed to his [Cope's] Mismanagement'.[18] Rumours of a court martial had been circulating since soon after the battle, and an East Lothian farmer-poet, Adam Skirving, had scored a hit with his new song about 'Johnnie Cope', which had played very much to that tune.[19] Robins would claim in his preface that he had held to this same view himself until he had heard the evidence presented at the inquiry. This is probably a literary device. Robins was a military engineer and ballistics specialist, as well as being politically active: he was rather more involved than the mere man-on-the-street he would have us believe him to have been.

The inquiry was not, as commonly believed, a court martial. It was an investigation, held by royal warrant, into the conduct of three named officers throughout the Prestonpans campaign. It was presided over by Field Marshal George Wade, who had served as Commander-in-Chief of the Forces until supplanted by the Duke of Cumberland for the final months of the Rising. At 73 years old, Wade had only sixteen months to live when the inquiry opened. He had not emerged from the war well himself, having twice failed to intercept the Jacobite army at the Border the previous winter. So frustrated was Wade at the difficulties he had faced in marching west from Newcastle that he had since commissioned yet another military road, a programme which did great damage to the Roman wall between Newcastle and Carlisle. Perhaps it was his own experience of Scotland, and more recently of being outmarched by the Jacobites, that encouraged Wade to press hard for Cope's vindication. Perhaps it was the reluctance of the king to abandon a man he had so recently raised.

Also on the board was Lieutenant General Charles, Lord Cadogan, a career soldier and a veteran of Marlborough's wars. Lord Cadogan had sat in the same parliament as Cope twenty years before, being five years his elder. Lieutenant General John Folliot, the absentee Governor of Carlisle Castle during its surrender to the Jacobites and the man responsible for the defence of London during the crisis of December, was also on the panel. So too was Lieutenant General Charles Lennox, Duke of Richmond, a grandson of the notoriously promiscuous Charles

---

18 Robins (ed.), *Inquiry*, p.iii.
19 Johnston, A.P. (ed.), *Rebellious Scots to Crush: An Anthology of the Arts as Engendered by the Battle of Prestonpans in 1745* (Prestonpans: Prestoungrange & Cuthill Press, 2008), pp.31-38.

II and who therefore shared a blood connection to Charles Edward Stuart. He was married to Cadogan's niece, and was a noted patron of the game of cricket. The final officer on the board of inquiry was Lieutenant General John Guise, who would one day bequeath his fabulous art collection to Christ Church in Oxford. Men of his own regiment had been present at Prestonpans, and so he no doubt had an interest in their performance.

The board of inquiry sat initially for five days from 10am until 3pm, hearing the testimony not only of the three named officers but of a great many officers of all ranks, as well as a number of civilian witnesses. Cope's correspondence with Tweeddale was presented; statements were read out; questions were asked and answered. Those who could not attend through illness, military service, or pressing business, sent written evidence which was read aloud after their handwriting had been authenticated. The sessions were held in public and any who wished to challenge what they had heard were invited to do so. Private rooms were made available should any such witnesses feel anxious about sticking their necks out in public. A great show of transparency was therefore being made, so much so that on 24 September the board reconvened specifically to hear the evidence of Richard Jack, the Edinburgh maths teacher who had claimed to be so vital a part of the artillery team. He had come forward to challenge some of the other evidence, but the professional military men lined up to rebut him point by point. They closed ranks against this audacious and perhaps misguided civilian, but although Jack's recollections seem to jar with those of most other witnesses, the interview shed light on some interesting details. Most of his opinions were brusquely disregarded.

The conclusion of the board was a unanimous exoneration of all three officers under investigation. Cope and his brother officers had all done their duty throughout the campaign and their behaviour was beyond reproach. So what had gone wrong at Prestonpans? Was Gardiner's faulty leadership the cause, or the inadequate training of the dragoon horses? Perhaps the unpreparedness of the army for irregular warfare had revealed important issues for review. Were the Jacobites to be credited with a boldness and ability beyond reasonable expectation, or was it the failure of the loyal clans to supply additional manpower which had led to the defeat? If the senior officers could not be blamed for failing to inspire or rally their troops, would that level of understanding extend to the rankers, who could in turn be forgiven for their dread of the Highlanders, their inability to prepare for the ferocity of the charge, or for their instinct for self-preservation once it became clear they could not win? No. The board's finding was simple and unequivocal: 'the Misfortune, on the Day of Action, was owing to the shameful Behaviour of the Private Men; and not to any Misconduct or Misbehaviour of Sir John Cope, or any of the Officers under his Command'.[20]

---

20 From the closing statement of the board, reported in Robins (ed.), *Inquiry*, p.100.

Clearly there were problems with the dragoons, although whether it was the horses or riders who were least fit for action is hard to say. There are question marks over Gardiner's fitness for command too, although the inquiry tactfully avoids speaking ill of the dead. Besides, the legend of Gardiner the Christian Soldier was already gaining currency. But by contrast, no cracks had shown in the infantry until the final moments. They had marched hard and far, maintaining their discipline throughout the campaign, keeping their morale high by most accounts until the very heat of the action.[21] That they broke at the battle is surely down to the perfect storm of circumstances they faced at the crisis point: the failure of the artillery, the flight of the dragoons, the efficiency and ferocity of the Jacobite attack. Even had they not fled it is doubtful that they could have won the battle alone, and the death toll would undoubtedly have been greater. Had Lord Grange's walls not blocked their rear, more of them might have escaped to fight another day. But whatever sympathy we can find for Sir John Cope and his officers, their willingness to allow their men to be blamed in order to preserve their own reputations leaves a grossly unpleasant taste.

The officers had closed ranks and had covered each other's backs even to the extent of using the same words and phrases in their evidence. The board, perhaps under pressure, did the same. After all, there was still a war on in Europe and nobody wanted to expose fundamental failings in the officer class. Had Cope been proven negligent it would have been impossible for his staff and his subordinates to then escape without censure, since they had signed their names to his decisions and supported his actions. Some had far weaker cases to present than the general's, and it is regrettable that Shugborough Whitney was not there to give his own evidence about some of them. Accordingly we must approach the inquiry evidence with caution, although inconsistencies and subtleties remain which reveal the potential weak-points in the evidence and encourage us to ask deeper questions than the board managed. There is much which is demonstrably true in the officers' evidence, and, with over forty witnesses called, the inquiry was certainly thorough. Sir John Cope's evidence has a convincing ring of truth throughout, but in highlighting his orders from Tweeddale to seek out the rebels in the Highlands he was clearly hoping to lay blame with the civilian rather than military establishment. The Secretary of State for Scotland had already fallen from office by then; there would not be another until 1885. In the end, however, the inquiry's findings would not save Cope either from the public or from the lasting stain of defeat.

Back in Prestonpans itself the dust had eventually settled. With the crisis past, for better or worse, the connected communities in this industrious pocket of East Lothian could concentrate on their more customary activities. Aided by a swift campaign to ensure that the battle was named after one of the nearby settlements

---

21 The only exception being the levels of desertion amongst the Independent Companies on the march northwards.

The Colonel Gardiner Monument at Bankton, viewed from the south. (Author's collection)

– Preston, Prestonpans, Cockenzie, Seton and Tranent could all make a claim – the location of the battle was not destined to become obscure, nor would the villages be denied their claim of association. The Jacobites tended instead to refer to the battle as Gladsmuir, claiming the high moorland to the south-east of the battlefield was near enough to fulfil the medieval prophecy of Thomas the Rhymer. A great battle would one day be fought to secure Scotland's fortunes forever and, as a popular 1615 edition of the verses put it, 'on Gladsmuir shall the battle be'. For the victors, Prestonpans seemed close enough to Gladsmuir to fit the bill; for the locals who petitioned the *Scots Magazine* on this issue, it was 'downright transubstantiation'. Had the Prince won his war then the Battle of Gladsmuir might well have become the accepted name. But he did not, and so the battle takes the name of the dominant settlement in the vicinity.

In the years following the battle the site of it began to change. Prestonpans continued to grow and develop as an amazing concentration of economic and industrial activity. Seton village, on the other hand, would disappear altogether, the residents relocated in order to improve the landscaping around the new house which replaced the old palace in 1790. Parts of the battlefield itself were enclosed within Alexander Carlyle's lifetime, although their fertility ensured that most of the field remained open as farmland. New farmhouses emerged therefore: Seton

West Mains, close to where the British line had formed for its final confrontation, and Thorntree Mains on the other side of the waggonway, where the army had lain down the night before. The latter survived until the middle of the 20th century, and took its name of course from that solitary hawthorn tree made famous by the blood of James Gardiner. It had quickly become the main landmark of the battlefield and was quickly added to maps of the area.

In the fields around Thorntree Mains low rises in the ground could still be discerned a generation after the battle, marking the last resting place of many who fell in the battle. Bones were found during drainage works north-east of the farm at the start of the 19th century, and again in this area in the mid-20th century. This area correlates with the 'burial place' identified on William Blakeney's sketch of the battlefield, which was informed by intelligence from Revered Cunningham of Tranent. Perhaps it was because of the battlefield burials that David Jack and Anne Bisset, who committed suicide in 1773 and 1774 in Seton and Tranent respectively, were interred in Thorntree Fields.[22] Unconsecrated it may have been, but hallowed ground nonetheless. Today the field is quiet, peaceful, and largely unvisited as it was later cut off by a railway spur. As such it is both one of the most atmospheric and most vulnerable parts of the site.

Cunningham's church at Tranent would not survive the 18th century, although fragments can be traced in its replacement. The gloomy interior and decrepit exterior meant nothing short of a rebuild would suffice, and in 1799 work began on pulling the old church down. The new one was certainly brighter, as large Georgian windows on the south side allowed light to stream in for the worshippers, many more of whom could now be accommodated in the elegant upper gallery on the north wall. That side of the building still retained one of its original pairs of buttresses, and the old north aisle was retained as an exterior memorial space. The new south wall lay directly on top of the old foundations, which can still be seen at the base. Another phase of renovations in the 20th century removed the gallery and facilitated matching windows in the north wall.

What happened to the grave of James Gardiner during these works is hard to say with certainty: some say that the original marble plaque inside the old church was lost, or that the extension of the south-west corner of the building intruded over his burial place. Robert Chambers heard that heavy rains once exposed part of Gardiner's body, partially covered by the building but still wearing his wig, but by the time that American cleric and travel-writer Andrew Bigelow made a pilgrimage to Gardiner's grave in 1817 the colonel was largely forgotten locally. Two passers-by proved totally ignorant; on calling at the manse Bigelow was then passed on to the church beadle who identified the burial spot. It was marked only by an earth mound, the beadle claimed, but it had been trampled down by the

---

22 Information from the *Tranent Mortality Book* 1754-1781, gathered by Alan Braby and Ed Bethune of the 1722 Waggonway Project.

workmen rebuilding the church.[23] Bigelow does not give any further detail on the location but it was clearly close to the south wall and that correlates with the tradition of the south-west corner. So there is no grave marker for James Gardiner, whose biography by Philip Dodderidge was a best-seller, and his name was almost forgotten amongst locals in Tranent. But on the ground beside the gate leading from the churchyard where Gardiner is buried to the manse in which he died, there is a curious inscribed stone: it is simply marked 1745. Enquiries as to its origins have so far proved fruitless.

This is not to say of course that Gardiner is uncelebrated. A large stone obelisk was erected by public subscription in 1853 in the grounds of his former home at Bankton. It is a mighty tribute, and has helped ensure that Bankton House has remained an iconic part of the battlefield area. The house was repeatedly gutted by fires in the two and a half centuries following the battle and was eventually left as a ruin. The exterior was restored in the early 1990s to its original appearance, and although none of the original interiors have survived, the doocot pavilion has been converted into a mini museum space telling Gardiner's story. The location of the obelisk in the grounds was well chosen, on a mound which ensures it can be seen from the adjacent railway line. The main route between Edinburgh and London opened only ten years before the monument was erected, and as the soot-blackened stone attests that it has been passed by many a traveller since. The obelisk was clearly placed for the benefit of Victorian rail passengers on their way to Waverley Station in Edinburgh, which is named after the hero of Walter Scott's immensely successful historical novel from 1814. The connection is no accident: in the story young Waverley joins the 13th Dragoons before falling in with the Highlanders, and one of the pivotal moments of the book is the death of Gardiner at Prestonpans. Those who erected the obelisk knew their audience, and those early rail passengers will have known the monument's significance.

West of Bankton, the new railway followed the line of the drainage ditch which had initially separated the two armies in 1745. In that sense its impact on the battlefield was relatively slight; it continues as the East Coast Main Line today, and the road runs parallel on the north side just as it did beside the ditch. Of course this was not the first railway in the area, as the waggonway had been in operation since at least 1722. The York Buildings Company had never really made a financial success of their Cockenzie operations, however, and eventually they sold out to the enterprising Cadells of Cockenzie House, who did. The waggonway rails were replaced with iron in 1815 and the route evolved in complexity. It shifted to the western side of Cockenzie House, feeding directly into the refurbished harbour where turntables allowed the coal to tip directly into waiting vessels. At Tranent the waggonway extended as the coal workings did, looping around to the back of

---

23 Bigelow, A. *Leaves from a Journal; or Sketches of Rambles in some parts of North Britain and Ireland chiefly in the year 1817* (Boston: Wells and Lilly; 1821), p.282.

the town. But the coming of the mainline, which it crossed over Gardiner's Bridge, and the increasing viability of coastal mines closer than those on the ridge, spelled the end for Scotland's first railway. The route is still traceable, and as a footpath it still runs from the heugh at Tranent and on through the battlefield towards Cockenzie. It is one of the most visited parts of the battlefield.

Improved drainage and pumping methods, as evidenced by the massive Cornish beam engine at Prestongrange, at last opened up the possibility of mining the coal seams closer to the Firth of Forth. Large mines developed on the shore between Prestonpans and Cockenzie, where Carlyle had once seen the prisoners gathered along the beach, around Riggonhead, and near Meadowmill in the epicentre of the battlefield. By the middle of the 20th century the battlefield was therefore under increasing pressure from a combination of industry, infrastructure, and housing. Prestonpans, having already subsumed Preston village, expanded eastwards towards the thorn tree. A mineral railway came to mark the eastern edge of the town, running north towards Prestonlinks pit, cutting through the edge of Throntree Fields beside the famous tree. This proved relatively short-lived, but when a major coal-fired power station was erected west of Cockenzie in 1959, a coal storage area was created over the Warren Parks site. It was fed by a new rail spur which cut diagonally across the battlefield, artificially separating the Thorntree Fields from the Waggonway Fields.

As for the famous thorn tree itself, it survived for not quite two centuries after the battle. As early as Andrew Bigelow's visit in 1817 there was a nearby row of sister hawthorns and there are plenty in the area still, but the original three-trunked icon still stood majestically alone. But time took its toll and eventually it was had to be held up by iron props. Photographs and engravings survive, but by 1924 only one of its trunks remained and it was clearly dead. What was left was deliberated cleared with the permission of the Earl of Wemyss, who owned the land and belonged to the family of Elcho of the '45. A large piece of the tree was donated to the Military Museum at Edinburgh Castle, now the National War Museum; another piece belongs to the Battle of Prestonpans (1745) Heritage Trust; two smaller fragments are in the museum store of East Lothian Council; and there are several trees locally which are said to have been grown from cuttings. But with the thorn tree gone so was the battlefield's principal marker, and so a cairn was erected in 1932 by the Society for the Preservation of Rural Scotland. With the mineral railway restricting access to the location of the original tree, the cairn was placed beside the road instead, a little east of the thron tree site and on the other side of the road. This smart but simple cairn was designed by William Davidson FRIBA; when bones were found by children in the Thorntree Fields area they were buried here in 1953. A large crowd turned out for the ceremony despite the rain. The service was led by the episcopal minister Reverend Lyford Pike.

In 1998 a further monument was erected closer to the actual site of the original thorn tree, in a children's play area on the boundary between Thorntree Fields and the eastern edge of Prestonpans. Sculpted by Borders-based artist Michelle

The *Battle Bing* viewpoint pyramid at Meadowmill. (Author's collection)

de Bruin, it takes the form of a triangular pillar illustrated with hawthorn motifs on two sides and an inscription on the third. Due to its location, the Thorntree Monument is the least well-known and most vulnerable of the Prestonpans monuments, but behind it is a considerable copse of hawthorns and tracks which lead straight out into Thorntree Fields beyond.

It was the closure of the Meadowmill coal workings which led to the battlefield's most striking monument, however. In the 1960s a large coal bing (spoil heap) beside the old waggonway line was sculpted into a pyramidal viewpoint, rising out of what was once the Tranent Meadows to provide panoramic views of the battlefield and beyond to Edinburgh or North Berwick Law. The land between this so-called Battle Bing and the restored Bankton House is now primarily taken up by sports pitches, which has the considerable virtue of preserving the openness of the ground. To the immediate east of the pyramid is a golf driving range and the 19th century Steill's Hospital, later St Joseph's school, around which there are still patches of ground which remind us of the marshy past. The summit of the bing serves as the main battlefield viewpoint, with recently update interpretation panels and a flagpole flying the standard of Charles Edward Stuart. Visitors are guided here by road-signs – in Gaelic of course, for the benefit of the Highlanders.

Across the wider battlefield there have been other changes. Preston House became a boys' school from 1781 (Schaw's Hospital), closing in 1832 and becoming increasingly dilapidated and ruinous thereafter. The surviving portions of this once magnificent house were demolished in stages from the 1930s until 1972 when no trace survived. The site is occupied by Prestonpans Community Centre and the adjacent buildings.[24] In 2008 the foundations of one of its pavilions were located in the grounds. Fortunately a fine cluster of other fascinating buildings does survive in old Preston: the ruined tower; Hamilton House; Northfield House; and Preston Cross.

Carlyle's church at Prestonpans still stands as well, albeit with some alterations to the original structure. The original manse has gone however. Cockenzie House can now be visited, and although its interiors are much altered from their original form the gardens are pleasant and there is a sense of history behind their walls. The farm at Riggonhead no longer exists, and although the nearby area where the Jacobites slept immediately before the battle became known as Prince's Park, it was all subsequently transformed by open cast mining. This too has now gone, and it is planned that a new town will be built here on the site of that crucial flanking march. It is to be hoped that the memory of that important association will be somehow preserved in the new developments.

But despite all of these changes, many of the key features of the battle have survived and much of the landscape is recognisable. Most importantly of all, the core areas of contact have remained open agricultural land ever since, particularly around Seton Mains and Seton West Mains. After the harvest, it is a joy to stand here and imagine the Highlanders charging across the rustling stubble. Metal detection surveys have produced important results in this area since 2008, confirming and enhancing understanding of the battle by identifying clear patterns of shot distribution which pinpoint the opening stages of the climactic confrontation. Further west, the thorn tree and Waggonway areas also remain open, although no longer farmed. Archaeological surveys in 2016 showed that large areas of this ground remain untouched, despite the encroachments of the subsequent centuries. But this is the most vulnerable part of the battlefield, sandwiched between the housing of Prestonpans and the former coal store of the power station, which itself no longer exists. The future of the western battlefield remains uncertain.

What is certain, however, is that interest in the Battle of Prestonpans is still very much alive. From the contemporary poems of Adam Skirving or the Jacobite William Hamilton, to the novels of Walter Scott and Robert Louis Stevenson, the battle boasts an enviable literary legacy which has kept its name on our lips. This bleeds into an artistic legacy too, not least in the form of the magnificent *Prestonpans Tapestry*: 104 metres of embroidery created 2009-10 by volunteers all around Scotland. The battle has been portrayed on film too, from the low-budget action of *Chasing the Deer* (1994), to the big-screen romanticism of David Niven's *Bonnie Prince Charlie* (1948). More recently, the book and television series *Outlander* have brought the battle to a broad new audience, even if the temptation of portraying a sleepy British army getting surprised out of the fog is as powerful

---

24 Statham, C. *Lost East Lothian* (Edinburgh: Birlinn, 2011), p.37.

to film-makers now as it was in Niven's day. Meanwhile, back on the ground itself, the Battle of Prestonpans (1745) Heritage Trust continues to research and interpret the site and its stories, and to campaign for the battlefield's protection.

Perhaps the last word on the Battle of Prestonpans should go to Captain James Johnstone, the Edinburgh merchant's son who charged beside Prince Charlie that morning. In the summer of 1746, after countless trials and sufferings in the wake of the final Jacobite defeat, Johnstone found himself once more on the coast of East Lothian. He had been rowing for Leith in the hope of finding a passage into exile, but his boat had drifted eastwards to Prestonpans. There he landed, a wanted man dressed only in rags, with his feet torn to tatters and fearing for his life. Returning to the battlefield helped put his life into perspective:

> I determined to pass the whole day on the field of battle, in order to tranquillise my mind and soften a little the rigours of our fate by reflections on the past… The remembrance of the glorious and inconceivable victory which we had obtained on this spot added to my extreme pleasure.[25]

May it do the same for us all.

---

25 Johnstone, *Memoir*, pp.198-99.

Epilogue

A year to the day since he had looked down upon his enemies from Birslie Brae, Prince Charles Edward Stuart took his final melancholy leave of Scotland. He had been on the run for five months, a wanted man surviving only through his own inner strength and the capacity for sacrifice and kindness that he had found in the Highlanders. From Loch nan Uamh, from virtually the same spot where he had first stepped onto the mainland, Charles returned to an exile which would last for the rest of his life. Many of his senior officers had already gone, some escaping more easily than others, but all bore the same burdens of loss and regret. Others would be in hiding for years to come, and most were ruined men. The Prince hoped that he might yet spur the French into action, but it was not to be. And whether he knew it yet or not, this experience had broken him. For a brief time Charles enjoyed the status of a celebrity in Paris, but his frustrations and political isolation made him volatile. When the War of the Austrian Succession finally came to a close in 1748 the peace terms insisted the Stuart Prince be expelled from France. Louis accepted and Charles Edward was arrested with silken cords. He went to Avignon at first, from which he began a dark and damaging period of disguises, futile gestures, and failed hopes.

Few of the officers who had charged at Prestonpans had fared even so well as this. James Drummond, Duke of Perth, never even made it as far as exile. He died aboard a French ship less than a month after the Battle of Culloden; his heart and body equally broken by the strains of the campaign and its brutal climax. Perth was only 33 and his death was a singular tragedy. His younger brother John had joined the Prince too late to serve at Prestonpans, but would not now be long in joining the Duke: he was killed fighting for the French at Bergen-op-Zoom in 1747. The following year it was the turn of Donald Cameron, Gentle Lochiel, whose support had been so crucial to the Prince's early hopes. Lochiel had been warmly received in Paris, where he was honoured with command of the new *Regiment d'Albanie*. But Lochiel's regiment did not long outlive its colonel: it was disbanded following the peace of 1748 having never seen action.

Other Jacobite leaders lived longer, but few were able to return to their homes. Lawrence Oliphant of Gask was one of the exceptions. Gask had commanded one of Strathallan's troops of Perthshire Horse. Strathallan himself had held his ground at Culloden and given his life there, along with many other veterans of

Prestonpans. Lord George Murray survived the final battle but was to end his days in the Netherlands. His role in the campaign had been controversial from the day he had first set foot into Charles Edward's camp, but he still has many admirers today. Murray and his Prince had parted badly, after barely managing to maintain civil relations to the end of the war. It took Murray longer even than Charles to escape from the Highlands, by which time his elder brother Tullibardine was already dead, aged fifty-seven, having been driven once more from his Atholl title. Murray travelled to Rome and laid his side of the story before King James, undermining Charles' role in the rising's successes and damaging the king's relationship with his son in doing so. Charles refused to meet with Murray when he arrived in Paris and they had no further dealings thereafter. Murray eventually settled in Medemblik, where he died aged sixty-six in 1760. The previous year Charles had referred to him as 'ye ruin of ye Affaire'.[1]

John William O'Sullivan probably died at around the same time as Murray, ending his days in such obscure exile that even the date of his death seems to have been forgotten. O'Sullivan had endured the same privations as his Prince in the heather, but soon after returning to France he resumed his military career. O'Sullivan visited Rome on Charles' behalf in order to present what amounted to an 'official' narrative of the war, revealing not only his own important contribution but also a positive review of the Prince's. After interviewing both Murray and O'Sullivan the old King Across the Water must have understood at least one thing about the Rising: the problems within the senior staff could not have helped their chances. As Charles subsequently cut himself off from almost everyone associated with the expedition, even his friendship with O'Sullivan came to an end. The latter married, rose to the rank of colonel, and then drifted into obscurity. John William O'Sullivan has since borne the brunt of an historical tradition which has repeatedly denigrated the Irish contribution to the '45, and his qualities have been overlooked and maligned in the rush to idolise Lord George Murray and romanticise the purely Highland perspective. Whatever his failings, he deserves better than that.

Also keen to tell his side of the story was David Wemyss, Lord Elcho. He spent the rest of his long life in France and Switzerland, where he achieved a level of comfort and respect that ought to have eased the bitterness he felt for what he had lost. To Elcho's apparent surprise, his high connections proved insufficient to secure him a pardon after the war, which only added to his increasing resentment of his former friend Prince Charles. Elcho campaigned bitterly for the Prince to pay back the money he had given to the cause on the road to Edinburgh, and his scathing comments about his former commander raised eyebrows in Paris. He accepted French commissions and eventually settled into continental society. Elcho died in 1787.

---

1   Elcho, *Short Account*, p.452.

Some of his companions in arms, like Tullibardine, were caught long before they had a chance to escape. These included both rich and poor. John MacNaughton, a watch maker from Edinburgh, was hanged at Carlisle for allegedly landing the fatal blows on Colonel Gardiner. He protested his innocence and in the fury of the battle it is probably impossible to know who in fact dealt the final strike. William Boyd, Earl of Kilmarnock, who had thrown in his lot with the Prince after being visited at Callendar House on the march to Edinburgh, was captured at Culloden. Kilmarnock was publicly executed in London along with Arthur Elphinstone, Lord Balmerino. Simon Fraser, Lord Lovat, who had once danced that jig at Lucky Vint's, also met his end on the block. His attempts to play both sides of the table had failed and the government meant to finish him. So many people attended Lovat's execution that the viewing stands gave way. Evidence against him had come from Charles Edward's former secretary of state John Murray of Broughton, who had himself been captured in the Scottish Borders and then chose to escape execution by turning King's Evidence. Lovat was probably doomed regardless of Broughton's evidence, but the cry of traitor will forever overshadow the Broughton's service to the Jacobite cause. After receiving his pardon John Murray chose to remain in England, where he died in 1777.

John Rattray, the Edinburgh surgeon who had attended the wounded at Bankton House, stayed with the Jacobites thereafter and was also subsequently captured. Like others, including Dr George Lauder and Robert Taylor, he cited the care he had given to the wounded at Prestonpans in his defence. Those prisoners who were sufficiently fortunate and literate were able to secure testimony in their favour. Rattray was doubly fortunate, as his golfing companions included Duncan Forbes of Culloden, Lord President of the Court of Session. He was released from captivity and returned to his practice. Rattray remains best known for his golf, and there is a campaign to raise a statue of him on Leith Links.

The peace which ended the War of the Austrian Succession did not long hold; it was born from mutual exhaustion rather than decisive conclusions, and the wounds festered on. Britain and France, having reversed their positions over Prussia, were locked in combat again by 1754. The Seven Years' War was even more global in scale than its predecessor, and the conflict drew into its cauldron many of the professional military men who had been involved in the Prestonpans campaign the previous decade. Some emerged as heroes, but not all.

Sir Peter Halket of Lee's Regiment, who as lieutenant colonel had negotiated the surrender of Cope's baggage train, was released by his Jacobite captors on parole. In exchange he vowed not to serve against them for the next eighteen months, a promise which the Duke of Cumberland expected him to repudiate. Halket refused and was dismissed from the service; only in 1751 was he able to return to office, taking command of his former regiment. Only a few years later Colonel Halket and his men were sent to North America along with the doomed Major General Edward Braddock. Born in Perthshire, Braddock was a competent career soldier who underestimated his enemy's strengths and overestimated his own. In the summer of 1755 he led an army roughly the same size as Cope's into mountainous and hostile terrain. Halket and his regiment, including its core of Prestonpans veterans, went with him, and on 8 July they were attacked by the French and their Native American allies near the Monongahela River. In the chaos Halket fell, his death witnessed by his son Lieutenant James Halket. The lad rushed to the aid of the father only to be shot dead at his side. Another son mercifully escaped from the carnage. General Braddock did not.

In the wake of Braddock's defeat the British government sent a new commander to North America with authority to force the colonial legislatures into cooperative action. The man chosen was John Campbell, Earl of Loudoun, who had fought at Prestonpans as Cope's adjutant-general. Soon after his escape to Berwick he had boarded ship and returned to the Highlands. Loudoun had then put himself at the head of his own fledgling regiment, for which Forbes of Culloden had been allocating commissions. At Inverness he assembled what loyalist Highlanders he could, enough to present a threat in the Jacobite rear. In December 1745 he detached Norman MacLeod to stop the Jacobites raising men in the north-east, but they were defeated in the oft-forgotten Battle of Inverurie. Two months later Loudoun himself led a column to Moy Hall in an attempt to seize the Prince. His men took to their heels when a handful of ingenious adversaries made enough noise to be mistaken for an army. The rather inglorious Rout of Moy was followed by the abandonment of Inverness to the Jacobites as Loudoun fell back. His presence nevertheless tied up Jacobite manpower in the crucial closing weeks of the war. Ten years later he was sent to North America with sweeping powers designed to restore the British colonial war effort in the wake of Monongahela. He did much to improve the administrative and logistical situation, but in doing so he alienated civil colonial interests. Then, while Loudoun was preparing an offensive against Louisburg, infamous events occurred at Fort William Henry. Loudoun was replaced, but he redeemed his reputation somewhat after helping repel Spain's 1762-3 invasion of Portugal. A magnificent portrait of Loudoun in Highland uniform hangs in the National Museum of Scotland.

The North American theatre also drew in Lascelles' Regiment, now the 47th Foot. As part of Wolfe's expedition to take Quebec in 1759 the regiment found itself making history on the Plains of Abraham. Here it achieved greater glory than it had at Prestonpans, participating in one of the British army's most celebrated victories. On the other side of the field, serving as an aide to the French commander Montcalm, was the Chevalier de Johnstone. This was the same James Johnstone, once aide to Lord George Murray, who had charged at Prince Charles' side at Prestonpans. He had later served as a captain in the Duke of Perth's Regiment, had survived Culloden, and made his way into a lifelong exile and service in the French Marines. Montcalm was killed in the battle for Quebec and the French defeat left Johnstone in a potentially vulnerable position. Fortunately the new British governor was the Scotsman James Murray, who was willing to turn a blind eye to the true nationality of this particular prisoner. Murray's home was at Ballencrief, just five miles from Prestonpans battlefield. Johnstone returned to France where he would later write a colourful memoir of both the '45 and his subsequent campaigns in Canada. He lived through the violence of the French Revolution, probably dying around 1800.

Peregrine Lascelles, meanwhile, had recovered from the humiliation of Prestonpans and had reached the rank of lieutenant general by the time his regiment approached Quebec. He remained colonel of the regiment that had fought at Prestonpans until his death aged 88 in 1772. A memorial tablet to Lascelles survives inside St Mary's Church in his native Whitby, the epitaph of which gives a generous assessment of his part in Cope's defeat: 'after a fruitless exertion of his spirit and ability, at the disgraceful rout of Preston-Pans, he remained forsaken on the field'. It tactfully does not mention that he fell over at the critical moment and then slipped away quietly. The fact that Prestonpans had to be mentioned at all at the conclusion of a long career suggests Lascelles had never fully shaken off the stigma of his escape.

Other senior veterans of Prestonpans were kept busy in the European theatre. The beautiful Mediterranean island of Minorca seems an unlikely confluence for their fortunes, but by one of those peculiar quirks of history several of our key players had connections there. In 1708 the island had been captured for Britain by an expeditionary force which included amongst its number both John Cope and George Wade. Four decades later Minorca was governed by William Blakeney, the gallant defender of Stirling Castle and early critic of Cope's deployments at Prestonpans. It was now the turn of the French to invade the island, and at no less a person than Charles Edward Stuart was initially offered the command. But the Stuart prince refused to be involved in a military sideshow in support of purely French aims, declaring that he would 'no longer serve as a mere bugbear'.[2] The expedition went ahead without him and the French immediately obtained the upper hand. The eighty-five year-old Blakeney was heavily outnumbered and was soon bottled up in Fort St Philip, around which he was forced to fight a far more determined siege than he had endured from the Jacobites. A naval relief force was despatched under Admiral John Byng, whose patrol squadron in 1745 had included HMS *Fox*, and battle was joined off the coast of Minorca on 20 May 1756. Badly mauled, Byng withdrew his ships to Gibraltar for repairs.

In command at Gibraltar was none other than Thomas Fowke, who had commanded the dragoons with so little distinction at Prestonpans. He and Sir John Cope were still in close contact a decade after their shared debacle, the latter even sending Cope the gift of a Spanish horse. Fowke had served on the general staff in Flanders in the closing stages of the War of the Austrian Succession and by 1754 he was a lieutenant general and Governor of Gibraltar. But when Byng's

---

2   Lang, A., *Prince Charles Edward Stuart: The Young Chevalier* (London: Longmans, Green & Co, 1903), p.391.

squadron had first arrived at this important outpost Fowke had refused to lend him the services of a regiment of marines. The newly-minted admiral's expedition was then a total failure, and despite their heroic defence Blakeney and his garrison were obliged to surrender after a 71 day siege. Blakeney secured excellent terms and the survivors were released to Gibraltar. Despite the outcome Blakeney returned to Britain as a hero. He died in 1761 at the age of ninety and was buried in Westminster Abbey. A statue of him was raised in Dublin, where a monument to Nelson would later stand. Both proved to be temporary.

General Fowke was court-martialled for his failure to support the Minorca relief and was suspended from the Army. King George was so irate at the island's loss that he pushed for a harsher punishment even than that, and Fowke was dismissed from the service. He had survived the Prestonpans inquiry without censure, but it may well have left a black mark against his name with king. Now, ten years later, he was up before a board once again and this time there was nowhere to hide; the government was actively seeking scapegoats. Fowke might have been dishonoured but he was at least luckier than Byng, who was executed by firing squad. George II could be unforgiving. Only when the king's grandson ascended the throne as George III was Fowke able to return to the army, retaining his former rank. He died in Bath in 1764.

Sir John Cope never commanded an army again after he was relieved at Berwick by Marshal Wade. Although he was officially exonerated of any wrong-doing, his public image was ruined and without an active command there was no opportunity to restore it. Cope did hold a number of posts, serving on a drill review panel at Horse Guards in 1749 and becoming Governor of Limerick. But in 1750 he sounded out Sir Robert Wilmot of Osmaston, Secretary to the Viceroys of Ireland, about an application for the governorship of Derry. The response, worded with considerable sensitivity, was that 'a Certain Ear is not yet so thoroughly reconciled to Certain Sounds as to receive them without starting'.[3] Clearly Cope believed he had lost the support of the king, interpreting this as George's 'determination never to grant… any further mark of his Royal favour'. A few years later he wrote to Fowke in Gibraltar that he was 'just as desirous not to be employed, as those who could employ [him] are unwilling to do it, so in *that* we are perfectly agreed'.[4]

The historical record offers few other glimpses into Cope's life after the Rising. His only legitimate child James had been born to his first wife in 1709 and had chosen a diplomatic rather than military career. During the events of 1745 James Cope was on the British staff in Hamburg, but in 1754 he had entered parliament. His career seems to have stalled, however, and two years later James Cope was discovered in his father's dining room at St James' Place in London hanging by his

---

3   Letter from Sir Robert Wilmot to Sir John Cope, London, 4 January 1750, Derbyshire Archives: D3155/C/1083.
4   Letter from John Cope to Thomas Fowke, 1753; sold at Bonhams in March 2011.

red garters. Sir Robert Wilmot was clearly a close friend of the old general, as it was to him that the servants had run when discovering that the dining room door was locked from within. After rushing to the tragic scene Wilmot sent word on to Bath, where Cope was taking the waters: 'touch gently', he begged the messenger, 'proceed gradually; lay open the wound with the tenderest hand'.[5] It must have been a heavy blow nonetheless.

Cope at least found a degree of comfort with 'a very good creature' called Mrs Metcalfe. They had two children together, although Cope's second wife Elizabeth seems not to have borne a grudge as she lived with Metcalfe's daughter even after her husband's death. Cope mentions the affair in correspondence with Thomas Fowke, suggesting that it may have been a relatively open secret. In his will both his wife Elizabeth and Sir Robert Wilmot were named as the trustees of a fund designed to set up Cope's illegitimate son, John Metcalfe Cope, in a career. They paid him the sum as an allowance and purchased him into the Army, but despite his father's obviously sensible precautions Metcalfe ran up considerable debts and had to sell his commission to cover them. In 1772 he successfully took the executors to court in order to take control of what remained of his inheritance.

Sir John Cope had died in the summer of 1760. He was buried in the charming St James' church in Piccadilly, close to his home. Whilst Wade and Blakeney are remembered in Westminster Abbey, and Lascelles can boast a fine memorial in his home town, there is not even a humble stone plaque to remember Cope. Even his fine house in St James' Place has gone, a victim of the Blitz, although the neighbouring Spencer House fortunately survived the attack. All the service Cope had given his country, from the battlefields of the Spanish Peninsula to the noble field of Dettingen, all counted for little after Prestonpans: he would be remembered for nothing else but that one chaotic morning. The only lasting memorials to Sir John Cope are a scribbled caricature and a couple of famous but equally unfriendly folk songs. *Hey Johnnie Cope* was written soon after the fighting stopped by Adam Skirving, whose grave can be found at Athelstaneford in East Lothian. Robert Burns later tweaked its verses, and the song epitomises the popular perception of Cope. Ironically the tune is most commonly heard today by those serving in the British army: it is played as the Reveille for six battalions of the Royal Regiment of Scotland. It has at least ensured Cope's name is not forgotten; small reward for what could be considered, Prestonpans aside, as a distinguished if not brilliant military career.

The victor of Prestonpans fared little better in his lifetime than his opponent. The taste of success made the strains of defeat even harder to bear, and time cast dark shadows over the flashes of brilliance which the young Prince had once shown. Charles Edward Stuart never commanded an army after Culloden, never again commanded the attention of the world as he had in 1745. The psychological

5 Sir Robert Wilmot, 4 August 1756. Derbyshire Archive: D3155/C/1874.

damage done by the failure of his life's mission, the mental and physical exhaustion, and the final catastrophic collapse of his cause, all played their part in the Prince's long and tragic decline into depression, paranoia, and alcoholism. Charles Edward Stuart was far from perfect: he could be stubborn, reckless, and hot-tempered; he bore grudges and was prone to bouts of lethargy and melancholy when events were not in his favour. But he was also a highly talented man with considerable potential: he was driven, courageous, charismatic, and engaging. He could also be courteous, patient, and understanding. If the Prince had not been all of these things he could not have carried men like Lochiel along with him, and his cultural legacy would not have proved so lasting. But he was also sensitive, both politically and personally, and tender-hearted. Like his mother, that made him fragile and volatile, easily wounded and quick to take offence. Charles Edward was a man of contrasts.

The Prestonpans campaign shows him at his best: from rallying the clans with the force of his personality, using his status and charm to overcome his lack of resources and experience; through to his decisiveness in the Corrieyairack, personal bravery at Prestonpans, and his care for the wounded in its aftermath. The crises within his senior command, in particular the incompatibility of Charles and O'Sullivan with Lord George Murray, had already shown as cracks but had yet to open as fractures; at Tranent the Prince had been able to smooth them over, showing himself to be flexible and willing to compromise. That would not last.

Charles Edward Stuart died on 31 January 1788, outliving many of his contemporaries. Today he is immensely famous and also astonishingly divisive, usually as he is seen as having gambled the lives of so many others for a cause which was, ultimately, personal. That is equally unfair to those who saw his cause as their own as it is to the Prince himself, a man who genuinely saw his peoples' happiness as being bound to his own. Perhaps that is an inevitable arrogance of royalty. But if we accept that this is how Charles Edward Stuart saw it – that he truly believed he could make them a free and happy people – then we should satisfy ourselves with the conclusion that it was a far nobler thing for him to have tried and failed, than for him not to have tried at all. Hindsight makes us blind, but in 1745 nothing was certain.

In fact after the Battle of Prestonpans, after victory at Gladsmuir, nothing seemed impossible at all.

Appendix I

Orders of Battle for the Opposing Armies at the Battle of Prestonpans

Jacobite Army[1]

Commander: Prince Charles Edward Stuart

Front Line (left to right)
Lieutenant General Lord George Murray's Division:
    Cameron: Donald Cameron of Lochiel, 600 men
    Appin: Charles Stewart of Ardsheal, 200 men
    Duke of Perth's: James Mor MacGregor,[2] 200-300 men
Lieutenant General James Drummond, Duke of Perth's Division:
    MacDonald of Keppoch: Alexander MacDonnell, 350 men
    MacDonald of Glengarry: Angus Og MacDonald, 400 men
    MacDonald of Clanranald: Ranald MacDonald, 200 men

Second Line (left to right):
Atholl Brigade: Lord Nairne, 350 men
MacLachlans: Lachlan MacLachlan, 100 men

Cavalry Reserve:
Perthshire Horse: Viscount Strathallen, 36 men

---

1 Numbers are approximate and are listed by regiment. Some regiments contained several clans.
2 As Perth was commanding a division, he did not lead his regiment at Prestonpans. Traditionally this task is said to have fallen to James Mor Drummond/MacGregor, although this is not universally accepted.

British Army[3]

Commander: Lieutenant General Sir John Cope
Brigadiers: Brigadier-General Thomas Fowke (cavalry); Colonel Peregrine Lascelles (infantry)

Front Line (left to right):
Hamilton's Dragoons: Lieutenant Colonel William Wright, 2 squadrons forward and 1 in reserve
Murray's Regiment: Lieutenant Colonel Jaspar Clayton, 10 companies
Lascelles' Regiment: Major John Severn, 8 companies
Guise's Regiment: brigaded with Lascelles' Regiment, 2 companies
Lee's Regiment: Lieutenant Colonel Peter Halkett, 5 companies
Gardiner's Dragoons: Colonel James Gardiner, 2 squadrons forward and 1 in reserve
Artillery: Major Eaglesfield Griffiths and Lieutenant Colonel Charles Whitefoord

Baggage Guard:
John Murray's Regiment (Black Watch): Captain Sir Patrick Murray, 1 company
Loudoun's Regiment: Captain Alexander Mackay, 3 understrength companies

---

3 Due to the uncertainties over the precise numbers, unit strengths are provided here as squadrons/companies.

Appendix II

Letter from Lieutenant Colonel Shugborough Whitney to Lieutenant Archibald Campbell, aide-de-camp to Major General Humphrey Bland

Edinr. Novr. 26th

Sir,
I was favour'd with yours of the 8th of Novr, which I could not answer sooner being then on the Hinge of removing to this place, & had only time to write a letter to the Genl [General] by last Post. To satisfy your curiosity as to the Regmt, I must tell you that in this Battle of ours we had only about 16, or 18 Men killed, & about thirty wounded. No officer killed except Col. Gardiner. Serjts Carrick & Haynes of poor Captn West's Troop that was, were both killed. Lieut. Crofton, Quarter Mr West, Burrows, & Young made prisoners, West and Young wounded. Belcher is perfectly well. I had just four men killed in my Troop, & about 8, or 9 wounded, none of which were your acquaintance.

I have had to deal with these savage Highlanders more than once. I find their fire is only a Bugbear, for not being acquainted with kneeling & stooping, the fire of their Center, & Rear Ranks, went over our Heads. Had all the Shot that they pour'd in upon my squadron been given according to Art, I think not one of us cou'd have escaped. I tell you this, that your Horse & Dragoons may promise themselves success whenever they attack these Myrmidons, tho by a complication of misfortunes I did not succeed to my wishes. These Rebels attacked us in three Columns. Its probably they'll deal with you after the same manner. I would not encourage the notion of keeping up our Fire, but whenever I discovered their design of making their rush, I would make the Grenadiers according to Custom begin about 60, or 70 yards distance from them, on a half wheel, & so from right to left, with the Platoons of the Battallion, keeping a heavy Platoon in the Center for their Front, to fire when within ten yards of them. I would intersperse the Cavalry with the Foot, allowing to each Battallion a Squadron, which upon the Column of the Rebels that I suppose must be ruined by the Foot, I would have marched out, wheel on their flank, & finish it. These are observations of my own, which you may keep to yourself as they would not stand the test of the superior wisdom of our Generals.

I always rejoice at your happiness in the favour of that excellent Man your Patron. From a motive of gratitude I shall ever be interested in his Felicity & good Fortune, having had many instances of his generosity, & friendship to me, among which his kindness to young Upton on my account is no small one, & I thank you for the friendly part you acted in his behalf. I wish you all imaginable success against these Rascals, who have risen in Rebellion against the best of Kings, & the best Constitution in the World. If you will take Sallust in your hand, & read the characters of his Rebels, I can assure you that the most part they'll answer exactly to these wretches who now disturb our peace, being generally men of profligate lives, & ruined Fortunes.

In that unlucky Battle near Preston I had the misfortune to lose a Brace of very good Geldings, now in the possession of My Lord Elcho. One is a mouse colour'd Gelding with a pretty large Star, & the near hind foot white as high as the fetlock, close upon fifteen hands high. The other a Bay about the same, with dapples exceedingly all over, with a large Start & a hind white foot. I think that as these cannot be call'd a prize in a lawfull war, but only consider'd as Stollen or Robbe'd by a Sett of Banditti, you may recover them for me, whoever may be the possessor.

I have had a good deal of trouble with my Arm. It was broke half way betwixt my Wrest & my Elbow. The small bone much shatter'd, the big one had two large splinters broke off it. I want now only the strength in my Arm & motion in my fingers, being pretty free of pain. My best respects always wait on your Genl. My Secretary makes his compliments to you. Be sure to tell me where you are on the receipt of this, & let me know every thing that occurs with you. Much do we long here for good news from England. Direct for me to the care of the Postmaster of Edinburgh. I am with perfect truth

Your most humble servt.
Shug Whitney.

Charles West is well & much your humble Servt.

Bibliography

Archival Sources

Henry Pelham Papers, Manuscripts and Special Collections, Nottingham University
Sir John Cope Papers, Manuscript Collections, National Library of Scotland, Edinburgh.
State Papers up to 1782, The National Archives, Kew.
Treasury Papers, The National Archives, Kew.
Wilmot-Horton of Osmaston and Catton Papers, Derbyshire Records Office.

Primary Sources

Bigelow, A., *Leaves from a Journal; or Sketches of Rambles in some parts of North Britain and Ireland chiefly in the year 1817* (Boston: Wells and Lilly; 1821).
Brown, I.G. & Cheape, H., *Witness to Rebellion: John Maclean's Journal of the 'Forty-five and the Penicuik Drawings* (Edinburgh: John Donald, 1996).
Burton, J.H., *Jacobite Correspondence of the Atholl Family* (Edinburgh: Abbotsford Club, 1860).
Carlisle, A., *Autobiography of the Rev. Dr Alexander Carlyle* (Edinburgh: Blackwood & Sons, 1860).
Chambers, R. & Forbes, R., *Jacobite Memoirs of the Rebellion of 1745* (Edinburgh: W & R Chambers, 1834).
Crichton, P., *The Woodhouselee MS* (Edinburgh: W & R Chambers, 1907).
Dodderidge, P., *Some Remarkable Passages in the Life of the Honourable Colonel J. Gardiner* (Derby: H Mozley, 1822).
Henderson, A., *The History of the Rebellion, 1745 and 1746* (London: A. Millar, 1753).
Home, J., *The History of the Rebellion in 1745* (Edinburgh: Peter Brown, 1822).
Johnstone, J., *A Memoir of the 'Forty-Five* (London: Folio Society, 1958).
Maxwell, J., *Narrative of Charles, Prince of Wales' Expedition to Scotland in the Year 1745* (Edinburgh: Maitland Club, 1861).

Murray of Broughton, J., *Memorials of John Murray of Broughton, sometime Secretary to Prince Charles Edward, 1740-1747* (Edinburgh: Edinburgh University Press, 1898).

Robertson, J. L., 'Log of the "Dutillet"' *Transactions of the Gaelic Society of Inverness*, Vol XXVI, (Inverness: Gaelic Society of Inverness, 1910).

Robins, B. (ed.), *Report of the Proceedings and Opinion of the Board of General Officers on their Examination into the Conduct, Behaviour and Proceedings of Lieutenant-General Sir John Cope, Colonel Peregrine Lascelles and Brigadier-General Thomas Fowke* (London: Faulkner, 1749).

Taylor, A. & H., *1745 and After* (Edinburgh: Thomas Nelson, 1938).

Various, *A List of Persons Concerned in the Rebellion* (Edinburgh: University Press, 1890).

Warrand, D., (ed.), *The Culloden Papers* (Inverness: Carruthers & Sons, 1927).

Wemyss, D., *A Short Account of the Affairs of Scotland in the Years 1744-46, with a Memoir and Annotations* (Edinburgh: David Douglas, 1907).

Secondary Sources

Aitken, J., *Acheson/Morrison's Have: What Came and Went and How?* (Prestonpans: Prestoungrange University Press, 2000).

Allan, A. Bonnar, J. & Prestougrange, G. (eds), *Prestonpans: a Social and Economic History across 1000 Years* (Prestonpans: Prestoungrange University Press with Burke's Peerage & Gentry, 2006).

Anderson, F., *Crucible of War: the Seven Years' War and the Fate of Empire in British North America 1754-1766* (London: Faber and Faber, 2000).

Burton, I & Newman, A., 'Sir John Cope: Promotion in the Eighteenth Century Army', *The English Historical Review*, 78: 309 (October 1963), pp. 655-668.

Cadell, R., *Sir John Cope and the Rebellion of 1745* (Edinburgh: Blackwood & Sons, 1898),

Chambers, R., *History of the Rebellion of 1745*, First American Edition (Philadelphia: E C Mielke, 1833).

Chambers, R., *History of the Rebellion of 1745*, Fifth Edition (Edinburgh: W & R Chambers, 1869).

Cruickshanks, E. & Erskine-Hill, H., *The Atterbury Plot* (London: Palgrave Macmillan, 2004).

Dorrell, N., *Marlborough's Other Army: The British Army and the Campaigns of the First Peninsular War, 1702-1712* (Solihull: Helon & Company, 2015).

Duffy, C., *The '45: Bonnie Prince Charlie and the Untold Story of the Jacobite Rising* (London: Phoenix, 2007).

Duffy, C., *Fight for a Throne: the Jacobite '45 Reconsidered* (Solihull: Helion & Company, 2015).

Gibson, J.S., *Ships of The '45: The Rescue of the Young Pretender* (London: Hutchinson & Company, 1967).

Gibson, J.S., *Edinburgh in The '45: Bonnie Prince Charlie at Holyrood* (Edinburgh: Saltire Society, 1995).
Henshaw, V., *Scotland and the British Army 1700-1750: Defending the Union* (London: Bloomsbury, 2014).
Hopkins, B., *A Pride of Panners* (Prestonpans: Prestoungrange University Press, 2004).
Houlding, J.A., *Fit for Service: the Training of the British Army 1715-1795* (Oxford: Oxford University Press, 1981).
Jarvis, R., *Collected Papers on the Jacobite Risings* (Manchester: Manchester University Press, 1972).
Johnston, A.P., *Blood Stain'd Fields: the Battles of East Lothian* (Prestonpans: Prestoungrange & Cuthill Press, 2013).
Johnston, A.P. (ed.), *Rebellious Scots to Crush: An Anthology of the Arts as Engendered by the Battle of Prestonpans in 1745* (Prestonpans: Prestoungrange & Cuthill Press, 2008).
Lang, A., *Prince Charles Edward Stuart: The Young Chevalier* (London: Longmans, Green & Co, 1903).
Livingstone, A. & Aikman, C (eds.), *No Quarter Given: the Muster Roll of Charles Edward Stuart's Army, 1745-6* (Aberdeen: Neil Wilson Publishing, 2001).
Lord, S., *Walking with Charlie: in the Footsteps of The '45* (Witney: Pookus, 2004).
Macaulay, M., *The Prisoner of St Kilda: the True Story of the Unfortunate Lady Grange* (Edinburgh: Luath Press, 2011).
Macdonald, N.H., *The Clan Ranald of Garmoran: a History of the MacDonalds of Clanranald* (Edinburgh: Norman H MacDonald, 2008).
MacKinnon, D., *Origins and Services of the Coldstream Guards* (London: R Bentley, 1833).
Margulies, M., *The Battle of Prestonpans 1745* Second Edition (Prestonpans: Prestoungrange & Cuthill Press, 2013).
McNeill, P., *Prestonpans and Vicinity: Historical, Ecclesiastical and Traditional* (Edinburgh: John Menzies & Co, 1902).
McNeill, P., *Tranent and its Surroundings: Historical, Ecclesiastical and Traditional* (Edinburgh: John Menzies & Co, 1884).
Miller, J., *The Lamp of Lothian, or The History of Haddington* (Edinburgh: James Allan, 1884).
Oliphant, J., *John Forbes: Scotland, Flanders and the Seven Years' War 1707-1759* (London: Bloomsbury, 2015).
Pollard, A.F., *Tudor Tracts 1532-1588* (Westminster: Archibald Constable and Co, 1903).
Ralton, A., *The Roads that led by Prestoungrange: a Journey through the Landscape* (Prestonpans: Prestoungrange University Press, 2005).
Ramsay, J. *Scotland and Scotsmen in the Eighteenth Century* (Edinburgh: William Blackwood and Sons, 1888).

Reid, S., *1745: A Military History of the Last Jacobite Rising* (Staplehurst: Spellmount, 2001).

Reid, S., *Like Hungry Wolves: Culloden Moor, 16 April 1746* (London: Windrow & Greene, 1994).

Sinclair, J.. *Statistical Accounts of Scotland 1791-99*, <http://stataccscot.edina.ac.uk/static/statacc/dist/home> (last accessed 25 February 2017).

Statham, C., *Lost East Lothian* (Edinburgh: Birlinn, 2011).

Struthers, J., *The History of Scotland from the Union to the Abolition of the Heritable Jurisdictions*, (Glasgow: Blackie, Fullarton & Co, 1827).

Thompson, A.T., *Memoirs of the Jacobites of 1715 and 1745* (London: Richard Bentley, 1846).

Tomasson, K. & Buist, F., *Battles of the '45* (London: Book Club Associates, 1978).

Tomasson, K., *The Jacobite General* (Edinburgh: Blackwood & Sons, 1958).

Van der Kiste, J. *King George II and Queen Caroline* (Stroud: Sutton Publishing, 1998).

Various, *Culloden: the Swords and the Sorrows* (Glasgow: National Trust for Scotland, 1996).

Wemyss, A., *Elcho of the '45* (Edinburgh: Saltire Society, 2003).

Index

Aberdeen 49, 88-9, 92-3, 104
Alloa 31, 96, 141
Anderson, John 25, 28, 147
Anderson, Robert 25, 29, 147, 155-7
Argyll, Archibald Campbell, 3rd Duke of 38, 40, 55-6, 71, 74, 78, 80
Argyll, John Campbell, 2nd Duke of 43, 61
Atholl, James Murray, Duke of xviii, 47, 67, 78, 84, 88
Atholl, William Murray, Jacobite Duke of (aka Marquess of Tullibardine) xvii-xviii, 61, 67, 70, 78, 88, 91, 184-5, 189, 190, 206-7

Balmerino, Arthur Elphinstone, Lord 191, 207
Bangley Brae 102, 116
Bankton House 25, 32, 51, 53, 98-9, 113, 132, 136, 146, 149-150, 153, 167, 169, 174, 190, 194, 200, 202, 207
Beavor, Capt. Edmund, 111, 193
Belhaven 104, 109, 113, 193
Beltonford 107-9, 114, 186
Bernera Barracks 49, 72, 74
Berwick-upon-Tweed 20, 48, 109
Birslie Brae 139-40, 143, 145-8, 170, 179, 205
Blackness Castle 50
Blair Castle 67
Blake, Capt. 173
Blakeney, Maj. Gen. William 50, 77, 92, 125, 180, 187, 189, 199, 209-11
Bland, Maj. Gen. Humphrey 164, 188, 215
Borrodale 70-1
Bowles, Maj. Richard 116-7

Brett, Capt. Piercey 69
British Army; units of: Black Watch xviii, 46-8, 55, 67, 73-4, 89, 130, 152, 171, 214; Gardiner's 13th Dragoons 51, 74, 84, 92-4, 105, 113, 130, 142, 149, 159, 164-5, 167, 175-6, 185, 189, 193-4, 214; Guise's Regiment 48-9, 74-5, 84, 89, 130, 189, 196, 214; Hamilton's 14th Dragoons 51, 73, 92-4, 99, 105, 116, 130, 149, 155, 158-9, 161, 166-7, 173, 175-6, 185, 190, 193-4, 214; Independent Companies 46, 197; Invalids 51, 54, 84, 111, 163; Lascelles' Regiment 48 51, 73-4, 77, 130, 167, 175, 189, 208, 214; Lee's Regiment 48, 74, 130, 141, 152, 159, 171, 175, 189, 190, 207, 214; Loudoun's Highlanders 73, 88-9, 130, 152, 171, 188, 214; Murray's Highlanders; see Black Watch; Murray's Regiment xviii 48-9, 74, 130, 167, 169, 173, 175, 186, 214; Royal Artillery 54-5, 81, 97, 102, 111, 126, 130, 140-1, 143-4, 152, 154-5, 158-9, 163-5, 175, 187, 194, 196-7, 214; Royal North British Fusilier Regiment 48, 73; Royal Scots 48, 74-5; Sempill's Regiment 47-8; see also Edinburgh City Guard, Volunteers
Brown, William 35, 191
Byng, Rear Admiral John 111, 209-210

Cadell, William 28-9
Cadogan, Lt. Gen. Charles, Lord 195-6
Cameron of Lochiel, Donald 71, 77, 144, 148, 157, 170, 173, 178, 180, 205, 212-3

Cameron of Ludvara, Allan 177
Cameron, James 177
Campbell of Inverawe, Captain Duncan 55
Campbell, Colin 35
Campbell, Lieutenant-Governor Alexander 74-5, 79
Carlyle, Alexander xiv, 31, 35-7, 52, 94, 97-8, 100-2, 104, 107-9, 112-121, 131-2, 134-5, 137, 139, 141, 145-6, 148, 152, 172-4, 178, 180, 186, 190-1, 194, 198, 201
Carlyle, Rev. William 31-2, 35, 94, 190, 203
Caulfield, Maj. William 82
Christie, Capt. 169
Christie, Lt. 186
Clare, Charles O'Brien, Viscount 66
Clarke, Capt. James 99-100, 173
Clayton, Maj. Jaspar 130, 175, 214
Cleghorn, William 107
Cochrane, Capt. Basil 171
Cockenzie 20, 24-9, 33, 38, 98, 100, 136, 146, 152, 159-161, 171-3, 180, 187, 189, 191, 198, 200-1, 203
Coltbridge 94, 96, 99, 168, 186
Cooney, Lt. 141, 162
Cope, Lt. Gen. Sir John xiv-xv, 214; background and early career 4-46, 49, 51, 66, 209; command in Scotland 46, 48, 51-56, 72; abortive march into Highlands 73-5, 77-79, 81-91, 95; and Prestonpans campaign 96-7, 100, 102-5, 107-111, 113-120, 123-127, 129-149, 151-5, 157-173, 176-9; aftermath of battle 182-8, 190-1, 193-197; later life, and death 209-211
Corrieyairack Pass 76, 80-3, 85, 212
Corstorphine 93-4, 120
Cowse, Adjutant Nicholas 99
Craig, Lt. 140-1, 152
Craigie, Robert 41
Crichton, Patrick 100, 127, 188
Crief 47, 78
Culloden, Battle of 88, 126, 130, 189, 193-4, 205, 207-8, 211
Cumberland, Prince William Augustus, Duke of 20, 40, 49, 102, 193, 195, 207

Cunningham, Rev, Charles 25, 175, 199
Cunningham, Robert 121-2, 133, 139
Cunningham, Surgeon Alexander 173

Dalnacardoch 79, 82, 88
Dalrymple, Sir Hew 20
Dalrymple, Sir James 133
Dalwhinnie 80-3, 86, 89
Davidson, Henry 25, 191
Dettingen, Battle of 20-1, 40, 44, 46, 48, 66, 133, 193, 211
Disarming Acts 55, 69
Dodderidge, Philip 52, 174, 179, 190, 200
Dolphinston 20, 22-3, 37-8, 98, 137, 139, 146-8, 150
Drummond, Capt. Adam 152
Drummond, George 120, 130-1, 160-1, 169
Drummore 20-1, 33, 102
Drummore, Hew Dalrymple, Lord, xiv, 21-2, 35-6, 38, 98, 110, 134-7, 139-140, 142, 152, 161, 166-8, 170, 187
Du Teillay 66-9, 71-2, 77, 82, 127
Dumbarton 49-50, 55
Dumfries 48, 185
Dunbar 20, 22, 29, 57-8, 96-7, 100-7, 109-114, 116-7, 141, 152, 183, 186, 193
Dunblane 89, 91
Dunkeld 59, 88
Dutch troops 89, 109-111, 182, 186

East Linton 107, 113, 115
Edinburgh 20, 23, 25-6, 32-3, 37, 41, 45, 47-8, 50-1, 54, 55-6, 58-9, 73-4, 78, 84, 86, 88, 92-8, 100-2, 105-9, 111-2, 114-5, 118, 220-1, 123-132, 135, 141, 146, 148, 152, 155, 159, 170, 174, 178-180, 183, 185-6, 188, 190-1, 193, 196, 200, 202, 204, 206-7, 216
Edinburgh Castle 50, 53, 73, 81, 94, 97, 102, 111, 123, 152, 154, 176, 194, 201
Edinburgh City Guard 94, 97, 101, 108, 120, 128
Elcho, David Wemyss, Lord xiv, 64, 112, 119-120, 125, 138, 143-4, 150, 154, 166, 172-3, 175-9, 191, 201, 206, 216

Elvingston 25, 132, 139
Eriskay 56, 70
Esk, River 20, 115, 123, 134

Falkirk 92-3
Falkirk, Battle of xiv, 120, 193-4
Falside 20, 22-3, 29, 139
Fifteen, the 25-7, 30-1, 39, 46, 49-52, 56, 60-1, 64, 67-8, 71-2, 76, 120, 147
Folliot, Lt. Gen. John 195
Fontenoy, Battle of 20, 40, 46, 48, 54
Forbes of Culloden, Duncan 41, 45, 54, 56, 73, 82-4, 88, 207-8
Forbes, Capt. 169
Fort Augustus 49, 74-5, 80-3, 85, 194
Fort George 49, 73, 81, 84, 89, 194
Fort William 49, 71, 74-5, 79, 82, 194
Fowke, Brig. Thomas xiv, 89, 93-4, 96, 98-100, 113, 159, 168-9, 186, 195, 209-211, 214
Fox, HMS 103, 111, 144, 152, 172, 184, 188, 193, 209
France 20-1, 27, 40, 46, 49, 52, 54, 59-61, 64-7, 69, 75-6, 82, 111, 115, 127, 163, 185, 193, 205-9

Garden, Francis 121-2, 133, 139
Gardiner, Col. James; early life and character 32-3, 51-3, 55; initial responses to rising & fall of Edinburgh 92-4, 98, 109, 112-3, 118; role at Prestonpans 130-2, 136, 141, 146, 149, 150, 152, 159, 196-7; death 168-9, 174-5, 179, 185, 190, 194, 199, 200, 207, 214
Garleton Hills 20, 102, 106
Garvamore 81, 83-6
George I 26, 30, 39, 59-61
George II 20-1, 39-41, 45-6, 49, 65-6, 72, 77, 88, 95, 110, 133, 184-5, 210
Gladsmuir 25, 35, 102, 109 131, 133; naming of battle as such xii, xvii, 188, 198, 212
Glasgow 48, 56, 70, 73-4
Glenaladale 72, 75
Glenfinnan 71-4, 77, 79, 82-3, 123, 128
Glenorchy, John Campbell, Lord 78-9

Gordon of Glenbucket, John 75, 86
Grange, James Erskine, Lord 30-33, 35-6, 136, 140, 197
Grange, Rachel, Lady (nee Chiesley) 31-32
Grant of Glenmoriston, Patrick 126
Grant, William 37-38
Granville, John Carteret, Earl 40-42
Griffith, Maj. Eaglesfield 50, 81, 111, 141, 144, 154, 162-3, 165, 175, 194, 214
Grosset, Walter 96, 98, 100, 141-6, 152
Guest, Lt. Gen. Joshua 51, 78, 88, 93-4, 97, 102, 123, 141, 176
Guise, Lt. Gen. John 196

Haddington 20, 25, 37, 51, 100, 102, 110, 114, 116-121, 130-1, 141, 186, 189
Halkett, Lt. Col. Peter 48, 130, 157, 169-171, 175, 194, 214
Hamilton of Redhouse, George 123, 188
Happy Janet, sloop 55, 73, 104, 110-1, 193
Hardwick, Ens. 189
Hawley, Lt. Gen. Henry 193-4
Henderson, Alexander 25, 153, 172, 191
Henderson, Andrew xiv, 174, 177-180
Hepburn of Keith, James 156
Highbridge, skirmish at 75-7, 79
Holyrood 58-9, 67, 73, 97, 106, 108, 112, 122, 190-1
Home, John xiv, 94, 98, 106, 109, 116-7, 127-8, 141, 176
Home, Captain William, Earl of xiv, 94, 110, 134-5, 140, 168-9

Industrial Revolution xii, 29, 38
Inverness 41, 49, 55-6, 73-4, 83-5, 88-9, 208
Inversnaid Barracks 49

Jack, Richard 111, 141, 145, 154, 164, 196
Jacobite Army; units of: artillery 77, 82, 84, 126; Atholl Brigade 112, 121, 126, 147-8, 150, 153, 155, 157, 161, 213; Camerons of Lochiel 77, 134, 143-4, 147, 157, 161-6, 170-1, 177, 193, 213; Duke of Perth's Regiment 91, 112, 126, 157, 189, 191, 208, 213; Grants of Glenmoriston 80, 126; Lifeguards 178-9, 191, 193; Macdonalds

of Clanranald 70, 72, 77, 126, 157, 166, 213; Macdonalds of Glengarry 126, 157, 216; Macdonalds of Keppoch 77, 126, 157, 177, 216; MacGregors 126-7, 157, 167-8; MacKinnons of Skye 126; Perthshire Horse 122, 126, 129, 131, 136, 139, 157, 205, 213; Stewarts of Appin 80, 126, 157, 177, 191, 213
James II & VII 41, 57-9, 61, 66, 108
James III & VIII 26, 57, 59-62, 66, 88, 102, 105, 188, 206
Johnstone, James (Chevalier de Johnstone) xiv, 108, 123, 127, 136, 156, 160, 177, 204, 208-9

Keith of Craig, Robert 35
Keith, George, Earl Marischal 61, 64-5, 67
Kelly, Rev. George 185
Kerr of Graden, Henry 142-5
Kerr, Cornet & Adjutant 98-100, 113, 116, 142, 164, 168, 175
Kerr, Lt. Gen. Lord Mark 182, 186
Kiliwhimen Barracks 49
Kilmarnock, William Boyd, Earl of 92, 207
Kinghorn, cutter 110

L'Elisabeth 66, 69
Laggan 81
Lammermuir Hills 20, 170
Lascelles, Col. Peregrine xiv, 48, 149-151, 157, 159, 166, 169, 186-7, 195, 209, 211, 214
Lauder 182
Leith 26, 48, 73, 85, 89, 94, 96, 130, 204, 207
Ligonier, Col. Francis 193-4
Linlithgow 51, 92-3
Linton Bridge 113-5, 117
Lion, HMS 69
London 20, 23, 28, 31-3, 37, 40, 45-6, 54-5, 57, 62, 83, 132, 173, 189, 191, 195, 200, 207, 210
Loudoun, Col. John Campbell, Earl of xiv, 73, 78, 85, 88, 130, 134-7, 140, 144-5, 149, 157-8, 161, 164, 169-170, 208
Louis XV 60, 64-6, 205

Lovat, Simon Fraser, Lord 22, 32, 36, 64, 88, 207

Macdonald of Boisdale, Alexander 70
MacDonald of Kinlochmoidart, Donald 69
MacDonald, Aeneas 65, 67, 69
Macdonald, Alexander ('Bard of Clanranald') 72
MacDonald, Angus Og 126, 213
MacDonald, Ranald 126, 213
Macdonald, Sir John 65, 77, 90, 128, 138, 153, 155, 179
MacDonnell of Keppoch, Alexander 126, 213, 76
MacDonnell of Lochgarry, Donald 85
MacDonnell of Tirnadris, Donald 75
MacDonnell, Archibald, 177
MacGregor, James Mor 72, 213
MacGregor, Malcolm 177
Mackay, Capt. Alexander 214
Mackintosh, Capt. Alexander, 85, 89
MacLachlan, Lachlan 126, 213
Maclean, Hector 55
Maclean, John xiv, 190-1
Mar, John Erskine, Earl of 26-7, 30-32, 43, 50-1, 60, 67, 71
McGhie, William 120-1
Molloy, Sgt. Terrence 86-8
Mossman, Maj. James 141, 162, 169
Murray of Broughton, John xiv, xviii, 64-5, 72, 85, 92, 106, 108, 121, 128, 142-3, 166, 174, 176-7, 179, 185, 207
Murray, Capt. Sir Patrick 189, 214
Murray, Col. Lord John 47, 67
Murray, Col. Thomas 48
Murray, Lady Aemilia 184
Murray, Lord George xiv, xviii, 67, 78-9, 89-90, 92-3, 128, 136-8, 142-4, 147-8, 155-7, 159-161, 169-171, 177, 180-1, 184, 189, 206, 208, 212-3
Musselburgh 19-21, 51, 94, 96, 98-9, 115, 123, 134-5, 137, 168, 181, 190

Nairne, John Nairne, Lord 112, 126, 147-8, 150, 156, 213
Napier, Francis Scott, Lord 94, 99-100, 105

INDEX 225

Netherbow Port 20, 97, 101, 112
Newcastle 48, 109, 176, 186, 188, 195
Newcastle, Thomas Pelham-Holles, Duke of 41, 185
Newhailes House 21, 133
Nineteen, the 39, 46, 49, 61, 64, 67-8, 72
North Berwick 20, 29, 98-100, 105, 136, 202

O'Sullivan, John William xiv, 65-7, 79, 85, 87, 90, 101, 108, 128-9, 143, 147-8, 153, 156, 162, 166, 168, 176, 178-181, 191, 206, 212
Oliphant of Gask, Lawrence 205

Paterson, Robert 188
Pelham, Henry 40-2, 78, 80, 187
Penicuik Sketches 126-7
Perth 26, 48-9, 56, 73-4, 88-9, 91, 189
Perth, James Drummond, Duke of 55, 63-4, 89-90, 128, 157, 159-162, 166, 172-3, 178, 205, 213
Pinkie 20, 115, 134-5, 137, 181-2
Port Seton 28-9, 136
Preston 23-4, 29, 32-3, 98-9, 113, 132, 134, 136-7, 140, 146, 155, 167, 170, 177, 198, 203
Preston House 29-32, 136, 149, 158, 180, 202
Preston, Lancashire 189; Battle of xii, 27, 51-2, 61, 93, 113, 186
Preston, Lt. Gen. George 51, 102
Prestongrange 36-8, 119, 201
Prestonpans (village) xvi, xvii, 19, 21-2, 24, 29, 31, 33-9, 51, 65, 77, 94, 94, 100-2, 112, 118, 120, 129, 136, 140-1, 146, 149, 152, 160, 172-4, 180, 187-8, 190-1, 197-8, 201, 203
Pyot, Rev. Alexander, 112-3, 115

Rattray, John 174, 207
Reid, Rev. Matthew 108, 115
Richmond, Lt. Gen. Charles Lennox, Duke of 195
Riggonhead 25, 29, 153, 156-8, 201, 203
Robertson, Rev. William 25, 35, 102, 107-9, 131

Royal Navy 60, 65-6, 104, 111, 185
Ruthven Barracks 49, 74-5, 81, 84, 86-8, 194
Rutledge, Walter 66

Scott of Scotstarvet, Capt. John 75-6
Seton 26-9, 33, 38, 136, 138, 149, 156, 169, 186, 191, 198-9, 203
Seton Palace 26, 28, 39, 132, 136, 155, 158
Severn, Maj. John 130, 174, 214
Sheridan, Sir Thomas 66, 70, 189
Sheriffmuir, Battle of 27, 43, 46, 61, 67, 71
Sherriff, Andrew 35, 191
Simson, Patrick 152
Singleton, Maj. 169
Skirving, Adam 195, 203, 211
Slochd, Pass of 85-6
Snugborough xiv, 81-3, 85
St Germains 25-6, 29, 36, 132, 134, 155-6
Stair, Field Marshal John Dalrymple, Earl of 21, 52, 133
Stewart of Ardshiel, Charles 80, 126, 179, 191, 213
Stewart of Invernahyle, Charles 165, 194
Stewart, Capt. John Coltrane 190
Stewart, Donald 167
Stewart, Lord Provost Archibald 93, 96, 100-1, 112
Stewart, Robert 177
Stirling 26-7, 48, 50-1, 56, 73, 77-9, 83-4, 91-3, 125, 155, 159, 180, 184, 187, 189
Stirling Castle 50, 74, 91-3, 209
Stranraer 48
Strathallan, William Drummond, Viscount 122, 126, 134, 137-8, 177, 179, 205, 213
Stuart, Capt. John 167-8
Stuart, James Francis Edward; see James III & VIII
Stuart, John Roy 88, 121
Stuart, Prince Charles Edward 39, 46, 55-6, 85, 182, 188, 196, 202, 207, 213; youth and early life 62-5; campaign in Scotland 66-72, 75, 77-81, 82-6, 88-94, 101, 106, 108-9, 112, 123; in Prestonpans campaign, 1246, 128-130, 133, 143, 146,

148, 154, 156, 160, 170, 175, 178-9, 181-2; subsequent actions during the '45 185, 190-1; later life, and death 205-6, 209, 212; assessment 211-2

Stuart, Prince Henry Benedict 62

Sweetenham, Capt. John 75, 77, 79, 82-3, 88

Tatton, Capt. Charles 189

Taylor, Robert 194, 207

Thorntree Fields xvi, 137, 152, 168, 180-1, 199, 201-2

Threipland of Fingask, David 177

Tranent 19, 23-5, 28-9, 32-3, 38, 131-2, 136-9, 143, 144, 147-8, 151, 153, 155, 157, 170-1, 174-5, 179, 190-1, 198-201, 212

Tranent Meadows 25, 29, 32, 136-7, 140, 142, 147, 202

Traquair, Charles Stewart, Earl of 64

Trotter, Surgeon William 173

Tullibardine, Marquess of; see Atholl, William Murray, Jacobite Duke of

Tweeddale, John Hay, Marquess of 20, 40-1, 54-56, 73, 77, 79, 83, 89, 102, 105, 107, 109-110, 134, 181, 183, 196-7

Volunteers, Company of Civilian 94-5, 97, 102, 113, 116, 118, 120-1, 130-1, 143, 152, 160, 169, 172, 188, 190

Wade, Field Marshal George 46, 49, 68, 80, 186, 191, 193, 195, 209-211

Waggonway, Tranent-Cockenzie 24-5, 28-9, 136-7, 143-4, 146, 148, 152, 154, 158, 168, 170-1, 175, 199-203

Walsh, Antoine 66, 71

Warren Parks 140, 152, 159, 171, 201

Wemyss, Capt. 169

Wemyss, James Wemyss, Earl of 64

Wemyss-Charteris, Francis 119-120

Whitburgh 25, 29, 156

Whitefoord, Lt. Col. Charles 102, 105, 111, 116, 119, 134, 144-5, 153, 162-3, 165, 175, 214

Whitney, Lt. Col. Shugborough 130, 159, 164-5, 175-6, 187, 194, 197, 215-6

Wright, Lt. Col. William 130, 175, 190, 214

York Buildings Company 27-8, 200

From Reason to Revolution – Warfare 1721-1815

http://www.helion.co.uk/series/from-reason-to-revolution-1721-1815.php

The 'From Reason to Revolution' series covers the period of military history 1721–1815, an era in which fortress-based strategy and linear battles gave way to the nation-in-arms and the beginnings of total war.

This era saw the evolution and growth of light troops of all arms, and of increasingly flexible command systems to cope with the growing armies fielded by nations able to mobilise far greater proportions of their manpower than ever before. Many of these developments were fired by the great political upheavals of the era, with revolutions in America and France bringing about social change which in turn fed back into the military sphere as whole nations readied themselves for war. Only in the closing years of the period, as the reactionary powers began to regain the upper hand, did a military synthesis of the best of the old and the new become possible.

The series examines the military and naval history of the period in a greater degree of detail than has hitherto been attempted, and has a very wide brief, with the intention of covering all aspects from the battles, campaigns, logistics, and tactics, to the personalities, armies, uniforms, and equipment.

Submissions

The publishers would be pleased to receive submissions for this series. Please email reasontorevolution@helion.co.uk, or write to Helion & Company Limited, Unit 8 Amherst Business Centre, Budbrooke Road, Warwick, CV34 5WE